Twentieth - Century
Embroidery
in Great Britain from 1978

Constance Howard

B T BATSFORD LTD   LONDON

Acknowledgment

ISBN 0 7134 4658 7

Typeset by Servis Filmsetting Ltd
Manchester
and printed in Great Britain by
R J Acford Ltd
Chichester, Sussex
for the publishers
B T Batsford Ltd
4 Fitzhardinge Street
London W1H 0AH

It has been suggested by Jane Warnick, a friend from the USA, that I should thank all those who have become fascinated with embroidery; otherwise there would have been little point in compiling the history. Without the interest and great output by embroiderers at all levels, what would there have been to write about in the twentieth century? As it is, there is far too much and, with the limitations on the size of each volume, selection and omission are inevitable.

My thanks go to all those embroiderers who have supplied photographs and slides of work, or who have allowed me to obtain photographs; to the Embroiderers' Guild for their help at all times; and to all those who have supplied information and opinions on their own work, which have enlivened the text.

Again I cannot give enough thanks to my daughter, Charlotte, for her patience in deciphering an almost illegible manuscript with its numerous alterations, for correcting poor English, illogical statements and other errors, and for typing and retyping much of the manuscript several times.

Thelma Nye has been both patient and helpful and I have learnt a great deal through her suggestions and corrections that have improved the manuscripts of the four volumes. I have never felt under pressure even with deadlines approaching when working with her.

Nick Nicholson is an excellent photographer and will endeavour to go to any place at short notice and to photograph work whenever it is available. I would like to thank him for the photography that he has contributed to this volume.

Introduction

Please note
For further references to embroiderers mentioned in this book, and other examples of their work, see *Twentieth Century Embroidery in Great Britain 1940 to 1963* and *1964 to 1977*.

Figures shown in brackets throughout the text refer to illustration numbers.

It is some time since I started to write the history of twentieth-century embroidery in Great Britain. During these years many students have received training, a number will have dropped embroidery altogether while others are becoming well known in their chosen areas of work. Inevitably, good artists will have been omitted from this history; I cannot know them all and the space is strictly limited. I could have produced a mammoth volume but the cost prohibits this; so I have purposely kept the text short in order to include as many photographs as possible.

The greater number of embroiderers actively practising the craft today, the diversity of styles, and the different levels of achievement by individuals and groups, have all contributed to what I hope is a wide collection of illustrations. Several different embroideries of sheep have been included to show a variety of approaches to one subject. Biographies are included in this volume, too, as the text is shorter than in *Twentieth-Century Embroidery in Great Britain 1964 to 1977*.

Contents

The late Seventies and early Eighties

Economically the world situation has not improved since 1978. Redundancy and cut backs in industry, with increasing unemployment, continue. Education, too, has received many reductions in university and other grants, leading to deployment of teachers and non-renewal of equipment. We have all been affected by rising costs in different ways but despite these frustrations and difficulties the interest in crafts has continued.

Promotion

Most of the comments on embroidery in *Twentieth-Century Embroidery in Great Britain 1964–1977* are equally true today and although no major changes have occured over the last few years, the scene is always moving. Allied crafts have been incorporated with stitchery, such as the making of handmade paper which reached a peak at the end of the seventies, and handmade felt which has grown in popularity since the end of the last decade. Painting with dye on silk, spray dyeing and dyed fabrics as backgrounds for embroidery are often used, while interest in patchwork continues. Smocking is gaining momentum and a guild group is suggested in *Embroidery* Volume 35, Number 1, Spring 1984.

There is an indication that design is becoming more realistic than in the early seventies with small naturalistic landscapes, figurative work and pictorial subjects. Geometric pattern and abstract compositions, as well as collage without embroidery, are still favoured, while machine embroidery continues to attract students. There is also an increased interest in hand stitching by groups of students, keen to develop the possibilities of this aspect of the craft of embroidery. Three-dimensional works in fabric and thread seem to be less in evidence than during the mid-seventies, although stump work has become popular, while padding and quilting are much in demand.

Exhibitions of embroidery throughout the country continue to create interest, whether as group shows, one-person shows or those containing a variety of crafts. New societies have been formed to hold exhibitions, some by graduates from colleges of art and polytechnics, while others have been formed by those interested in meeting together to exchange ideas and opinions, with exhibitions a further consideration. Promotion has been fostered by such places as the Rufford Art Centre near Newark, also by the Lady Lodge Centre in Peterborough where, in 1983, embroidery was included in its activities for the first time, although quilting and patchwork courses had been held there since the end of the seventies, with workshops, lectures and exhibitions. Another centre, Quarry Bank Mill in Cheshire, also holds courses in textiles, a number being on aspects of embroidery. Museums, too, are more frequently showing the work of embroiderers.

1984 – Millicent Spiller. *The Rose*. A panel with the rose in pinks and reds using fabrics as lightly and as freely as possible, overlaying transparent materials, to obtain a variety of delicate colours. Limited stitching is added to give texture and tone. *Photograph by Hawkley Studios*

Education

In the polytechnics and the colleges of art offering the BA honours degree courses in embroidery and textiles, more applications for places are received than are available. Adult centres and higher education establishments, such as the London College of Fashion, all cater for embroidery, the latter college specialising in embroidery for industry as well as training students for the City and Guilds of London Institute examinations which are attracting more part-time students, with a consequent increase in the number of classes. It appears that embroidery as an art at a high level of attainment, as a craft for leisure, and as a theraputic occupation, has validity and does not diminish in popularity.

Colleges of art and degree courses

The degree courses in the polytechnics and colleges of art, each with their particular qualities, aim to develop individual approaches to embroidery. In 1976 a degree was granted to Glasgow School of Art by the Council for National Academic Awards. In 1979 embroidery was approved as a subject in the School, which is the only place in Scotland where it may now be studied as a main subject at degree level; Dundee College of Art offers it as a second subject, but it is no longer a part of a degree course in Aberdeen or Edinburgh.

Comments by heads of departments

Heads of departments in establishments recognised for the BA honours degree in embroidery have written accounts of their aims in their courses. In 1979 Anne Butler Morrell, describing the Manchester BA course, said that the subject is regarded as a legitimate art form rather than a conventional craft and the result of three years' study produces a great variety of work. In the first year, history and methods, lectures and demonstrations, are a basis for further development with students experiencing a wide range of materials, while in the second year, work of a more specific nature is undertaken, often with a particular purpose. In the third year, students are free to pursue their own inclinations which are of major concern, as is the thought behind the work. (*Embroidery*, Volume 30, Number 3, Autumn 1979.)

Ruth Elsey, describing the degree course in textiles at Trent Polytechnic, established in 1975, says that it is broad, including embroidery, print, weave, knit and lace. These subjects are taken by all students in their first year. The course is general rather than specialised but by the third year students need to be self-motivated, with their own projects. If they decide to study embroidery this may be developed in more depth during the second and third years when they carry out set projects, often several at a time in the second year; in the third year solving their own problems. (*Embroidery*, Volume 31, Number 1, Spring, 1980.)

Patricia Foulds at Loughborough College of Art emphasises the fact that students do not make their final choice of study until the last term in their first year. Instead, they spend the first year developing assurance in the use of colour, texture, materials and image, with drawing a fundamental part of the course. In the second year, importance is given to the creative use of hand and machine embroidery rather than to their technical aspects and, in the third year, students are given complete freedom in which to express ideas in their own ways. The importance of an original approach to embroidery is stressed, with students encouraged to discover its possibilities as a fine art and as a decorative and a functional medium. (*Embroidery*, Volume 31, Number 2, Summer 1980.)

Joan Cleaver in 1980, discussing later developments of the Birmingham Polytechnic degree course in embroidery, said that there is much more emphasis on drawing now than when the diploma course started, with students specialising in one of the options offered in woven and printed textiles, embroidery or fashion, after a term of preliminary study. Subjects such as the history of textiles, the history of fashion and analysis of materials, are common to all textile courses. She thinks that the students now have more commitment and singlemindedness in their work, that they are less interested in teaching as an aim than in the past, and that the course has changed over the years, although the basic aims and objectives are still concerned with the education of the individual designer. An innovation on the course has been the introduction of business methods, with students having to write briefs on some of their projects. Joan Cleaver feels that at present there are more opportunities than previously for a graduate student to become established as a designer craftsman. (*Embroidery*, Volume 31, Number 3, Autumn 1980.)

Writing on the Degree Shows in 1981 Diana Springall mentioned both Manchester and Goldsmiths, commenting on their different approaches. She compared work by two students who had obtained first-class honours degrees. In Manchester, design for industry and for objects with a purpose were predominant, with excellent craftsmanship; while at Goldsmiths the bias was towards fine art, with personal statements but little awareness of the craft or technique of embroidery. She felt that the complementary viewpoints in the individual approaches produced work of richness and variety. (*Embroidery*, Volume 32, Number 3, Autumn 1981.)

Glasgow School of Art

Crissie White has written an account of embroidery at Glasgow School of Art during the late seventies and early eighties. Expressing her own point of view on the subject, she says that since her appointment as head of the department in 1974 she has realised that new attitudes to embroidery were encouraged by a small group of people 'infecting each other with enthusiasm which finds different expression in each generation'. Changes had taken place in students' choices of subjects, from the study of natural forms, patterns of growth, man-made objects and buildings, to rainbows and windows; with an interest in glitter, feathers, stretch fabric and unusual materials. 'The present seems to be dominated by a craze for patterns of decay, rust-eaten metal, rotten wood and flaking paint, demolition might be added to this list.' She says too that 'The present day is of breaking down, rather than of building up, by tearing, cutting, bleaching and burning, using acids to reduce fabrics to pulp, and to reconstruct as felt or paper. The increase in the use of dyes has enabled students to produce various colour effects in a personal way'. In 1983 she noticed more interest in the use of the human figure as subject matter for design, also the use of mirrors, lenses and other means to produce distortions: another facet of the times and an extension of the interest in optical effects of the sixties. She suggests 'that when the preoccupations of students in other establishments appear, the change of expression could reflect a greater influence than a student might be exposed to in a teaching programme. This is only seen in retrospect'. She concludes saying that 'there is a desire among leading students to rebuild, making their own materials when what they want is unavailable' and 'alongside the so-called destruction of fabric and material' she is hopeful of the future.

London College of Fashion

The Embroidery Department is organised by Anthea Godfrey. There are now courses for the City and Guilds examinations in embroidery, courses for students training for industry, also for fashion embroidery, where the students are designing garments specially to be embroidered. Anthea Godfrey says that the aim of herself and her assistants is to produce thinking embroiderers not technicians as such. The industrial course is hoping to provide industry with a new injection of original ideas and to train students to research and develop these quickly. This has been a struggle with an 'old fashioned' industry, with low pay and often poor working conditions, but now firms are applying to the College for students. She has high hopes for the future of embroidery and its value to industry and to the individual.

General Certificate of Education

The Associated Board for the General Certificate of Education has helped to raise standards of embroidery in schools, but there is no longer a separate paper for the subject in the art and design syllabus. At O level, provision is made in option one of the design paper, first set in 1979, while at A level, embroidery may be chosen as a part of the art and craft papers. The syllabus for domestic science at present provides for separate papers on embroidery at both O and A levels. The Certificate of Secondary Education in many areas includes embroidery as a subject for examination.

Embroidery is included in the O and A level syllabus for London University. In textiles at O level a choice may be made, while at A level, for the paper on craft history, three areas may be studied: printed and dyed textiles, hand weaving and embroidery. The instructions state that candidates should be aware of embroidery as a creative form in its own right.

The Joint Matriculation Board also includes embroidery in the craft-design and practice papers at O and A levels, both of which include history and methods. The design papers require that at each level a part of the design is worked.

The Oxford and Cambridge O and A level examinations for the School Leaving Certificate do not include embroidery in their syllabus.

City and Guilds of London Institute examinations

Many part-time classes in embroidery are being held in adult education centres, with a number of students studying for the City and Guilds examinations in embroidery. Each centre has its particular approach to the craft which is assessed by an external examiner, with students setting up shows of their work for this purpose.

Two exhibitions of work by past and present students were held in January 1982; one at Brunel University, of embroideries from Jan Beaney's classes at Windsor and Maidenhead Adult Centre, the other at Foyle's Gallery, of embroidery by students at the London College of Fashion. These produced the different ways in which the Windsor and Maidenhead Adult Centre work produced an imaginative outlook, a restrained use of colour, carefully planned design – as a whole an understatement; while that from the London College of Fashion, also inventive, was exhuberant, overflowing with pattern and stitchery. Technical expertise was excellent in both exhibitions, each of which was of embroideries by past and present students.

Embroiderers' Guild and other courses

Classes in aspects of embroidery are advertised in *Embroidery* by the Embroiderers' Guild, by members of the Practical Study Group and by the New Embroidery Group. Allied subjects include courses in drawing, dyeing and painting on fabric, and the study of particular aspects of design: some are for one day only, others are residential. Branches of the Guild also arrange courses, as do independent establishments such as Stitch Design.

Television series 'Embroidery'

Another educational venture was by the BBC who promoted the television series of talks on embroidery, produced by Jenny Rodgers. Jan Beaney presented the programme while Diana Springall wrote the book accompanying the series, for which practical examples were made. The first showing of the film was in the autumn of 1980, having been considered in April 1979. The reasons for the series were to encourage those with some technical knowledge to try an experimental approach to embroidery, also to show the beginner the possibilities of the craft and the excitement in creating individual pieces of work. In an attempt to interest everyone, historic, foreign and contemporary embroideries were shown, including examples by beginners, students and professional embroiderers. A number of well-known artists were included in the series, some televised in their own studios where they talked about their work and their aims in using embroidery as a means of expression.

Textile development assessment

In *Crafts* magazine, March/April 1983, in an article entitled 'Through the Eye of the Needle', Ann Sutton 'undertook' to assess the development of textiles since the early seventies. Commenting on 'soft art' she said that 'Over-constructed (and unfashionable) dress decoration ran riot. The embroiderers pulled out the stops too far (to state their case?), before settling down to something quite healthy. So *embroidery* stopped being a dirty word – the embroidery departments in the colleges saw to that. And, significantly, the best fine-art textile department, at Goldsmiths, managed to achieve this status, while still under the name of "embroidery"'.

In conclusion, she thought that 'the only salvation of what remains of Britain's fine-art textile reputation is to come via Goldsmiths' College embroidery degree course. It is the only one where the fine art approach is not tucked into a design course – Goldsmiths is uncompromising and is producing artists'.

The Royal School of Needlework

During the late seventies and early eighties the Royal School of Needlework organised classes in a variety of embroidery and lace techniques. The two-year apprenticeship course continues but another venture, the Youth Training Scheme, was inaugurated in October 1983 to give a broad base of skills in embroidery and needlework. Drawing and design are studied, museum visits arranged, and insight into workroom procedure, management and business studies, office and computer skills are all included in the scheme. Some students have entered the two-year apprenticeship course from the scheme, others have gone into the Design Room.

Conservation, the carrying out of private commissions and of designs by outside artists, continue at the School.

The Wemyss School of Needlework

The Wemyss School of Needlework still carries on, having originated during the latter part of the nineteenth century. Although it has now only a small number of part-time staff, repairs to old quilts and tapestries are undertaken, also work for clients wanting embroideries started for them or wishing for partially worked embroideries to be completed. (*Embroidery*, Volume 34, Number 4, Winter 1983.)

Stitch Design School

Stitch Design, a school of embroidery, was set up as an independent enterprise in February 1983 by Julia Caprara and Barbara Marriott. This is situated in the developing area of the Dockland in London and provides part-time tuition for students not wanting to study for examinations, as well as for those who wish to take the City and Guilds examinations in embroidery. Exhibitions of work by '62 Group members and others are arranged, and lectures and meetings are held there from time to time.

Women's Institutes

The Federation of Women's Institutes continues to promote crafts throughout the country. From notes given to me by Barbara Moss, the headquarters of the Institutes at Denman College near Abingdon, offers 13 textile crafts, excluding tailoring and dressmaking, for their curricula. National certificates are obtainable in hand and machine embroidery as well as in a number of other crafts; while all teachers employed there hold the National Federation of Women's Institutes Teaching Certificate, the City and Guilds Certificate or an equivalent qualification. Regular classes are organised by the Institutes, also day schools and visits to exhibitions and lectures; also local and regional shows of members' work are held there.

Ecclesiastical embroidery

Embroidery for the Church gained impetus during the seventies with well-known artists specialising in ecclesiastical work. Beryl Dean, Pat Russell, Judy Barry and Beryl Patten are among those in England who have carried out many commissions. Barbara Dawson and Isabel Clover have specialised in this field too; while in Scotland Kathleen Whyte and Hannah Frew Paterson are well known for their embroideries for the Church. Groups of women, often unskilled, but willing to carry out the designs of others, under guidance, have been formed to embroider kneelers for their parish churches. These ventures have led to more ambitious projects being undertaken when greater skill is acquired. The cathedrals, too, have their particular groups of stitchers who carry out whatever is required, often a certain amount of conservation being involved, usually under the supervision of a skilled organiser with some knowledge of the subject.

Exhibitions of ecclesiastical work held in a number of cathedrals and churches since 1978, articles written on designing for the Church and the interest taken by some churchmen in commissioning artists to design and carry out embroideries for these buildings, have resulted in a diverse number of individual examples being created.

The Very Reverend Peter Moore, Dean of St Alban's, in 1978 emphasised certain points in an article entitled 'Working for the Church' in *Embroidery*, Volume 29, Number 2, Summer 1978. He mentioned the enrichment of many churches with the making of hassocks in needlework and that an advantage was that this could be a co-operative undertaking with different levels of skill. An important point was the contribution made by amateur workers. Peter Moore felt that imagination was a part of creation and that an artist is one who creates things. He mentioned symbolism and thought that the cross had been misused and abused for too long and that 'it is quite a struggle to re-authenticate its validity'. He said that texture could be abstracted from an object to make a pattern that was not obviously related to the original form. Attention could be paid to the shape of articles and materials used for the Church with decoration of secondary importance. Permanence, too, he felt was questionable, saying that 'in this matter of design there is an opportunity for experiment. But before experiment there must be discussion. What is good design? The only certain thing that can be said is that you cannot talk about a design outside the context of where it is for. This will have a great influence on its scale'.

Exhibitions of Church embroidery

The East Kent Branch of the Embroiderers' Guild in 1978 arranged an exhibition of twentieth-century Church embroidery in Canterbury Cathedral: the aim 'to show the wide variety of design and technique' inspired by the differing tastes and traditions of Christian people, here and overseas. Well-known artists submitted examples of embroidery, among these Judy Barry and Beryl Patten, Pat Russell, and Beryl Dean whose five copes for the ceremony of the enthronement of the Archbishop of Canterbury were on show. The Silver Jubilee cope from St Paul's Cathedral and a fair linen cloth by her were also exhibited. Ione Dorrington's cope, commissioned by St Katherine's, Hatcham, as a gift to Australia, was shown; also embroidery by Barbara Dawson for Manchester Cathedral.

Several exhibitions were held in cathedrals and churches during the late seventies and early eighties. In the summer of 1979 'Church Art and Craft' was the title of a show in Rochester Cathedral, while in May 1980 'Embroidered Vestments' was staged in St Alban's Abbey. A great deal of work both historical and contemporary was shown, with well-known ecclesiastical embroiderers contributing to the show. Again, in July–August 1981 another show of both 'Embroidery Old and New' was arranged by the East Kent Branch of the Embroiderers' Guild, in the Chapter House of Canterbury Cathedral where group work and individual pieces were on view; the screen design by Doris Anwyl, depicting the four seasons, was among these (145).

Cathedral commissions

In 1978 the Sarum Group, affiliated to the Mid-Wessex Branch of the Embroiderers' Guild, was formed by Jane Lemon and her students, to produce embroideries for Salisbury Cathedral. After a show held in November 1978 a number of works was completed for the Baptistry, the Audley Chantry Chapel and the Cathedral School Chapel. The 'Energy' frontal (37), for the High Altar, was completed in February 1982 designed for all seasons but basically in red, rather than the green stipulated by the Sarum Rites. A lenten frontal has also been made with conventional figures representing 'the congregation as rock-like people'.

Ruth Tudor designed and worked a frontal in machine and hand embroidery for a church in Antony, Cornwall. The community is rural, this being reflected in her idea of depicting the seasons surrounded by four arches containing a landscape that is continuous but with the colours changing with each season. Five festal copes for Winchester Cathedral (60) were completed by March 1979. These copes were to be worn on Royal occasions, the stipulation being 'not modern please'. Moyra McNeill and Barbara Siedlecka combined ideas for Winchester basing them on the architecture of the Cathedral, celebrating its 900th anniversary. Barbara Siedlecka drew out the ideas, suggesting that smaller decoration could be based on the twelfth century Winchester Bible. The scheme was presented to the Cathedral in 1977. Limited time in which to execute the work meant simple construction, so gold cords and braids and heavy, stiff fabrics, silks and velvets were employed, mounted on a linen base as a 'rigid splendour' was required.

Judy Barry and Beryl Patten were commissioned in March 1979 to design and carry out five embroidered copes for Chester Cathedral (153), to be worn by the Dean and Canons for festivals and special occasions. The chosen scheme was based on the idea of trees and plants mentioned in the Bible, with plain copes in different colours having embroidered orphreys and hoods. A final presentation of designs was made in May 1980 (151). Each cope is decorated with a different symbol; the 'Chester' cope relating to the City and its county is decorated with corn. In scarlet, this cope makes a focal point for the vestments worn together.

In 1979 Hannah Frew Paterson was commissioned to design and embroider a screen to go behind the communion table in Cardross Parish Church, Dumbartonshire. The design, composed of several panels, was completed in 1981 (108). In 1984 she designed and executed a pulpit fall, *The Cup*, using multi-coloured silks on gold fabric, with padded gold leather to give a relief effect (295).

In 1980 Beryl Dean completed a cope for the Archbishop of Canterbury (89). She had been asked in 1974 to design copes to be worn by the Dean and Chapter of Canterbury Cathedral for the enthronement; she also designed a cope for the Archbishop but as Dr Coggan received another one, this design was not executed. In 1980 she decided to complete the set of vestments with the cope which was worn by Dr Runcie on the day after his enthronement as the Archbishop. These vestments are decorated with a variety of crosses, the ancient Canterbury cross being given prominence.

Recent commissions by Beryl Dean in 1983–4 include six different designs for 600 kneelers for Chelmsford Cathedral with three different arrangements of colour to reflect the jewel-like stained glass windows of the South wall, with the kneelers to be seen on a light stone floor. The Essex Handicraft Association is working the canvas embroidery. Beryl Dean has also designed the hanging for the east end of the Cathedral, in 'vibrant, glowing colours' in patchwork squares, with former students assisting in its construction. (279.)

In another recent commission – vestments for the 'Cathedral of the Forest' in Newland, Gloucestershire – her designs are 'influenced by ferns, grasses, rocks and snails, and colours of the old glass'. The pulpit fall design evolved from brocade hangings in the church. Embroidery for the Lady Chapel was undertaken by her former students. Sylvia Green designed a patchwork frontal in blues and greens, also a dossal and two kneelers, echoing the colours of the window above. (*Embroidery*, Volume 35, Number 1, Spring 1984.)

Pat Russell was closely involved with the preparations for Wells Cathedral's 800th anniversary celebrations and for the 900th celebrations at Worcester Cathedral where she has been appointed Design Consultant. Many of her designs are kept 'beautifully simple', their effect relying on choice of fabric and carefully organised colour combinations. She says that 'for richly embroidered work she uses a wide variety of fabrics in freely stitched appliqué, embellished with machine embroidery, couched yarns and braids. Designs are such that they fit in with and enhance their particular surroundings and are "right" for the services in which they are used'.

Dress In the late seventies and the early eighties machine embroidered fabrics and garments have become fashionable. The introduction of hand embroidered blouses and dresses from such places as India and Hong Kong may have furthered the interest in embroidered clothes, with fine shadow work on cotton shirts and the most intricate embroidery on silk blouses. Quilted jackets, machine stitched, have also been imported as well as accessories such as bags and belts embroidered with metal threads, sequins and beads. Fabrics in cut work have been in vogue while smocking on clothes for adults and children has revived. Elaborately embroidered evening wear has been seen in the exclusive boutiques, from Britain, France and Italy. Quilted waistcoats (238, 239), known as vests in the USA, patchwork and embroidered examples, short casual jackets with embroidered areas, additions of lace, and plain and patterned fabrics used together have become a part of the early eighties scene. Susan Rangeley is now producing jackets and accessories such as small quilted bags, and combining hand painted floral decoration with semi-detached flowers and leaves, stitched by machine, all in delicate colours of pale lavenders, pinks and blues, with variously shaded greens for the leaves (43, 180, 181).

Zandra Rhodes showed exotic garments at 'Aditi', an exhibition at the Barbican in London, in 1982, which was a part of the Festival of India. She designed the garments to be decorated with embroidery, having been commissioned by the Handicrafts and Handlooms Export Corporation of India to design a *couture* collection with an Indian theme (182 and 301 colour plate 7) to demonstrate the skills of Indian craftsmen, who embroidered the garments. She said that she had tried to show the use of traditional crafts of 'an excellence which we in the West are in danger of losing'. (*Embroidery*, Volume 33, Number 4, Winter 1982.) In her later collections she has used beads, sequins, diamanté and embroidery on a number of her chiffon creations, with her own printed patterns. Metal threads incorporated in the embroidery have been features of some of her exclusive 1983 models.

Robin Giddings, since the late seventies, has been perfecting his technique of machine embroidered lace-like structures, worked on the Irish machine. He is incorporating fine silk fabrics and metal threads in his kimono-shaped garments and is producing embroidered fabrics on the Schiffli machine. He is also carrying out commissions for private clients. At the Waterloo Gallery in October 1984 some of his embroidery for dress, executed on the Schiffli machine, was shown as well as his lacy garments worked on the Irish machine.

Lucy Goffin, on talking about fashion to Rozanne Hawksley who interviewed her for *Embroidery*, Volume 33, Number 2, Summer 1982 said it was her concern to make garments rich and beautiful. 'I'm interested in making detailed coats and covers, quilted in various thicknesses, using pleats, tucks and unusual buttons, with free hand embroidery as surface embellishment' (76, 77.)

Materials and threads

The Needlewoman Shop in London closed in July 1979, since when more mail order firms are supplying materials and threads as well as equipment for embroidery. Fabrics made of natural fibres, particularly silks from India and China, are more easily obtained now than in the mid-seventies. Pure cottons, including calico, are always popular, particularly the unbleached calico, while Welsh flannel is used as a basis for pattern darning and backgrounds of surface stitchery. Linen is generally imported. Fabrics composed of natural and synthetic fibres, or wholly of synthetic fibres, have improved in quality over the last decade and are more easily handled for embroidery than when first seen on the market. Threads still include tapestry and crewel wools, knitting yarns, both natural and synthetic. Weaving yarns also are used for embroidery, while silk threads are imported. Stranded cotton, perle cotton, coton-à-broder, soft cotton and machine embroidery cottons are available, but also imported are synthetic threads, from India and Japan, obtainable for both hand and machine embroidery. Metal threads are mainly synthetic as Jap gold is no longer imported.

Embroidery and felt

During the mid-seventies onwards, felt-making in colleges of art became increasingly popular. Embedded with brightly coloured pattern, stamped to give raised effects or stitched into to give 'chunky' embroideries, it was used to make clothes and hangings as experimental articles. This coincided with the craze for handmade paper, and both crafts flourished, having been practised in America for some time. Embroidery on paper, stitchery through both paper and handmade felt was seen in exhibitions by the '62 Group and in degree shows. Felt accessories such as boots and hats appeared, small pieces were framed, edges left uneven with threads sometimes embedded.

As the early eighties have progressed the felt pieces have become larger, with wall hangings 'splashed' with coloured pattern, while finer examples are being made into clothing and accessories, sometimes embellished with embroidery and quilting. Commercial felt has been popular for embroidery and toy-making for many years, but handmade felt has a more personal quality, with colours and patterns merged together. Embroiderers were 'inspired by examples of felt seen in 'The Frozen Tombs of Siberia' exhibition at the British Museum in 1978. These were of the fifth and fourth centuries BC and included felt garments, saddle covers and saddle cloths, all embroidered. An exhibition, 'The Art of the Felt Maker', at the Abbott Hall Museum in Kendal, was arranged by Mary Birkett who wrote the introduction to the show 'Fibre Art' which took place in March 1984 at the Bury Art Gallery in Lancashire. She says that 'it is the first exhibition of the work of contemporary felt makers staged in Great Britain'. Among exhibits was a panel in commercial felt by Diana Springall, in raised felt and rouleaux (82), while Rozanne Hawksley showed two garments – a machine embroidered sleeveless coat, and one based on peasant costume, with embroidery designed by Eirian Short, worked by hand by Rozanne Hawksley. This was a commission from Peter Walter, the marketing manager of the Lancashire felt manufacturers BCW in Bury, the reason for the venue of the exhibition. Students from colleges of art and polytechnics entered a number of felt articles, among these a third year degree student at Goldsmiths' College, Victoria Brown, showed hats created to drape over and fit the head. Other hats were decorated with embroidery. Also she exhibited a handmade felt coat, covered in silk through which small holes had been pierced in parts to reveal the brightly coloured felt. The garment was machine quilted (291).

Embroidery on paper

During the second half of the seventies an interest in handmade paper developed, increasing in popularity in the early eighties; schools of art, adult evening classes and children in schools produced a variety of thicknesses and sizes of sheets. Embroiderers, making their own paper, combined it with fabric and stitchery (255), also with screen printing and painting. (257.)

Commercial embroidery

This includes kits of all kinds, for canvas work and surface stitchery, smocking, quilting and patchwork 'packs'. A number of these kits have improved in standards of design and sometimes are a starting point for an embroiderer.

Some firms specialise in embroidery and beading for television, the theatre and the screen, and for high class garment decoration, among these Stanley Lock and Spangles; while embroidery for the Church is designed and carried out by such firms as Watts and Wippells.

Embroidery is a viable means of decoration for exclusive fabrics, for *couture* garments and for high-class articles in interior decoration. It has also been used in advertising certain products, for greeting card reproductions, and as prototypes for plastic products such as the patterning of napery and curtaining. Julia Caprara is producing garments for exclusive boutiques, Robin Giddings has designed embroidery for fabrics, worked on the Schiffli machine, and is carrying out his lace-like technique in the embellishment of fabrics and accessories. Barbara Siedlecka has carried out advertisements for Jaeger Wools using embroidery and knitting (35); some backgrounds for commercial advertising on television show embroidered decoration from time to time. Eugenie Alexander has produced posters, window displays and magazine covers in collage and embroidery, and Verina Warren is designing kits and Christmas cards for commercial reproduction.

The '62 Group

The Group has retained its momentum since its inception in 1962, with exhibitions that were often controversial, and an experimental approach to embroidery and the combining of mixed media; all of which have helped to broaden people's attitude to the craft.

Exhibitions of work were held in Greenwich, Central London, and Cardiff during 1979, resulting in members of the group giving their views on their approaches to work. Mary Maguire says that she never knew what the finished product would look like . . . 'it is of an intuitive nature . . . partially in response to the materials that I use. I like to create a feeling of preciousness and richness from what is considered "a load of rubbish"'. Renate Meyer, originally a painter, explained that she began to experiment with threads in order to improve her drawing and design, 'using a reel of cotton, unwinding it over a sticky surface I drew with a trail of thread'. She decided that her work looked flat and unsubstantial so started to do soft sculpture (67). Irene Ord felt that she could best express her thinking about surface design, with a non-functional context, by using the qualities of texture, pattern and colour of fabrics and threads. She used systems based on squares and overlapping grids, with gradations of colour and permutations of thread, fabric and stitching as additional themes (62). Verina Warren's interest was in the combination of embroidery with other media and from painting on fabric, she began to incorporate the painting with card rather than with fabric as the mounts round her work were important. She has discovered many ideas for further development, using dyes with hand and machine stitching (65). (*Embroidery*, Volume 30, Number 3, Autumn 1979.) The conclusion reached by members of the Group was that exhibitions should be held in centres other than in the London area. In the summer of 1980 a show was held at the Usher Gallery, Lincoln, while in Winchester, in 1981, the first show in a college of art was arranged. Among exhibits Kate Hobson Wells' tryptich of a landscape using dye and stitchery by hand and machine was shown. Among new members, Polly Binns' work combined woven and embroidered forms with porcelain, and Wendy Hawkin's work contained printed and stitched handmade paper (126, 127). The review in *Crafts*, January/February 1981, by Jeanette Kilner said that landscapes predominated and that although there was a lot to look at much of it was good enough to remain memorable.

Manchester Polytechnic at the end of 1981 presented an exhibition by the Group which, according to reports, was well received. It was featured on television programmes and written up in the *North-west Arts* newspaper. Few pieces of work were rejected and Isabel Dibden in her report stated that variety in style, subject matter and scale were noticeable as was the high standard achieved.

For its twentieth anniversary, 'Sign and Symbol' at Hampton Court in April 1982, there was an attempt to work to a theme. Katherine Virgils in her review of the show said 'what makes work "good" is not just the application of materials but the ironic situations in which they combine. One sees the strength of both aspects in Mary Maguire's *Roundle* (54 (a) (b)). What seems at first glance a coherent surface, on closer inspection breaks up into a swarming mass where fish hooks jostle with diamanté for attention. The juxtaposition of materials is taken even further in the "found objects" constructions of. . . Rozanne Hawksley which test to the limits the inclusion in an embroidery show. . . . What does emerge overall from this exhibition is the dilemma of the artists working in and out of several disciplines and mixed media, which focuses again on the problem of modern embroidery's eclectic nature. What worries me in general, realising the dangers of this eclecticism, is the cultivation of styles independent of any deeper reasoning, such as the regularity with which threads and ripped edges are appearing. This can be accepted and appreciated in the exquisitely simple handweaves of Alexa Wilson. . . . In other words the actions of tearing/pulling seem to have neither aesthetic nor constructional reasons, but only mimic notions of content/process found in fine art.

'If contemporary embroidery's ambitions are to deal in an enquiring manner with both its technical boundaries and its artistic aspirations . . . it must subject itself to a much more comprehensive and questioning inspection by both its makers and viewers.' (*Crafts* September/October 1982.)

My opinion was that the show was partially successful, that the general impression was of quiet, monochromatic work. Some examples showed symbolic content, others appeared to have none. Small fragments with frayed edges and machine stitched textures were gimmicks and samplers rather than works with any depth. The symbols of death by Rozanne Hawksley were among significant exhibits although they contained little or no stitchery. (*Embroidery*, Volume 33, Number 2, Summer 1982.)

The exhibition at the Seven Dials Gallery in London in the autumn of 1982 was important as it was the twentieth year of the Group's existence. With this in mind the artists showing work were able to present major examples with related studies as a series of 'small one-man shows'. (*Textile Aspects* 62 Group, 1982). According to both members and non-members of the Group this show was one of the most successful put together, with lively, experimental work. A variety of styles was seen at the Bath show in April 1983. Among works, Julia Caprara exhibited large hangings in which rug hooking was combined with stitchery (226, 227), and Renate Meyer arranged a table with every kind of fancy cake which, although carried out entirely in fabrics, I thought were a part of the private view refreshments. Linda Gomm showed freely-hanging strips of dyed silk and one example in which both free forms and a rigid, decorated background were combined (213). Beverley Clark's *Snake Piece* (221) used a smocking technique to gather together the tightly knit folds of printed fabric to form a large, snake shaped wall decoration. Figurative subjects and abstract compositions were also shown.

In *Crafts* May/June 1984 Sara Bowman wrote about the '62 Group, saying that 'it is the most important professional group in the United Kingdom. . .concerned with promoting embroidery as a valid art form. . . . Recent '62 Group exhibitions have broken the traditional boundaries of embroidery and shown a depth of vision and freedom usually associated with the realms of fine art'. Sara Bowman quotes Julia Caprara, chairperson of the Group, who says that 'members are encouraged to develop their own ideas according to their vision. What holds the Group together is the conviction that in working with textiles and threads the artist inherits a rich tradition of techniques and materials that is unique in the visual arts'. She states too that 'increasingly links are being forged with industry . . . Elaine Waller, Robin Giddings and Julia Caprara all work with fashion designers' (101, 102).

In 1984 a selection of work was shown at the Clarendon Park Festival; while a travelling exhibition, first seen in Belfast at the Arts Council gallery was scheduled for Wales and England. The highlight of the year was to send work to Tokyo, by invitation. An exhibition opened at the Hanko department store after which it travelled to the Kyoto Craft Museum.

Other groups

Groups already established continued to flourish; the **New Embroidery Group**, the **Practical Study Group** and the **Beckenham Textile Studio** each increased their membership, as did the **Embroiderers' Guild**. Barbara Siedlecka took charge of the Beckenham Textile Studio when Alison Barrell retired in 1978.

The **Society of Designer Craftsmen** held group shows of members' work in different places where mixed crafts were exhibited together. A scheme was inaugurated, too, whereby individual members could have work selected to be shown in smaller galleries during the summer months. Exhibitions were arranged of licentiates' work that had been given distinction during assessments for the BA Hons degree, which was shown in London during the autumn. Two shows mainly of textiles and ceramics were mounted at the Seven Dials Gallery in 1984 and at the same Gallery, now Smiths, in 1985.

The **Red Rose Guild**, which has always accepted embroidery and is a group of craftsmen pursuing different crafts, held annual exhibition in 1976 at the Whitworth Art Gallery in Manchester and from 1977–1980 at Manchester Polytechnic. From 1981–1983 the group exhibited in Stockport Art Gallery and in Manchester again in 1984 at the Royal Northern College of Music. Small shows were displayed in other towns, including London.

In 1976 the **Lace Guild** was formed as so many people were interested in the subject. It had its first exhibition at Sandersons in London in 1978, after which shows were held in different areas including the Bowes Museum, Barnard Castle, Co Durham; and Birmingham, Poole and Edinburgh. At the Royal School of Needlework a selection from the last two shows was held in 1982.

The Quilters' Guild was formed in August 1979 at the British Crafts Centre, its aim being 'to promote the craft of quilt making, to bring quilt makers together and to encourage and to organise selective exhibitions of quilting and patchwork'. Since its inception this Guild has held several large exhibitions (page 22).

Fibre Art, a group to which embroiderers can belong and with which they can exhibit, was started in 1980 'as an exhibition group dedicated to the formation of all forms of creative expression in the realm of fibre'. The first show was at the Roundhouse in 1980, with a number of shows following. (*Embroidery*, Volume 35, Number 3, Autumn 1984.)

North West Craftsmen was inaugurated in March 1980, for artists working in the north west, to promote sales and to encourage the development of original designs and high-quality craftsmanship. A panel selects work for exhibition which is chosen for creativity and craftsmanship, and an annual exhibition has been staged at the Royal Northern College of Music. This is proving a successful group.

The Embryo Group was formed in 1980 by Pauline Hann MA and Angela Taylor DA who studied together at Duncan of Jordanstone College of Art, Dundee. The aim in forming the Group was that membership should be open to art graduates of the College for exchange of ideas and to provide exhibition facilities. They were concerned particularly 'that embroidery should be recognised as a valid art form in its own right'.

To quote from the Dundee Creative Embroiderers, now Embryo: 'Our members are artists first . . . who have in common that they are working in the same medium . . . and drawn from a variety of disciplines; ie printed textiles, drawing and painting, illustration, print making and woven textiles. . . . Membership ranges from those who left College last year, to those who left over 25 years ago'. The result was a great variety of work seen in the three successful exhibitions in Scotland, with plans for shows further afield. In 1983 Marion Stewart, senior assistant in embroidery and women's crafts in the College of Art, who had encouraged the Group from its inception, was made Honorary President.

An extract from an article by Janet Ray in *The Scotsman*, July 1983, says: 'British embroiderers have won well-deserved kudos in recent years and Hannah Frew . . . is not boasting when she claims "We're leading the field in embroidery". . . . Yet defining a Scottish style within the British context is difficult. . . . Crissie White . . . says simply that embroidery is currently in a "baroque period" and in her view, this means "anything goes". She observed too that "embroidery tends to grow up around a group of people and flourish as much as their enthusiasm for it". Glasgow and Dundee both possess colleges of art where embroidery has been a subject of some standing, and where in Glasgow Kathleen Whyte developed the craft towards fine art. In 1957 she formed the **Glasgow School of Art Embroidery Group** which has exhibited regularly for many years in the United Kingdom. **Embryo**, formed in 1980 in Dundee, and the **New Scottish Embroidery Group** in Edinburgh, are the most recent.

'Through the Eye of a Needle', held at the City Art Centre in Edinburgh in 1982, was the first exhibition of the New Scottish Embroidery Group, the members, often trained in art rather than embroidery, being selected by invitation. Kathleen Whyte reviewing this exhibition said that the standard was uneven 'particulary so in the area of sensitivity to the textile qualities of threads and fabrics'. Both abstract and realistic approaches were seen in the exhibition and among the exhibitors Kathleen Whyte mentioned Jennifer Hex whose works she said 'were beautiful and sympathetic'. (*Embroidery*, Volume 34, Number 1, Spring 1983.)

Another new group, **The Creative Needlework Association**, organised by Gawthorpe Hall, held its first weekend conference in February 1984. The response showed that there was considerable interest in the subject of embroidery. The group attending the conference was appreciative of the lectures and visits; Audrey Walker, Joan Edwards and myself gave lectures while, at the Embroiderers' Guild, Rosemary Ewles talked about the historic collection. During the final summing up, pertinent questions were asked and a general eagerness to discuss problems and the solving of these in schools, the place of embroidery in education and other areas, were points for further discussions. Other conferences have since been held.

Exhibitions

Exhibitions of embroidery only, or as a part of a craft show, have multiplied from 1978 onwards. Professional artists, amateur embroiderers and students have presented shows of varying sizes and standards while embroidery has been accepted in some fine art shows. Groups already mentioned have held shows in London and in the provinces. They attract crowds of enthusiasts, as do those exhibitions in colleges, polytechnics and adult education centres, which have been instrumental in maintaining interest in the craft and have helped to develop awareness of current trends. Experimental work, whether appreciated or not at the time of showing, has stimulated controversy and thought on the future of embroidery, the reasons for its popularity, and discussion on 'what is embroidery and where is it going?'.

In a volume of this length it is possible to mention only a few of these shows, but some of the major ones, with reviews written at the time, may be useful in gauging the progress of embroidery, development of styles and the broadening of approaches to the craft, such as the greater use of dyes and mixed media, or the absence of stitchery in some work. To note the reaction of viewers to *avant-garde* and experimental embroidery, which is important in any creative activity, is an education in itself.

In the summer of 1979, at Charles de Temple's shop in London, two embroiderers shared a 'Craftsmen of Distinction' exhibition with another artist Anne Sicher who painted on silk. A reviewer (*Crafts* September/October 1979) thought that the exhibition 'was a beautifully presented glimpse into the dreamy world of silks', the intention having been to use silk entirely for the work. Of Lucy Goffin it was said that 'her work is intriguing. She uses heavy Assam silk to make jackets, waistcoats and tabards which are intricately embroidered. . . . The fine stitching and multitude of colours and prints mean that her garments reflect the East'. Also 'an unusual touch is added by the crests embroidered on her garments, giving the name of the designer and the year of creation. This superb attention to detail makes her garments works of art in their own right'. The garments could be worn or hung flat on a wall, as they consist of detachable pieces, are geometric in concept with embroidery worked sometimes on both sides of the shapes (76, 77).

Sue Rangeley combined hand painting and spraying with dye and quilting for her 'delicate and beautiful cushions and bags with intricate embroidered and applied flower and butterfly designs, in misty, seashell colours'. (43.)

Glasgow School of Art (Modern) Embroidery Group held an exhibition 'Small is Beautiful' in May/June 1979. At the Whitworth Art Gallery, Manchester, in the summer of 1979, an exhibition of Hungarian Costume was shown which contained embroidered garments from the sixteenth to the twentieth century, giving inspiration for present-day ideas. During this time, too, a contemporary show 'Gardens in Flower' was arranged at Doddington Hall, Lincolnshire. Four of the nine exhibitors invited were embroiderers: Lillian Delevoryas, Millie Stevens, Diana Springall and Verina Warren. A review (*Crafts* November/December 1979) said that the show could have contained more exciting work. Cherry Ann Knot, the reviewer, writing about Millie Stevens' 'quiet little embroideries with intensity and control', said they reflected her training as a painter, while Verina Warren was moving in a new direction, away from sugary landscapes to a 'cooler, often moonlit quality'.

Another exhibition at Doddington Hall, 'A Celebration of Embroidery Gardens' took place in August 1984. The review mentioned Mary Cozens Walker's large three-dimensional topiary embroidery, *Lillian in a Bush*, which contrasted in scale with that of Verina Warren whose work was meticulous, with colours evoking moods. '*Blue Frosted Garden* looked icy cold . . . perhaps bathed in moonlight.' Dyes on wet fabric created 'subtle backgrounds' that suggested ideas for Elizabeth Ashurst's machine embroidered and quilted panels, while embroideries by Thomasina Beck evoked an 'old world quality'. (*Embroidery*, Volume 35, Number 4, Winter 1984.)

At the end of 1979 artists from the 401½ Studios and Fosseway House showed work at the Commonwealth Institute. A variety of crafts was displayed, including embroidery by Sue Rangeley, Diana Harrison and Philippa Bergson. During this time, too, the Associated Board held an exhibition at Foyle's Art Gallery of O and A levels embroidery which included course work, design sheets and practical examples selected from the examinations.

Historic textiles attract attention and in March 1980 an exhibition of Irish Patchwork, 1800–1900, at Somerset House, showed some less usual techniques, including appliqué of printed chintz flowers and some early topstitched machine patchwork.

In 1980 a retrospective exhibition of embroidery from 1894–1920 was held in the Glasgow School of Art. This featured work by Jessie Rowat (later Newbery) and Ann Macbeth and also included examples by both well-known and lesser-known embroiderers of the time. The show was a revelation to many, with its wealth of ideas and colour, and Kathleen Whyte commenting on it said that 'it showed the work of a unique period . . . the glowing silk panels . . . gave a shock of delight'. She commented also on the multitude of shades and gradations of colour in shell-like effects of light and shade. 'We can only sigh and say, where have all the threads gone?' (*Embroidery*, Volume 31, Number 4, Winter 1980; *Twentieth-Century Embroidery in Great Britain to 1939*.)

At the Embroiderers' Guild exhibition at the Commonwealth Institute in the autumn of 1980, several professional embroiderers, who possessed workshops, were invited to participate. As well as embroidery by Verina Warren and Sue Rangeley, examples for Diana Springall's BBC book were exhibited. Panels predominated in the show, a number of these using straight stitch only but, as Nora Jones remarked, 'a straight stitch accurately placed is far from easy, but it is expressive and conveys meaning'. Mixed media were prominent with printed, dyed and painted fabrics combined with stitchery, while traditional techniques of hardanger, patchwork and quilting, some embellishing dress, were shown. Three-dimensional examples included a realistic cauliflower by Sheila Read and a tomb effigy by Ruth Tudor. Landscapes and garden subjects continued in popularity; patchwork and ecclesiastical embroidery were also shown. Concurrently with this work a selection of historical embroideries from the Guild collection was on view at John Barkers of Kensington. Reviewing the exhibition in the January/February 1981 issue of *Crafts* magazine, Isabelle Anscombe mentioned the popularity of landscapes and gardens and said that design and problems of aesthetics were now a part of embroidery. Among works that interested her were *Leek* by Wendy Lees, and Rozanne Hawksley's mass of stocking heads. She found the show varied and surprising.

At the end of 1980 the Glasgow School of Art Modern Embroidery Group 3 held an exhibition in Glasgow.

Michael Pinder, in his review of the exhibition by Members of the Red Rose Guild of Craftsmen held at Manchester Polytechnic in November 1980, said that the show had intellectual and, even more importantly, emotional integrity and that 'a gradual but continuous policy of raising standards of selection is paying dividends'. (*Crafts* March/April 1981.)

The first exhibition by the Quilters' Guild was held at the Seven Dials Gallery in March 1981, with traditional and contemporary quilts shown. The reviewer found most of the quilts in the traditional category disappointing and said that 'what keeps a craft alive is experiment and imagination; traditional techniques and patterns are not enough . . . it is not enough simply to exploit shape and colour. She found *Stitched Stripes* by Esther Barrett the most original exhibit in the show. Where some of the patchwork was reversed, showing paper templates and raw edges and tacking cotton among the ideas, the whole piece became 'a sampler of patchwork techniques'. Pauline Burbidge's *Pyramid I* was mentioned as giving a 'vivid and attractive effect'. (Lucinda Gane, *Crafts* July/August 1981.)

Diana Springall showed past and current work, including paintings, at Foyle's Art Gallery in the spring of 1981, with embroideries mainly in felt, in monotone, with rouleaux a main feature (82). Later in the year at the British Crafts Centre 'Stitchery' was presented, with 15 embroiderers invited to participate. Among works shown were hand embroidered, heavily textured hangings by Hannah Frew Paterson (140), a hanging by Anne Butler Morrell in hand and machine stitching on felt in brilliant colours, and landscape in hand stitching by Eleri Mills (83, 84, 85). Verina Warren combined dye with machine embroidery in her landscapes (65), while Michael Brennand-Wood (222) showed his trellis-like constructions. Kimono-shaped lacy forms, machine stitched by Robin Giddings (130) and hangings composed of small silk shapes held together by machine insertion stitches by Jane Happs (117) floated from the ceiling. I showed a small landscape in monotone with stitchery that completely covered the fabric (40).

The review of this exhibition in *Embroidery*, Volume 32, Number 2, Summer 1981, remarked that 'every technical aspect of the stitch is exploited extending the bounds of embroidery as far as they dare – using the stitch as a decorative application to pictorial designs and also as a means of constructing a surface'. Michael Brennand-Wood and Jane Happs were mentioned as using threads as visible elements of the structure, for their own decorative quality and a means of joining together such materials as wood, paper and fabric, while 'Phyllis Ross exploits the virtues of the machine, stitching two silk fabrics together in parallel lines, corded with coloured threads giving a shaded effect'. Her work was mentioned as purely aesthetic.

In December 1981 a retrospective exhibition of embroideries by Marjorie Kostenz was held in the Gunnersbury Museum, London. Her work is distinctive in style, with heavily textured areas, thick black outlines couched down with brilliant colours of thread and the application of beads and sequins, which, combined with tweeds and other textures of fabric, contribute to the individual quality of her work. The designs are pictorial, often based on her experiences in Provence and mainly of figurative or landscape subjects. (See *Twentieth-Century Embroidery in Great Britain 1940–1963*, page 59.)

At the beginning of January 1982 one of the first exhibitions of the year was held at the Oxford Gallery. I selected the artists, each with as different an approach to embroidery as possible, with among these some members of the '62 Group and the New Embroidery Group. Irene Ord, who belongs to the former, showed large square panels of silk, each dyed a different colour, containing small applied silk squares, all machine stitched (158). Linda Gomm, also a member of the '62 Group, had etched grids into large plastic squares over which embroidered and dyed squares of fabric were slung on pegs. Eleri Mills and Verina Warren both contributed embroideries based on landscape while Vicky Lugg's aerial views of potted plants showed fine detail (141). The kimono-like garments by Robin Giddings now incorporated metal threads and brightly coloured silk fragments in the machine lace patterns that he produced on the Irish machine (130). Audrey Walker's panel *A Little Bowl of Cherries* (159), and a *Bunch of Strawberries* by a student at the London College of Fashion, were both realistic in concept (148).

Joan Crossley Holland, the Director of the Oxford Gallery, in an article 'Super Stitchers' in *Embroidery*, Volume 33, Number 1, Spring 1982, said 'The needlework of happy stitchers shows awareness of painting and collage, but seldom contributes an experience particular to its medium: sometimes even in the fashion field, it loses sight of style in favour of technique. I wonder what area stitchers will claim as their own . . . who will explore new frontiers'. She mentioned work of several exhibitors but said 'the promise shown in the untitled, unfinished, unresolved but rampant stitched and dyed panels of Jane Denyer (277 and jacket cover) stems from a powerful personal vision. That quality in my opinion is what makes collecting crafts worthwhile'. 'The Maker's Eye', another show of crafts, including some textiles, was held at the Waterloo Gallery in London in the spring of 1982. Selected craftsmen chose exhibits; some were pre-war artists who tended to look for craftsmanship, while those of the post-war period favoured the arts in their selection. Enid Marx, one of the pre-war artists and a textile designer, painter, graphic designer and industrial artist, said 'skill is something which I greatly admire, particularly skill to make things which are attractive to use. . . . I personally have no space for bottles which will not hold water. . . . As an old hand I would like to add a final plea to the young craftsmen and women; craft is for quality not quirks. Doing your own thing is not enough'. (From the Catalogue of the show.) Zandra Rhodes and Pat Russell were among the few exhibitors selected to show embroidery in this exhibition.

The Fibre Art group held an exhibition in Lincoln in 1982, the reviewer mentioning the term 'fibre art' as useful in that the divisions had merged between weaving, embroidery, sculpture, painting and paper making, but it was sometimes used, too, to describe 'some strange creations'. (*Embroidery*, Volume 33, Number 2, Summer 1982.)

The Commonwealth Institute showed a collection of Guatamalan costume at the end of 1982 after it had been to the Whitworth Gallery in Manchester. The brightly coloured woven and embroidered patterns and stylised figurative and geometric motifs, the structural joining together of seams with embroidery, contained ideas that, from what is said, embroiderers found inspiring.

'Quilting, Patchwork and Appliqué', coming from the Minories in Colchester, an exhibition which included both historic and contemporary examples, was staged at the Waterloo Gallery in London for six weeks from February 1983. Present-day work included quilts by Pauline Burbidge (168, 169), Diana Harrison (135), Sue Rangeley (180, 181), Phyllis Ross (237), Mary Fogg and Michelle Walker. Colours were often brilliant, and techniques included cathedral patchwork, Italian quilting and sprayed and dyed examples.

Several exhibitions by the Quilters' Guild have taken place since. About the one in London in October 1983 the review said that many of the quilts were straight from books or copies of traditional examples, while colours were harsh with little attempt to experiment in design, to show a contemporary feeling or to use new ideas. (*Embroidery*, Volume 34, Number 4, Winter 1983.) A second national exhibition was held in Cardiff in April 1984, after which it toured. In *Crafts* July/August 1984, David Briers reviewing the show said that 'the immediate impact of the Quilters' Guild exhibition was elating'. He was surprised to find that works he covered were by people without an orthodox art and design training and were 'as compelling as any similar sized paintings seen on these gallery walls for many a year'. The quilts he disliked were by people with 'full-blown art college training', often third-hand derivatives of well-known painters' works. They were entered in the show as quilts or hangings, the latter, to him, giving 'a negative response'.

Exhibitions were held, too, by the Practical Study Group, at the Embroiderers' Guild in December 1982 to January 1983 being reviewed in *Embroidery*, Volume 34, Number 1, Spring 1983. This said that 'a lot of work was of the exploratory level and had not been developed fully', but 'as an exhibition was successful in showing experimental pieces by practising teachers'.

Another show, 'From Paper to Thread', by the Group, at the Embroiderers' Guild in the spring of 1984, was reviewed by Audrey McLeod, a painter. She said that the exhibition 'explores those regions of design between idea and realisation with sketches and design sheets shown with the finished works. . . . Design is in the doing and not a mechanical progression towards a preconceived solution. . . . Embroidery comes happily into its own in the precision of Daphne Nicholson's *Activity* (236). That design is integral with the making is shown in the manipulation of fabric surface into tucks, pleats and free smocking by Dorothy Tucker and in the machined grids and cut surfaces by Vicky Lugg'. (*Embroidery*, Volume 35, Number 2, Summer 1984.)

In March 1983 The School of Art, Goldsmiths' College, held an exhibition of textiles, drawings, paintings and constructions by the staff of the Embroidery Department. A review in *Crafts* May/June 1983 said that the exhibition 'offered a typically heterogenous range of work, the most convincing . . . linked to the concerns of the department. . . . Christine Risley's large machine embroideries were interesting. . . . Her work is neither figurative nor symmetrically abstract. She has developed into the Miró of machine embroidery (223), though simply because of the obsessive look of stitchery it is difficult not to be reminded of Outsider Art. It is hard to imagine that chance could play much part in embroidery, but Christine Risley's work makes this a refreshing possibility. Audrey Walker's *There's a rainbow round my shoulder and a sky of blue above* (colour plate 9) was a pretty piece which recalled traditional patchwork but managed to dissolve into an effect of landscape. Eirian Short's honest work illustrates the limitations of needlework and tapestry as a vehicle for landscape and indeed for any sort of conventional representation (143, 209).

'. . . Margaret Hall works figuratively but on a tiny, humorous scale (236) exquisitely pastiching sources as varied as Japanese prints and Elizabethan portraits. . . . Michael Brennand-Wood's three pieces looked assured. In *Untitled II* he had toughened up his fragile structures with a coating of sand and paint, a reminder of how restrained and inventive his formal exploration of embroidery structures has been.'

In the summer of 1983 Joan Edwards arranged a show at the Embroiderers' Guild of work by individual embroiderers from 1900 to 1940. The stitching in a number of examples was very fine, completely covering the background fabric. Colours were delicate and styles were varied although mainly pictorial. According to the information on the show, design and technique were 'hotly discussed during this period'.

The exhibition in 1983 by the Embroiderers' Guild at the Harris Art Gallery and Museum, Preston, had a varied reception. I found the show overcrowded and according to one visitor 'too many items were overworked . . . obviously contrived and dated so that they had lost the emotional freshness and vitality of good embroidery. . . . The conclusion was that 'the exhibition is not up to the standard one has come to expect of the Guild'.

The New Embroidery Group continued to hold shows in a number of galleries during the early eighties. An ambitious venture was at the Seven Dials Gallery in London, in October 1982. Two shows, one in the summer of 1983 and one in the summer of 1984, were held at Leighton House in Kensington. As the gallery is small work displayed was limited in size and amount. The comments on the recent show were that 'the work is better than that shown last year, it has more punch, is less pretty and stronger in design'. Some embroidered garments, including decorated hats, embroidered cushions, and several three-dimensional articles with wit and humour, were on view. Moyra McNeill in her review said that the show was a skilful combination of fabric and thread.

Dorothy Tucker reviewed a show by Helen Pincus at The Ice House, in the summer of 1984 where her work was based on the structure of music theme. She said that the panels, although small in scale, showed a 'series of apparently geometric designs of stunning textural surface . . . with wrapped rods of varying thickness . . . some panels kaleidoscopic in colour or very restrained'. An innovative use of diamond mesh sheet was incorporated in many of the panels. (*Embroidery*, Volume 35, Number 4, Winter 1984.)

The exhibition at York City Art Gallery in October 1983 contained mainly ecclesiastical embroidery, with a small section of secular work and a few historical examples. According to the review in *Embroidery*, Volume 34, Number 4, Winter 1983, the standard was variable. Among exhibits were Beryl Dean's chasuble for the Cathedral of the Forest, Ione Dorrington's cope for St Peter-le-Poer, Muswell Hill, London (colour plate 3), and one cope from the Chester set by Judy Barry and Beryl Patten.

One of the Winchester copes (60) by the Beckenham Adult Centre staff was also shown, as was Joyce Conwy Evans' cartoon for the altar frontal for Canterbury Cathedral (162). Kneelers were exhibited from different places and among secular exhibits were landscapes by Verina Warren (65). I showed two small landscapes in monotone with raised stitchery (40). The reviewer felt that selection should have been more vigorous and that there was little innovative design, but suggested a future show. (*Embroidery*, Volume 34, Number 4, Winter 1983.)

A fourth exhibition by Embryo was held in Dundee in November 1983, mainly of small framed works. Among these Rosemary Campbell's landscapes in layered and stitched transparent fabrics were mentioned as successful, as was the embroidery of Pauline Hann (196) whose *On the Crest of a Wave II* (266, 267) gave a dazzling effect (*Embroidery*, Volume 35, Number 2, Summer 1984.)

In 1984 an exhibition of textiles was arranged to coincide with the Bath festival; the theme was 'Maze Makers' to which a number of well-known embroiderers contributed; among these were Pauline Burbidge, Jean Davey Winter, Isabel Dibden, Sian Martin, Christine Risley, Verina Warren and Kate Hobson-Wells.

'Material Evidence' at Camden Arts Centre in January–February 1985 was a retrospective exhibition of work by artists who had trained at Goldsmith's School of Art in the Textiles Department, during the period 1974–84. In the *Quarterly Journal of the Guild of Weavers, Spinners and Dyers*, Spring 1985, the review said that the work was very varied both in ideas and materials, also that 'stitchery, the distinguished tradition of Goldsmiths' College, was still evident; embroidery has been the basis for all its textile work from 1954–1974. However, since then the BA and diploma students of the College's textile department have been encouraged to combine and experiment freely with textile techniques and materials. However the principal concerns of Goldsmiths' textile Art course are not of definition and evaluation by craft, but are to do with personal expression. Idea and intention come first, and then the most appropriate choice of medium to carry out that expression follow'. She said that although some exhibits could have been worn, the exhibition was mainly of non-functional works of art.

Another review of the exhibition mentioned that 'Makers are not just uncertain about what to call their work, in many cases they seem quite deeply uncertain about what it is. . . . It is nothing new and nothing bad, for an audience to find any kind of creative work baffling or challenging, it is the apparent bafflement of some of the creators that matters'.

Jane Happ's and Phyllis Ross were mentioned as showing good work, as were others; but – 'Between the good art and the good craft, the refusal to acknowledge the difference, or to substitute for it any other criteria for discrimination, opened up a gap.' (*Crafts* May/June 1985.)

Community work

Several community embroideries commenced before 1978 were completed during the period 1978–84, while others have since been undertaken. Among work now completed is *Bunyan's Dream* (56, 57) designed by Edward Bawden CBE RA and carried out co-operatively by members of the Bedfordshire Music and Art Club: this was commenced in September 1977 and on view in July 1980.

The New Forest Embroidery (110, 111) was commissioned in 1979 in commemoration of the Forest's 900 years of age. The work was financed by local industry and Belinda Montagu was asked to design the hangings. These were worked by some 55 embroiderers, supervised by the designer. They hang as three panels between the windows on the wall of the Verderer's Court in the Queen's House in Lyndhurst.

The Maidenhead Charter Hanging (178) was designed by Jan Beaney and Jean Littlejohn and worked by 70 people, taking 20 weeks to complete. The occasion was to commemorate the 400th anniversary of the town's charter and was on view in March 1982, (*Embroidery*, Volume 33, Number 2, Summer 1982.)

Another community embroidery is the *Croydon Hanging* (281) designed by Moyra McNeill and worked in six months by the 50 members of the Croydon Branch of the Embroiderers' Guild. The hanging was completed in March 1984, having been devised and executed to commemorate the centenary year of the Borough of Croydon. It hangs in Teberner House, Croydon.

A community project promoted by Liberty and thought up by Kaffe Fassett who designs and carries out canvas embroidery schemes, produced 'a phenomenal' result. The aim was to give everyone in the country the opportunity to work a 6-in. (15cm) square on canvas with the theme *Count Your Blessings* 'to make a positive statement to counteract the gloom surrounding much of contemporary life'. The idea was broadcast on the Pebble Mill at One programme by BBC Television. Those who responded to this represented 'a wide cross section of people and many subjects; among these birds, animals, houses, churches, sports and activities, such as knitting and car racing. A screen designed and constructed by Robert Buis of 14 panels with 784 squares had been made up and eventually will be housed in Chatsworth House. Other squares, of which over 2500 were received, have been made into hangings; one for Pebble Mill, and one for the Wool Marketing Board who sponsored the project. Two hangings were made up of children's work. (*Embroidery*, Volume 35, Number 4, Winter 1984.)

The Wisborough Tapestry is a communally worked hanging in tent stitch on canvas, carried out by villagers of Wisborough Green. The idea was suggested by Pamela Warburton as a lasting commemoration of the Queen's Silver Jubilee in 1977. It was designed by Mr Pat Gierth and under the auspices of the Wisborough Green Trust was executed over eight years with more than eighty people helping to stitch it. It was unveiled in the Parish Church of St Peter ad Vincula, Wisborough Green in March 1985 (298).

Community banners

According to Rozsika Parker in her book *The Subversive Stitch*, published by the Women's Press in 1984, 'the most recent radical movement to employ embroidery is the Women's Peace Movement. Large, brightly coloured embroidered and appliquéd banners have been produced since 1978, to be carried on marches and, more recently, attached to the perimeter fence at Greenham Common air base, where the women camp in protest against cruise missiles'.

Embroiderers' Guild

From December 1975 until 1980 the Guild was without a proper home. The Wimpole Street lease expired in 1975 and with no permanent premises forseeable, the Guild moved temporarily to Greycoat Place, where there was little space so classes could not be held and visitors could be seen only by appointment. Messrs J & P Coats provided accommodation for a limited period at their Bolton Street premises, where a small study centre was established in the spring of 1977, while administration continued at Greycoat Place. By the summer of 1978 the Guild was offered a permanent place at Hampton Court Palace, and in December 1979 were given temporary rooms at the Palace until repairs had been completed in the new quarters. Again, with a lack of space, visitors were discouraged, although a few classes were organised; but on 10 June 1981 the new headquarters of the Guild were officially opened. Since then full activities have been resumed and early in 1984 another apartment, currently under repair, was offered to the Guild to give the much needed space for expansion.

The Young Embroiderers' Society, which was started by Lynette de Denne in 1974, was successful for several years, then discontinued. In 1981 a revival was discussed and this new Society is now flourishing at Hampton Court. Groups in other areas have also started classes for young embroiderers.

What might be termed a communal effort came to fruition in June 1984 with many people involved. This was an idea conceived by Jennifer Harrison and Jane Lemon to hold an 'International Festival of Embroidery'. This became a reality with the help of a number of sponsors and the co-operation of the Embroiderers' Guild, and in June 1984 the Festival was held at Clarendon Park near Salisbury. An extensive programme of events was planned including demonstrations, lectures and classes; examples of embroidery and lace from the Guild collection were displayed, also modern ecclesiastical embroidery and a selection of '62 Group work. Embroideries from Europe were shown in this country for the first time, and the Young Embroiderers' work created interest. Audrey Walker, in reviewing the show, said that she wondered 'just what is it about embroidery that fascinates women to such an extent?'. She commented on the overcrowding when she visited the Festival on the first Saturday of its opening and in conclusion said that "More" is not necessarily "better" and although the occasion obviously gave a great deal of pleasure to a lot of people there is a reverse side to that particular coin. . . . The Guild has a superb asset in its historic collection on which it could capitalise to far greater effect. Dare I suggest that "big" events could be more selective and specialised . . . that distinction could be drawn between those which are primarily educational, those which are concerned with entertainment and fund-raising and those who seek to promote the very highest aesthetic standards'. (*Embroidery*, Volume 35, Number 3, Autumn 1984.)

Opinions Audrey Walker, in the foreword to the catalogue of the embroidery degree show at Goldsmiths' School of Art in 1978, wrote: 'The history of textiles is amazingly rich and reveals fascinating variations in their cultural significance. Out of the surfeit of possibilities the students must learn to select, to refine and re-define. This is a slow process and likely to last a lifetime if done honestly. Stitching, weaving, knitting, dyeing, printing are the activities they may be engaged in and the context in which they build a visual language, but the processes are subordinate to the chief concern – the development of concepts'.

In her editorial in *Embroidery*, Volume 29, Number 3, Autumn 1978, Nora Jones said that degree shows that year contained far more stitchery than 'some people would have us believe and was noticeable in the hangings and the three-dimensional work on display'. This comment was made as there was unrest among the more traditional embroiderers that stitchery as such was disappearing. Previously some of the experimental work produced by the '62 Group and in some degree shows had been criticised for containing little or no embroidery, although on closer examination this assumption was not strictly true, as stitchery had been used with more thought, limited too, in order to say what was intended. In earlier decades of the century, among amateur embroiderers, the delight was in stitching, employing a number of stitches instead of one or two only. By the 1980s the aims of many amateur embroiderers were to learn to draw and to design before stitching, this contributing to the gradual rise in standards as well as in appreciation of the craft. Exhibitions, day courses, residential courses, as well as books, have helped to give a broader outlook to embroidery, as have experiments employing non-embroidery materials such as card, plaster and metal, combined with fabric as collage, these again suggesting ideas for more stitchery.

Diana Thornton, a young embroiderer, in an article on note books, defined the creative mind as 'that which is capable of assembling a piece of work in such a way that interesting and original relationships are established . . . the need to find new and unusual relationships between materials . . . is a constant challenge to those who attempt to create art'. (*Embroidery*, Volume 30, Number 1, Spring 1979.)

Other excellent articles were written by the honours degree students. In 1979 Helen Wright, a student from Loughborough College of Art, talking of work sheets said that a note book was often the most lively part of an embroiderer's work, but as the pages could only be seen singly it was a good idea to tear these out and to staple a number of pages to a large piece of card so that the progress of ideas could then be followed. As an extension of the sketch book and as a means of display, the sheets mounted on card could act as inspiration. (*Embroidery*, Volume 30, Number 2, Summer 1979.)

Lorna Tressider thinks that embroidery is at present very diverse, with personal approaches as well as work produced in colleges of art and polytechnics where there are, inevitably, collective styles. These she feels range from 'fine art', where the stitching is almost lost and she would not call embroidery, the decorated frame that is no longer a regular shape, to the image covered with sequins and knots. In the past embroidery has been for dress and domestic purposes; much of it today is in the making of pictures and wall decorations as well as three-dimensional constructions. What will 'last and live' is difficult to say but she feels that the embroiderer must still use the skills of the needle and not rely on passing fashions where the craft, at times, is almost lost.

Richard Box showed a collection of work in March 1980 and had some useful things to say. He believes that 'there are many advantages in making several studies of one subject'. He found it better to work on more than one piece at a time in order to understand his subjects more fully. In his flower paintings he tried to obtain different aspects in each study, such as the character of flowers and their relationship to their surroundings, or the rhythm and growing patterns, colour and light, omitting naturalism. The composition and the media of its execution also concerned him in 'making a picture which is an object in its own right'. He has recently been translating some of these paintings into fabric with machine stitchery, as near to the original works as possible. His attitude is experimental, his early pieces being based on Wagner's operas, Greek myths and legends while, later, his ideas have developed into embroidery and collage from his paintings of flowers and trees. (Colour plate 12.)

Nora Jones, in her editorial in *Embroidery*, Volume 30, Number 4, Winter 1979, remarked on the importance of looking, mentioning Richard Box as 'a professional painter and expert in embroidery and collage, who finds that a series of works on one subject has "a stimulating cross reference". His paintings are complete in themselves but the collages based on the same subjects are the result of the former although each medium demands different things'.

Again in her editorial in *Embroidery*, Volume 31, Number 1, Spring 1980, Nora Jones points out that 'craftsmanship – or good technique – is important and satisfying, but it does seem that it commands less respect in the field of textiles than in . . . furniture or musical instruments. . . . We may be at the beginning of a period when craftsmanship – the ability to handle stitches and to make up well and a sensitivity to fabric – will have a strong appeal. There has to be a spark, a subtle difference, without it, craftsmanship can look tired and stale'.

For *Embroidery*, Volume 34, Number 2, Summer 1983, I wrote an article tracing the last 50 years of embroidery and commenting on the changes that had taken place during that time. Santina Levey, Keeper in the Department of Dress and Textiles at the Victoria and Albert Museum, in her foreword to this issue said that at its best the magazine had 'balanced the sometimes conflicting interests of tradition and innovation' and 'has encouraged its readers to look about, to vary their approach and to find stimulation and sources of creativity outside their normal channels'.

Embroiderers

Susan Aikin in charge of embroidery at Ulster Polytechnic feels that today the craft has a highly personal approach, making maximum use of the wide range of threads and materials available. She feels that drawing or visual research has again become an important basis of both ideas and design. At present she finds that bold colour and large scale works are popular, also that embroidery is gaining acceptance by the public as an art form in its own right, partly as there is an increasing interest in the subject by some galleries. (193.)

Doris Anwyl, teaching at a day centre for the disabled, finds that collage with very little stitching is the best means of approach to maintain interest without too much hard physical work. She feels that the area, for the young disabled person in particular, needs developing and that embroidery and collage are two of the most rewarding means of increasing imagination, initiative and independence. Group projects are successful, as hidden talents come to light during the process of drawing, designing, cutting, and in choosing suitable colours and fabrics that are appropriate to the subjects chosen. (145.)

Alison Barrell continues with landscapes that have become three-dimensional, having invented ways in which to achieve these. An example is *Winter Hill*, a *papier mâché* form covered in a variety of white fabrics (See *Twentieth-Century Embroidery 1964–1977*, figure 127). Her later experiments involve mixed media using wire, resin and the properties of metal (burnt, tarnished and beaten) together with fabrics and threads. (7, 33.)

Since the partnership of **Judy Barry** and **Beryl Patten** began in 1973, they have completed many ecclesiastical commissions, sharing the work equally and evolving a distinctive style. (*Twentieth-Century Embroidery 1964–1977* page 88.) In a craft supplement to *The Crafts and NW Arts* 1983, Gerry Harris, writing about their work says that they 'upset many of the familiar preconceptions concerning ecclesiastical embroidery . . . while respecting liturgical traditions and conventions, their designs are contemporary and original: employing mainly machine embroidery . . . to provide vestments, altar cloths and hangings that are unusual and, above all, economical. . . . Commissions come from churches of all denominations. . . . On accepting a commission and before producing any designs Judy and Beryl visit the site. . . . They are concerned that their designs harmonise with and complement the surroundings. . . . They seldom use furnishing fabric or synthetic fibres, finding that natural fibres wear better. . . . They regard themselves as craftspeople in the artisan tradition with a skill used to serve others'. (151, 152, 153, 165; and colour plate 4.)

Anne Bingham believes strongly in the value of the City and Guilds courses as a creative study. They fulfil an important need in the community, offering adult part-time students a structured, testing course that helps to develop their creative potential and build confidence through learning and achievement. This is necessary for the mature student who, having raised a family and been away from the demands of industry for several years. (258, 287.)

Michael Brennand-Wood has developed a personal approach in the use of fabric and thread, making painted grids of different sizes in wood. Over these grids, designed as regular or irregular structures, dyed fabrics and threads are wrapped, tied and twisted to form wall decorations. A review in *Crafts* magazine November/ December 1980, reads 'his work has no category . . . it is atmospheric and tangible and suited as much to the rarefied atmosphere of an art gallery as it is to a community centre. He makes the most of whatever he uses and whatever situation arises, choosing to study embroidery as it might give him time to experiment. He also studied bobbin lace and discovered that he could obtain sound, texture and movement by hanging paper cubes on the ends of threads and became interested in embroidery and in the movement of thread to make stitches. He is concerned with the situation in which his work is placed as well as in its appearance'. (222.)

Audrey Brockbank continues to use old shirts as a basis of design, developing a more abstract concept. She incorporates seams, buttonholes and various parts of the garments into compositions, using paint, dye, machine and hand stitching. An interest in weaving of ikat-dyed strips of fabrics which she makes into garments, have an affinity with her collages where folded areas such as parts of collars, frayed and cut edges, are also incorporated.

Recently she has been using paper garment patterns with fabric, their fragility contrasting with the fabric. She works on several compositions at a time, with ideas often developed from an interest in atmospheric effects, beaches and landscapes. (29, 228.)

Pauline Burbidge's patchworks, according to *Crafts* July/August 1979, are works of art in their own right; in vivid colours and geometric patterns they are destined to be collectors items. Her work is pictorial or geometric, sometimes the two overlapping. She started with small designs for cushions using natural forms as a basis, then designed geometric, brightly coloured patterns while other pieces, with carefully placed tones, have a three-dimensional appearance. She dyes her own fabrics to obtain the exact colours she requires; her technique is meticulous, her later work showing complicated repetitive geometric shapes that appear three dimensional, combined with areas of patterned fabrics, freely arranged. (169.)

Anne Butler Morrell's great interest is in promoting hand stitchery. She is at present researching into the origin of embroidery stitches; visiting archaeologists to discuss with them their fragments of stitchery finds, and to ascertain the use of stitches, why they were done, and their similarities and differences in various parts of the world. Her book on hand stitches, *The Batsford Encyclopaedia of Embroidery Stitches*, published in 1979, demonstrates this interest. (9, 128, 187, 248.)

Rosemary Macmillan Campbell says that drawing is her source of ideas and is fascinated by natural forms. Through her teaching she has become interested in using traditional techniques freely, such as beadwork, metal-thread embroidery and shadow work. Machine embroidery, spraying and painting with dye are often used but her drawing suggests her choice of technique. A member of the Embroiderers' Guild said 'Rosemary Campbell excels in her choice of mixed media . . . and in the intelligence of her designs'. (*The Scotsman*, 1981.)

Julia Caprara has a workshop at Stitch Design where she is embroidering garments on coarse net, using rags, ribbons, lace and braids darned into coarse mesh fabric, a development from her interest in textures. Her latest works contain textured surfaces but are in brilliant colours contrasting with delicate ones, using rag-hooking techniques, appliqué and fine hand and machine stitching. She continues to use anything that expresses her ideas, saying that technique has always been secondary to content in her work. (42, 72, 101, 102, 226, 227; *Twentieth-Century Embroidery 1964–77* pages 88–89.)

Joan Cleaver thinks that embroidery should always have a sense of purpose as in the past: *Opus Anglicanum* depicted Bible stories, while Elizabethan embroidery was a part of the architecture and the furniture of that time. She mentions the fact that embroidery for fashion can underline a mood or emphasise a line but that the important point is having a convincing thought to express, with an understanding of scale, materials and colour. Drawing to her is also important as a means of developing a theme, and of recording information that could lead to a whole series of embroideries. She says that many of her students produce 'one-offs', the most successful being those who can take an idea and get some mileage out of it.

Heather Clarke-Martin worked for some time on 'see-through' embroideries which included cut work, lace and the use of transparent fabrics. After spending two years in Papua, New Guinea, her return via Indonesia has rekindled her interest in 'see-through' work inspired by Javanese puppets (*Textile Aspects* '62 Group, 1982.)

A great interest in Romanesque and Mediaeval architecture has influenced **Isabel Clover** in her embroidery, which is mainly ecclesiastical, and for East Anglia where she finds the churches give her scope for rich colour and texture. It is also a challenge for her to work to a given space. She draws her designs with care, most of them for large scale commissions; natural forms and symbolism being a basis of ideas for many of these. Appliqué in various fabrics, enriched with padded gold kid, beads and cords are favourite methods of work. (61, 87.)

Elspeth Crawford regards embroidery as 'painting with cloth and thread' and continues her interest in the ideas, colours and embroideries of primitive and peasant textiles. Her more recent work echoes some of these in her use of brilliant colours, her rag tassels and fringes, and fragmented fabrics patched together in her evocative but simplified floral shapes. These influences are seen in the vitality of her work. She also uses figurative ideas and continues to paint. (265.)

Jean Davey Winter is keen on the dichotomy between hard and soft materials. She has produced plaster forms into which she has embedded fabrics, paper, wire and threads, finding that the soft fabric in comparison with the hard plaster fascinates her. Recently she has made paper which is often printed and stitched into by hand and machine, and is also draped or folded into subtle shapes. (176, 177, 255, 257.)

Barbara Dawson has worked freelance since 1983 but still does some lecturing and teaching. In her research on a book she is writing on *White Work* she has found that the fabric on which embroidery is worked affects the technique chosen and that the integration of background and stitches depends on the choice of fabric. She has also come to the conclusion that personally-made threads by twisting, spinning and plying can give rise to inventive techniques and innovative pattern that has individuality. (86.)

Beryl Dean has sufficient commissioned work to last for years and at present (1984–85) is embroidering a cope in dense black and dark gold, graduating to light, shining gold at the top. When completed it will be known as the 'Resurrection Cope'. She remarked on the advancement of ecclesiastical embroidery in this country, saying 'I contrast it with 1955 when my idea was to try to do something about introducing a contemporary approach to the subject and I designed many things that students helped to execute. I felt that unless people saw modern things they couldn't do them themselves?' In 1958 she put on an exhibition of this work, but couldn't find modern church embroidery in England with which to illustrate her first book. She acknowledged the support of Dorothy Allsopp without whom none of this would have happened, neither could she have carried out the work without the techniques learnt at the Royal School of Needlework. The changed outlook on ecclesiastical embroidery has stemmed from the 1955 classes which she started at the Hammersmith College of Art and Building. Quoting from a recent book review, it said 'Beryl Dean's outstanding technical skill and view of embroidery has completely altered much ecclesiastical embroidery during the last thirty years'. (89, 279 and colour plate 6.)

Isabel Dibden says that there must be an understanding of what embroidery is and the purposes for which it could be used. At present she feels that the craft is in the doldrums; that time and money are lacking; that everyone wants immediate results, and that students seem unable to spend long, hard hours on a piece of work, endeavouring to get it right. She is impatient, too, once she has started an embroidery, with the pace of life a continual rush from one thing to the next at breakneck speed. She would like to do less but do it well. Her geometric design quilts are often in brilliant colours, using patchwork and machine embroidery. (120, 252.)

Marjorie Dyer says that she inclines more to fabrics than painting. Her great interest is in colour and its relation to tonal values, 'so I work also in black and white, but have an interest too in the mingling of primary colours'. She finds that she can achieve real texture, less easy in painting, also she likes the considered, mathematical working out of a set problem which is a challenge.

Joan Edwards retired in 1978 from the Victoria and Albert Museum in order to continue with freelance work. She is now publishing her own booklets on particular aspects of embroidery – people, styles, periods and subjects of interest not hitherto studied in depth. These booklets are the outcome of her interest in research into the history of embroidery.

Maria-Theresa Fernandes enjoys working on a large scale using mixed media. Some of her compositions consist of a series of equal-sized frames put together, often ten or twelve to create a complete work. She draws her ideas constantly from landscapes, interpreting these freely in machine and hand stitching. She uses dyes, a mixture of fabrics, rug hooking over metal mesh and anything that expresses what she wants to say. Her early work often appeared 'shaggy' with ends of threads trailing across the surface of the fabrics. During her visit to the USA she became impressed by the vastness of the country and this has affected her later designs which show increasing areas of space. She incorporates wrapping into her compositions, with colours often co-ordinated as warm or cool schemes. (16, 17, 18, 243.)

Hannah Frew Paterson says that 'Recently I have been exploring larger scale stitchery using hand spun, thick silk threads, and weaving the particular background required for the work in hand. This in time has led to a closer integration between weave and embroidery. Most of my interest lies in the use of natural fibres, threads and materials and in producing good colour compositions'. A private commission in 1977, *Sea and Sand*, explored the three-dimensional properties of fabric and thread, the latter related to the movement of water. Lately she has been working entirely with stitchery, to express her ideas. Her most ambitious work is *The Cardross Panel* (107). a tryptich incorporating many ideas. (108, 140, 295 and *Twentieth-Century Embroidery 1964–77* page 90.)

Robin Giddings, who trained as an embroiderer developed a method to make lace-like structures worked on the Irish machine, stitching on to vanishing muslin. He says: 'My experiments with guipure lace have led to my creation of wholly personal embroidered structures. I have tried to create from formal, or clearly defined shapes, delicate and skeletal forms: sometimes using mosaics of fabric, densely or openly; at other times letting a very airy web of threads carry the design; so that when folded as a garment it will form changing patterns of light and shade'. On the Manchester MA course for textiles he experimented with design on the Schiffli machine, translating his intuitive drawings into more elaborate structures.

In 1982 Robin Giddings was awarded a Crafts Council grant for equipping a workshop in order to continue making his embroidered creations. Since setting up his studio he has carried out work for dress designers and individual clients and continues to experiment with his lace techniques, making accessories and working on commissions. (130.)

Lucy Goffin was trained in ceramics but preferred to work in textiles, using natural fibres and natural dyes such as indigo. She gained knowledge of construction when employed by a theatrical costumier and is now designing and making unique garments. She is fascinated by clothes as flat patterns that unbutton to become wall decorations, also in concealed features such as hidden pockets and details.

Lucy Goffin does not consider her clothes follow a fashion in the sense of the 'fashion world', but that they are a gradual development of ideas and skills that enable her to become more fluent in her media. She is now less concerned with jackets but is making things for rooms rather than for bodies. This new direction involves some change of scale in her designs, but she maintains that the two areas work for both the body and the room. (76, 77.)

Linda Gomm uses a variety of techniques and mixed media. She develops a theme as a series of abstract wall decorations, often with geometrical progressions. Etched plastic grids, plastic rods, dyed silk in strips that float freely, resin and glass fibre are all employed in her work. (213.)

Esther Grainger, since her retirement, spends much time now in designing and carrying out embroidered collage hangings, unglazed and unframed and larger than earlier work that was mounted under glass. She dislikes glass which reduces the textures of the fabrics so she works in dark colours that appear less susceptible to dirt. Her ideas develop from artifacts such as the Balinese God, the Mayan Stela or from architectural sources such as *Moissac Remembered*, illustrated in *Twentieth-Century Embroidery 1940–1963* figure 143 page 148. She feels that the collages combine the rhythm of craft with the flexibility of painting and the seductive quality of fabrics. (12, 112, 113, 119; and colour plate 5.)

In a profile on **Margaret Hall**'s work in *Embroidery*, Volume 34, Number 4, Winter 1983, the writer says she 'must surely do the finest hand embroidery of anyone in Britain today. Using goldwork techniques, she meticulously couches threads over padded shapes to create sculptured figures that seem to change appearance according to the position of the light'.

Margaret Hall thinks that 'embroidery is one of the hardest media to learn' and her results are always complicated. She dislikes framed embroideries that 'ape painting' and 'has tried various ways to overcome this by making padded frames and *papier mâché* ones'. She uses machine embroidery to cover the surface of a fabric completely with pattern, the direction in which she stitches giving light and shade and colour changes. (270.)

Jennifer Hex says that she prefers not to commit her thoughts to paper but to let her work speak for itself. At present she is exploiting the qualities of silk and linen threads, using simple stitches; the subject matter usually derived from nature. (93, 94, 95.)

Kate Hobson-Wells works primarily as a painter and draughtsman, her embroideries developing from sketches and paperwork, and combining painting on canvas with machine and hand embroidery. Her work is often on a large scale, with several panels adjacent in a series, or a triptych to expand the image, and to express space and the freshness of the open landscape. From a distance the embroidery functions as painting. Only on close inspection, or by the play of light across the fabric, are the details of stitch, texture and hand work to be appreciated. It is this aspect of the work that she hopes will give delight to both the viewer and the maker; its attributes slowly appearing with nearer proximity. Her recent work is on a small scale with garden and landscape subjects. (144.)

Polly Hope's subjects are wide, fantastic, mythical and present day. Recently she has made portraits with glass fibre features and stuffed bodies. John Russell, art critic, says: 'Polly Hope has an unsleeping fancy and contagious high spirits'.

Edward Lucie Smith, in an article in *Art in the 70's* published by Phaidon in 1980, describes Polly Hope's hangings as 'flamboyant, padded, quilted and appliquéd. . . . Her work can be thought of in two ways . . . as something that falls within a traditional craft orbit and which, despite its much more ambitious scale, can be compared to seventeenth-century stumpwork; or else as something which responds to other aspects of modernism . . . through extending the idea of collage and through making a feminist statement by its choice of technique. . . . They [her collages] restore to art a kind of innocent, guilt-free playfulness which has become increasingly rare'. (6, 78.)

Constance Howard An article on my career by Anne Butler Morrell was published in *Crafts* in March/April 1982, stating my aims in trying to raise the status and standards of embroidery from the fifties to the seventies. It traced briefly the development of embroidery, with particular reference to Goldsmiths' School of Art during that time. Audrey Walker says in this article 'Due to her pioneering spirit and incredible energy the Department had grown, in 25 years, from a mere gleam in her eye to a place of international prestige in the teaching of embroidery as an art form. The case she made for embroidery to be viewed as a serious art medium no longer needs special pleading. Instead, it takes its rightful and distinctive place as one of the most expressive ways to realise an idea visually – not only within the textile arts but in the broader context of art generally'. (40, 271, 272, 299, 300 and *Twentieth-Century Embroidery 1964–77* page 59.)

Edith John, now retired, retains her original aims, which are to discover through experiments the fluidity of stitches and to encourage others to do the same. She is interested in discovering new ways of developing and combining different techniques as opposed to keeping them in separate compartments. (282.)

Nora Jones died in June 1981. She had been the editor of *Embroidery* since 1964. A tribute to her by Audrey Tucker praised her high standard of journalism, her knowledge of historic and foreign textiles, also her indefatigable energy in visiting degree shows. Her interviews with established embroiderers and the giving of space in the journal to young embroiderers was a part of her policy. With her sense of humour and her perceptiveness her editorial comments were apt and informative, her training in embroidery at Bromley College of Art having given her a good grounding in the subject. Her own work was mainly in the field of ecclesiastical stitchery. Her book, *Embroidery*, was published in 1978 by Macdonald.

Margaret Kaye continues her work for the Church, and has designed and made frontals and smaller items since her retirement. From 1978 she has worked in paper collage making small drawings and paintings of abstract landscapes – all with some degree of collage, often adding details with pencil, chalks and paint. Without previous drawing, her collages contain stitching where necessary and employ whatever fabrics will express what she wants to say. She builds these up step by step, her ideas developing as she progresses, but her selection of fabrics and colours form a basis for her ideas. (109, 191.)

Janet Ledsham has recently developed three-dimensional forms with threads knotted and interwoven to give fine mesh textures, and with loose threads hanging to give an effect of movement. Her work is hand stitched, with thread direction and colour important to her to create the qualities she finds in marsh and woodland in the County of Antrim. As her work is often done on location some of the embroideries have the appearance of sketches freely interpreted. She uses handmade paper and stitching combined with handmade felt and makes collages of transparent fabrics laid one over another, all treated with great individuality and expertise. (97, 106, 107, 114, 142, 183.)

Wendy Lees has had varied experiences as an artist and as a teacher but says that the commission for Elvin Hall, London University, Institute of Education, was her most formidable undertaking. She trained as a printmaker and fabric printer, now combining print and embroidery. She has been interested in dance and movement for some time and has designed a number of panels and hangings on this theme, many of them a combination of print, fabric and thread. Her work is generally for wall decoration, using appliqué, surface stitching by hand and machine, and print. (214, 215.)

Malcolm Lochhead's later work consists of freelance design for the interiors of shops and houses. He is involved in ecclesiastical embroidery, too, designing a commission for the Chapel of St Andrew, Glasgow Cathedral, dedicated to the nurses of Scotland and promoted by the Nursing Association. He has designed church furnishings and costumes for the stage and television, as well as canvas embroidery.

Madeleine Mainstone, Director of the Education Department of the Victoria and Albert Museum, died in October 1979. Joan Edwards paid a tribute to her foresight and enthusiasm, saying that Madeleine Mainstone had from 1962 developed the Department considerably and also had a particular interest in embroidery. Through her interest in the subject, Joan Edwards was asked to teach in the Department, conducting the Ten-week Courses in embroidery (*Twentieth-Century Embroidery 1964–1977* page 10) which proved very successful and were received with enthusiasm. (*Embroidery*, Volume 31, Number 2, Summer 1980.)

Enid Mason carries out machine embroidery, often on an old 201K Singer machine, and teaches courses for the Women's Institutes on the subject. She finds that textures and colours are often her starting point in design, rather than subject matter. She believes that the different methods of embroidery should be taught and understood properly, before free, experimental work is undertaken. (188.)

Kirsty McFarlane is interested in a number of embroidery techniques and likes to design so that materials and methods of work shape the finished piece of embroidery. Her range of styles is superficially dissimilar but her use of certain techniques is seen throughout her examples. She derives her ideas usually from natural forms, very seldom working from the figure, depending on the Scottish surroundings for inspiration and says that she cannot imagine working anywhere else. Traditional methods of working interest her and she enjoys solving technical problems. She weaves rugs, wall hangings and tapestries as well as carrying out embroideries.

In January 1982 she became Weaver in Residence at the Paisley Museum and Art Gallery, the first such appointment of this kind and one which involves an exhibition at the end of each year. (71, 115.)

Moyra McNeill says that in her training verbalising about reasons for their work was not encouraged, they just drew and embroidered, somewhat haphazardly. This tends to mark her work, but she has a compulsive interest in fabric and thread, and their endless combinations. Two themes have been of continual interest to her: one the spatial relationship of canopies of summer leaves, their spaced trunks below; the other the motor car, a symbol to her of modern life – a deceptive image, time saving, essential but often the reverse. She feels that butterflies reflect her embroidery, flitting impulsively from one influence to another, and provide inspiration for her book *Machine Embroidery: Lace and See-through Techniques*, Batsford 1985. (14, 138, 199, 281.)

Renate Meyer, originally a painter, now works in three dimensions, making water colours of her ideas before carrying them out as soft sculptures in fabric and threads. Her work is often symbolic; her apple sculptures based on a sphere expressing the life cycle. About her fancy cakes, more real than reality, she says: 'I enjoy the humour and ambiguity of enticing food coupled with dire warnings on what will happen to you should you consume it.' (*Textile Aspects* 62 Group, 1982.) Her fabric stones have arisen from her interest in small, geometric, three dimensional shapes. (9, 67, 148 and colour plate 8.)

Lesley Miller often works three dimensionally, using stitches and threads that completely cover the fabric ground. Since 1978 she has been working on small commissions using the knitting machine for woven backgrounds with applied knitted pieces in relief, combined with free embroidery. She has also been concentrating on machine embroidery, with some appliqué and surface stitching, working on silk. (46 and *Twentieth-Century Embroidery 1964–77* page 90.)

Many younger embroiderers became known during the second half of the 1970s.

Eleri Mills became Artist in Residence at Alsager College, Crewe. She said 'to me embroidery is an art form which maintains the freedom of painting, yet has a wealth of traditional techniques which act as an endless inspiration'. The Welsh agricultural background is the source of many of her ideas. She likes the element of growth and starts at the bottom of an embroidery, working upwards, saying that the secret is never to hesitate or unpick.

She works mainly from landscape using hand stitching and dye, often with fabric stretched over card shapes, and straight stitches worked over one another giving an illusion of depth. Her colours are based on those of moorland scenery, with stitching sometimes minimal but expressive. The combination of very fine threads worked freely, with areas of coarse threads massed together, create a sense of distance seen in much of her work. In an exhibition held in 1980 in the Royal Northern College of Music, a *Crafts* magazine review said that she had 'a feeling for infinite expanses of nature, very rarely using man-made objects. . . . She makes careful studies and samples, good in their own right'. (2, 83, 84, 85, 249, 250.)

Betty Myerscough has been working on commissions for large hangings and prefers to carry out this type of work. She feels that there is a need for them in modern buildings. (58, 59.)

Annwen Nicholas works from her colour sketches and drawings of landscape, using the property of fabrics with machine embroidery to produce atmospheric effects in which her interest lies. Her sources of inspiration derive from the Derbyshire hills, Cheshire, Snowdonia and Anglesey.

E K Norris has been fascinated by embroidery since childhood, when she went through all the traditional techniques. She became tired of copying from books, realising that this knowledge was not enough. She says that her most rewarding pieces have been in using gold metal threads for ecclesiastical commissions, but she finds all kinds of embroidery equally absorbing. There is never enough time for what she wants to do. She is intrigued too by the history of embroidery and finds the experimental outlook in using threads and fabrics exhilirating and thinks that whichever way the craft develops in the future it will be enthralling.

Jane Page has always had an interest in fabrics and threads, in their relationships and what could be accomplished entirely with stitchery, the mingling of textures and colours, the direction and depth of a stitch, and the effects obtained. She finds that traditional techniques are adaptable to present-day design for garments and accessories. She works entirely in threads with hand stitchery, using no dyes or applied fabrics. Most of her work is derived from drawings of her surroundings, often becoming abstract or geometric pattern when simplified as design and translated into stitchery. She is interested in working on fine canvas using near tones of colour to obtain merging effects. She has executed a number of ecclesiastical embroideries in which gold thread worked solidly gives tone by the direction in which the gold is laid. (74, 75, 131; and *Twentieth-Century Embroidery 1964–77* page 90.)

Dorothy Reglar has continued as a freelance fashion designer. Since visiting Greece and Turkey her interest in peasant costume has increased and she has incorporated some of the ideas she has seen into her own creations. She uses few types of stitches for embroidery. Recently she visited India where she gathered more ideas which she is again incorporating into her garments. (290 and *Twentieth-Century Embroidery 1964–77* page 91.)

In *Crafts* June/July 1978, an account of **Zandra Rhodes** and her creations said that her work was 'delicate and exotic, bold, subtle, in fact contrasting'. The strength of her work lies in the fact that the printed patterns and the garments are designed together, and although the patterns are limited, the blocks are interchanged to suit whatever shapes she has in mind, thus giving quite different effects. The fabrics are gathered, pleated and layered in tiers, mainly chiffons or fine silks, with one-colour prints. Embroidery in metal threads and silk with beads, sequins, pearls and diamanté, decorate many of the garments. Embroidery is by hand, finely worked in silk threads. (182, 301 and colour plate 7.)

Christine Risley's work at present consists of richly patterned and coloured fragments that are placed closely together to form a sumptuous, ornate and lavishly stitched and appliquéd textile. The units are an amalgamation of reality and fantasy, things seen, felt and remembered. She would like her work to be a total expression of what she is, so that it is read as being a visual multi-faceted image of experiences that for many reasons cannot be conveyed by words, but are evocative when expressed visually. Her method is to stitch a number of separate motifs, then to assemble them on another fabric, rather as in a jig saw puzzle, adding machine embroidery to connect them until the richness she requires is obtained. (115, 216.)

Phyllis Ross has been designing and executing quilts since she made them while a student at Goldsmiths' School of Art in the late seventies. She uses white satin or white jap silk for these, stitching the patterns, usually geometric in style, by machine, padded, quilted or corded. Sometimes the colour is monochromatic; sometimes the stitching is in various colours – the Italian quilting in brilliant colours threaded under the white silk giving a surface of delicate tints; or lines of straight stitching in colours on the surface of the silk are modified by sheen and direction. The basis of her design is repetition of geometric forms; the movement of water and waves having a strong influence on her work.

In an exhibition of 'Textiles Today' in Cambridge in 1981, selected by Marianne Straub, Phyllis Ross was praised for her 'finely quilted surfaces that express space and movement and colour development'. Some of her hangings worked in narrow strips, are stitched in delicate colours of pink, green and pale blue Italian quilting with the twin needle on white jap silk, the stitching giving an undulating movement. The joining of strips at intervals serves to emphasise this movement. (237.)

Pat Russell obtained a bursary from the Crafts Council in 1978, to experiment with letter forms with different tools and materials, including work in fabric and machine stitching. She now designs almost entirely for ecclesiastical robes and furnishings for cathedrals and churches in the South of England. (4, 163, 164 and *Twentieth-Century Embroidery 1964–77* page 51.)

The Very Reverend Peter Moore, Dean of St Alban's, in a commentary on Church embroidery said, about a design derived from orchards that it 'has resulted in a fascinating pattern of colours whose relationship to the original is not at first hand, easy to discern . . . but what does it matter . . . or take the patterns formed by lettering: these can be of quite extraordinary beauty and yet be unrecognised as lettering. . . . Does this matter? Certainly not in some examples of Pat Russell's where form and colour yield a beautiful pattern derived from calligraphy'. (*Embroidery*, Volume 29, Number 2, Summer 1978.)

Jennifer Shonk, in *Textile Aspects* 62 Group, 1982, says that her work is erratic, both in output and content, owing to other commitments, so she does not follow a theme in depth. Her visual ideas develop before she has time to carry them out as a practical proposition. She works mainly figuratively combining design and execution, her drawings becoming part of the embroidery, paper and fabric merging with applied fabrics and stitchery to embellish them. (164, 244.)

Eirian Short continued with her themes during the seventies, working out ideas on each of her subjects until, as far as she was concerned, their possibilities were exhausted. In the summer number of *Embroidery* in 1983 she gave some of her reasons for returning to naturalism or realism towards the end of the decade. She said that in the fifties flat pattern was the accepted style, evolved from reality often as a vignette surrounded by space; her outlook until 1967 was that embroidery did not contain perspective or shading. She had now changed and her work is as realistic as possible with shading to show roundness. In *The Clump* (143) her idea was that one could walk through the roundness of the trees. Her new approach came from seeing 13 foxes hanging from a tree in Wales – a scene which she felt she had to embroider. She used straight stitches, layer upon layer, to obtain the effect of her drawing. The landscape element gradually took over and although she felt that her work would be unacceptable to those embroiderers whose preference was for flat pattern, she says 'every artist should work according to his own convictions and not be swayed by fashion or by adverse criticism; also that photographs on their own are never really satisfactory. The selection and understanding that come through drawing are vital'. (24, 143, 209.)

Lilla Speir, during the late seventies and the early eighties, has concentrated on work that has a functional place in society, rather than using embroidery as a fine art medium. She has tried to avoid her studio developing as a cottage industry and to retain the 'one off' quality in her work in spite of producing many quilts, cushion covers and other domestic articles. In her exhibition at Broughton Castle in 1980 she showed domestic embroideries and in other exhibitions has maintained the balance between large hangings and quilts and very small, pictorial embroideries. (241.)

Millicent Spiller, trained as a painter, says that she finds pleasure and delight now in interpreting her drawings and paintings into fabric and threads, but that her work succeeds or fails according to whether her first encounter with her subject remains true or intense enough to communicate something of what she has seen or felt to the onlooker. She is interested particularly in natural phenomena, in plants and their growth (Frontispiece), the delicacy or brilliance of colour, in atmosphere and mood as seen in *Winter Sea* (92).

Ann Spring works mainly in silk and cotton materials, folding, pleating, rolling and curving shapes to give shallow relief effects. Most of her work is hand sewn, geometric, often repetitive in design; her colour is sometimes near in tone to give subtlety, sometimes strongly contrasting in tone and colour. There are no raw edges visible and fragile materials are often padded and quilted. The results are similar to relief sculptures. (240 and colour plate 10.)

Diana Springall trained as a painter but is equally interested in embroidery. Much of her work is developed from drawings of rock strata, bark and other natural forms. She has devised a method of work that gives a sculptural effect consisting of felt or fabric rouleaux stitched over cord. These are manipulated into a variety of designs sewn on to a background and are in monochrome; tones being obtained by the relief structures. Other examples of her work in patchwork or appliqué are often brightly coloured. Lately she has been designing from figurative subjects. Her book *Twelve British Embroiderers* was produced in Japan and published towards the end of 1984. In spite of devoting considerable time to the chairmanship of the Embroiderers' Guild from which she retired in 1985, she continues to embroider and to paint. (49, 82, 157.)

Margaret Swales, a former student of Birmingham College of Art, Birmingham Polytechnic, works within a broad range from small, machine embroidered pictures of floral and landscape subjects to large-scale commissions. Local landscape, natural forms and contrasts of texture give her inspiration. She has executed some ecclesiastical work, and recently been involved in embroidery for interiors. (205.)

Lorna Tressider's work resolved itself into using the aesthetics of drawing and painting combined, with an emphasis on the play of light. She uses domestic scenes as subjects, trying to make her embroidery 'more real than reality', so her work has a strong pictorial quality. She uses the Irish machine with variegated and shaded threads for subjects that often involve still life, floral forms and plant life. She has recently carried out ideas based on things seen through glass, using machine embroidery. (36.)

Dorothy Tucker is interested in the stitch as a mark and as a means of expression, as well as a way of building up surface decoration and texture. She finds the relationship between drawing and embroidery a challenge, and the subtlety of the embroidered surface, with the combination of printed and woven pattern, an intriguing design problem. She makes drawings and careful studies for her designs, finding that examples of embroidery with a purpose, such as the decoration of garments, involve a particular use of materials and processes, with the limitations again presenting a challenge. (4, 5, 129.)

Stephanie Tuckwell says: 'My embroidery stems from drawings and paper collages. I generally begin with a series of watercolour studies of an object such as a fish, a stone, a crumpled tin can, . . . anything which I find exciting for its surface qualities. These I interpret through the use of monoprinting/spraying/painting/stitching with a Bernina and/or Cornely/manipulating the materials, . . . and from the resulting variety of colour, shape and texture I build my collages'. (From the '62 Group Newsletter, July 1983.) (166, 167, 173, 288.)

Ruth Tudor works mainly in machine embroidery, using figurative subjects in many of her examples. She has been inspired by mediaeval ecclesiastical sculptures and has produced three-dimensional, machine stitched, portraits based on fourteenth-century paintings and manuscripts; also an effigy of a mediaeval woman on a tomb, as well as imaginative nymph-like creatures, using fine fabrics, subtle colours and machine embroidery with some hand work. She is more interested in architecture as such, rather than in ecclesiastical work, often incorporating ideas drawn from religious buildings, but developed as secular embroideries. (216, 217, 218.)

Audrey Walker uses direct experiences for her designs, evolved from detailed drawings and paintings of landscape and related subjects. Her aim is to achieve a 'mysterious effect which evokes atmosphere and the character of a place through the use of fabrics and threads'. To obtain the quality of real textiles she says that she 'finds this a wonderful adventure and very challenging'. Her recent work involves a great deal of machine embroidery, overlaid in parts with hand stitching, or work entirely in hand stitching with fine techniques in contrast to her bolder embroideries, often in wools, as seen in her earlier works. By the direction of stitch she obtains effects of light and shade, as seen in *A Little Bowl of Cherries* (159). Her textures mixing hand and machine embroidery give a variety of surfaces that she finds fascinating. (Colour plate 9 and *Twentieth-Century Embroidery 1964–77*, page 92.)

Mary Ward says she tries 'to create calm, static, two-dimensional geometric compositions that develop movement by subtle colour changes and varying perspective as the viewer moves'. By this means her aim is to stimulate optical effects of lenses, prisms and mirrors. She uses mainly straight stitching or buttonhole. Circles of stitching appear in many of her works, often 'floating' from the background, an effect achieved with tones and colour. (105.)

Verina Warren's early examples show pattern painted to the edges of the frames on card mounts. Later, space became important, with empty fields, more sky and fine detail in machine embroidery. She uses spray-dyed areas that appear translucent in contrast with the density of machine embroidery with detailed, painted insets and wrapped silk borders instead of gold threads, and has gone through several phases during the late seventies and early eighties. Stewart Warren dyes some of the fabrics while Verina Warren carries out the stitchery and, since the late seventies, they have worked together earning their living from embroidery. Recently, a more naturalistic approach to landscape has developed, with more painted areas stitched over by hand and machine, that from a distance merge with the dye, and with mounts also painted to extend the landscape further. Poetry has been a source of inspiration in some of these works. Another venture is in painting and stitching in silk. (65; see also *Twentieth-Century Embroidery 1964–77*, page 92.)

Stewart Warren promotes Verina's designs in other areas. Working with a small textile firm, her designs now appear as quilted cushions, whilst the printing of Verina's embroideries in the form of cards and notelets has developed into the production of a limited edition.

Crissie White in the seventies commented on the continued development and change in the area of structured textiles, also the desire of students to 'do their own thing', concentrating on personal development rather than facing the problems of designing for commissioned work or for industry. She continues her interest in patchwork.

In a new edition of her book *Design for Embroidery* published in 1983, **Kathleen Whyte** says 'Art is about values and embroidery, like any other creative activity, provides a medium for training the senses to recognize them. It develops . . . a visual sense . . . it provides opportunities for discriminating choice, sharpening the critical faculty, and creating standards of quality. . . . 'At the present time the demarcation between one form of expression and another is breaking down . . . the concept of "embroidery" has widened greatly . . . but . . . the more an art form stretches out to experiment or to become involved in ideas belonging to other media, the more it is necessary to investigate its own foundations'.

Previously commenting on new samples for the Embroiderers' Guild, for which she was the supervisor, with members of the Scottish branches working them, she wrote 'stitches alone are like words in a dictionary. They need a thought or theme to make them speak'. Her aim was an organised tone and colour sequence, with a planned arrangement of stitches, requiring a simple choice with the colour combinations. (*Embroidery*, Volume 31, Number 1, Spring 1980.) (85, 133, 296 and *Twentieth-Century Embroidery 1964–77* page 92.)

Anna Wilson finds teaching stimulating and is concerned with inspiring students to make personal statements, also to keep stitching articulate and lively. Her own work has grown from small panels to those of a considerable size during the mid-seventies but she is now interested in small, richly stitched, almost encrusted embroideries worked by hand, often for domestic settings.

Carrie Robertson Wright says that the starting point for her embroideries are 'scraps of landscape' taken from small sketches. She is fascinated by borders, frames and windows, revealed in the construction of her work. She uses various techniques and frequently dyes her own threads as the correct colour for her ideas is important to her. She uses natural fabrics such as silk and cotton. (224, 225.)

Looking ahead

From information gained by research, from opinions of individuals and from reviews of exhibitions, it would appear that embroidery is a vitally alive craft/art. There is still controversy over its status but the important consideration is that its standards have been maintained. Changes in styles, in uses of techniques, in emphasis at certain times on particular aspects of embroidery, are inevitable, such as the making of banners during the latter half of the nineteenth century; the interest in wall decorations during the late thirties onwards; and now the craze for patchwork and quilting. Interest in ecclesiastical embroidery since the early sixties has increased as it did in the same period in the nineteenth century. Figurative design; design based on natural subjects; geometric design and, today, computer patterns used in design, come and go as do fashions in dress, interior design and other fields of creativity.

Much experiment, the use of mixed media and machine embroidery, are particular to the twentieth century. An awareness of environment, of colour and texture and a wider interest in art, the plea for more education in this subject and in the crafts generally, have been conductive to the raising of standards of appreciation of all forms of art.

Design and drawing are still the essentials from which aesthetic appreciation and embroidery with meaning can develop. There is, however, a lack of understanding of the meaning of design by the general public who know 'what they like', but is this good enough? Embroidery continues to be a subject omitted from conversations by many artists and groups of artists. Why? By looking ahead these questions should be seriously considered.

To quote Kate Walker, from *The Subversive Stitch* by Rozsika Parker, is a fitting ending to this history. 'Passivity and obedience, moreover, are the very opposites of the qualities necessary to make sustained effort in needlework. What's required are physical and mental skills, fine aesthetic judgement in colour, texture and composition; patience during long training and assertive individuality of design (and consequent disobedience of aesthetic convention).'

Summary from 1978

Prominent people

Dorothy Allsopp	Beryl Dean	Beryl Patten
Judy Barry	Patricia Foulds	Sue Rangeley
Jan Beaney	Hannah Frew Paterson	Zandra Rhodes
Pauline Burbidge	Bill Gibb	Christine Risley
Anne Butler Morrell	Anthea Godfrey	Pat Russell
Richard Box	Lucy Goffin	Eirian Short
Michael Brennan-Wood	Diana Harrison	Barbara Siedlecka
Valerie Campbell-Harding	Constance Howard	Diana Springall
Isabel Clover	Eleri Mills	Audrey Walker
Joyce Conwy Evans	Moyra McNeill	Verina Warren
Jean Davey Winter	Bruce Oldfield	Crissie White

Events

1979 The Quilter's Guild formed

1979 Glasgow School of Art became a centre for the BA Honours Degree in embroidery

1979 The *Chester Tapestry* completed

1980 Fibre Arts formed

1980 Embroiderers' Guild moved to Hampton Court Palace

1980	Embryo Group, Dundee, inaugurated
1980	The North West Craftsmen Group formed
1980	The New Scottish Embroidery Group, Edinburgh
1980	The Embroiderers' Guild exhibition, Commonwealth Institute
1981	The official opening of the new headquarters of the Embroiderers' Guild, Hampton Court Palace – June
1981	July wedding of the Prince of Wales to Lady Diana Spencer
1981	The Young Embroiderers' Society re-commenced
1981	The Falklands War, May to July
1981	'Stitchery' – an exhibition at the Crafts Centre of Great Britain
1982	'Superstitchers' – Oxford Gallery, High Street, Oxford
1983	Stitch Design, an independent Textile Art Centre opened in March
1983	Preston, Harris Gallery, Embroiderers' Guild exhibition
1983	Quilting, Patchwork and Appliqué – exhibition at the Waterloo Gallery
1984	Exhibition of felt articles – Bury Art Gallery
1984–85	Coalminers' strike from March to March
1984	Creative Needlework Association formed
1984	Festival of Embroidery, Clarendon Park – June
1985	Celebrations of VE Day, forty years on
1985	'Material Evidence' – textiles by students trained at Goldsmiths' School of Art 1974–85, Camden Arts Centre

Main types of embroidery from 1978

Continuing interest in ecclesiastical embroidery
Mixed media prominent, using dyes, painting on silk, batik
Quilting and patchwork increasing in popularity
Little embroidery seen on so-called embroidery at the beginning of the 1980s, but signs of a return to stitchery later
Collages of fabric, paper and thread
Stitchery on handmade felt and paper
Commercial embroidery on clothes end of 1970s – cut work, sequin and bead decoration, often 1920s influence in design
Embroidery on clothes, batik plus embroidery, patchwork and appliqué using contrasting textures of lace, satin and calico. Quilting fashionable
Increase in the number of classes for the C & G examinations

Books since 1978

1978	*Textile Crafts*, editor Constance Howard, Pitman
1978	*Needlework*, Bridgeman and Drury, Paddington Press
1978	*Embroidery – New Approaches*, Jan Beaney, Pelham Books
1978	*Embroidery*, Nora Jones, Macdonald Guidelines
1979	*Constance Howard's Book of Stitches*, Batsford
1979	*Encyclopaedia of Embroidery Stitches*, Anne Butler, Batsford: paperback 1983
1979	*Quilting*, Eirian Short, Batsford
1979	*Creative Needlecraft*, Lynette de Denne, Marks & Spencer
1979	*Faces and Figures*, Valerie Campbell-Harding, Batsford
1979	*Traditional Smocks and Smocking*, Oenone Cave (reprint), Mills and Boon
1980	*Canvas Embroidery*, Diana Springall (new edition), Batsford
1980	*Figures on Fabric*, Margaret Swain, A & C Black
1980	*Dictionary of Canvas Stitches*, Mary Rhodes, Batsford

1980 *Embroidery and Nature*, Jan Messent, Batsford: paperback 1984

1980 *Embroidery*, Diana Springall, BBC publication

1981 *Embroidery for Religion and Ceremonial*, Beryl Dean, Batsford

1981 *Twentieth-Century Embroidery in Great Britain to 1939*, Constance Howard, Batsford

1982 *Smocks and Smocking*, Beverly Marshall, Alpha Books

1982 *Church Embroidery*, Beryl Dean, Mowbray

1983 *Twentieth-Century Embroidery in Great Britain 1940–63*, Constance Howard, Batsford

1983 *Patterns for Canvas Embroidery*, Diana Jones, paperback, Batsford

1983 *Design in Embroidery*, Kathleen Whyte, new edition, Batsford

1983 *Strip Patchwork*, Valerie Campbell-Harding, Batsford

1983 *Advanced Embroidery Techniques*, Beryl Johnson, Batsford

1984 *Twentieth-Century Embroidery in Great Britain 1964–77*, Constance Howard, Batsford

1984 *Batsford Encyclopaedia of Embroidery Techniques*, Gay Swift, Batsford

1984 *Embroiderd Boxes*, Jane Lemon, Batsford paperback

1984 *Ideas for Canvas Work*, Mary Rhodes, Batsford paperback

1984 *Embroidery and Animals*, Jan Messent, Batsford

1984 *Every Kind of Patchwork*, Valerie Campbell Harding, Batsford

1984 *Smocking – Traditional and Modern Approaches*, Oenone Cave and Jean Hodges, Batsford

1984 *The Subversive Stitch*, Rozsika Parker, The Womens' Press

1984 *Needlework School* – Practical Study Group, Winward Press

1985 *Embroidery for Fashion*, Gisela Banbury and Angela Dewar, Batsford

1985 *Embroidery and Architecture*, Jan Messent, Batsford

1985 *Stitches – new approaches*, Jan Beaney, Batsford

1985 *Using Simple Embroidery Stitches*, Anne Morrell, Batsford paperback

1985 *Machine Embroidery; Lace and See-Through Techniques*, Moyra McNeill, Batsford

1985 *Textures in Embroidery*, Valerie Campbell-Harding, Batsford paperback

1986 *Twentieth-Century Embroidery in Great Britain from 1978*, Constance Howard, Batsford

Search Press Books on a variety of techniques

Batsford Embroidery paperbacks
Catalogues and pamphlets from exhibitions
Magazines: *Crafts* and *Embroidery*

1 1978 – Linda Callinan. A panel by a student at Loughborough College of Art and Design. It is based on football, emphasising the money aspect. Worked in machine embroidery over screen printing

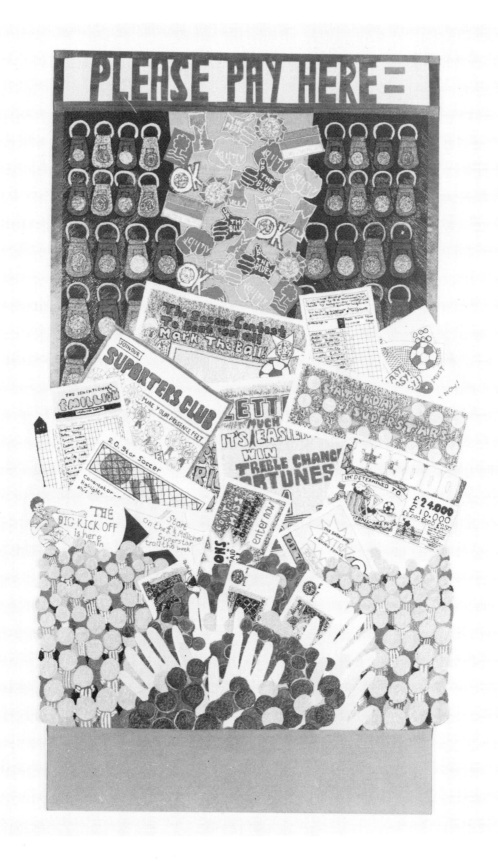

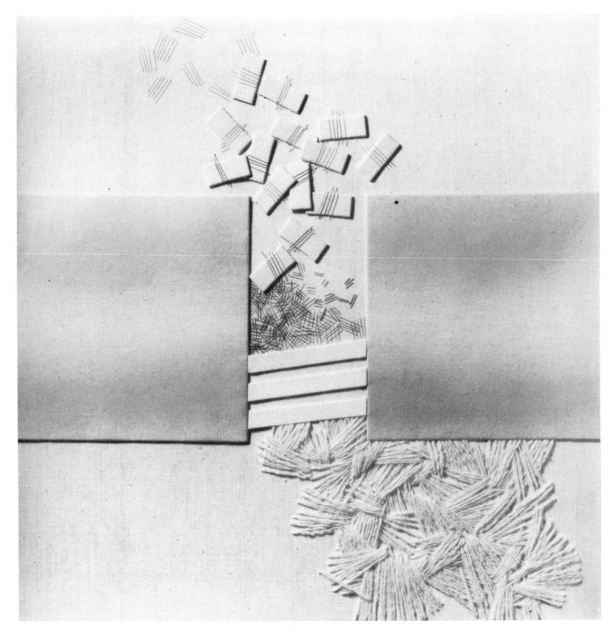

2 Above: 1978 – Eleri Mills. A panel 20½ in. (52 cm) square. Fabric shapes are stretched over card and applied to the background; with blue and green dyes sprayed over the large area. Small fabric covered rectangles of card are secured with dark or light threads. Straight stitches are in fine black and fawn threads and in heavy cream threads.
Photograph by Hawkley Studios

3 Right: 1978 – Leslie Buckingham. A panel by a student at Loughborough College of Art and Design. Spray dyed and worked in hand and machine embroidery

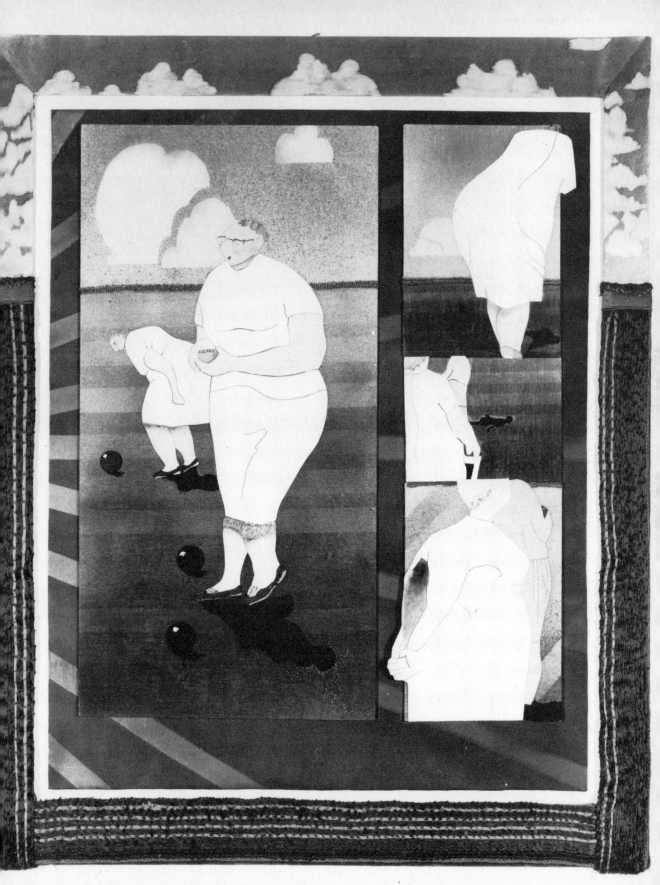

4 1978 – Dorothy Tucker. *Lavender,* **54 in. × 45 in. (137 cm × 114 cm). The background is a mid-blue with mauve, purple and blue rags for flowers, and hand dyed threads for stitchery. Grey-greens are used for the stems and leaves.** *Photograph by John Hunnex*

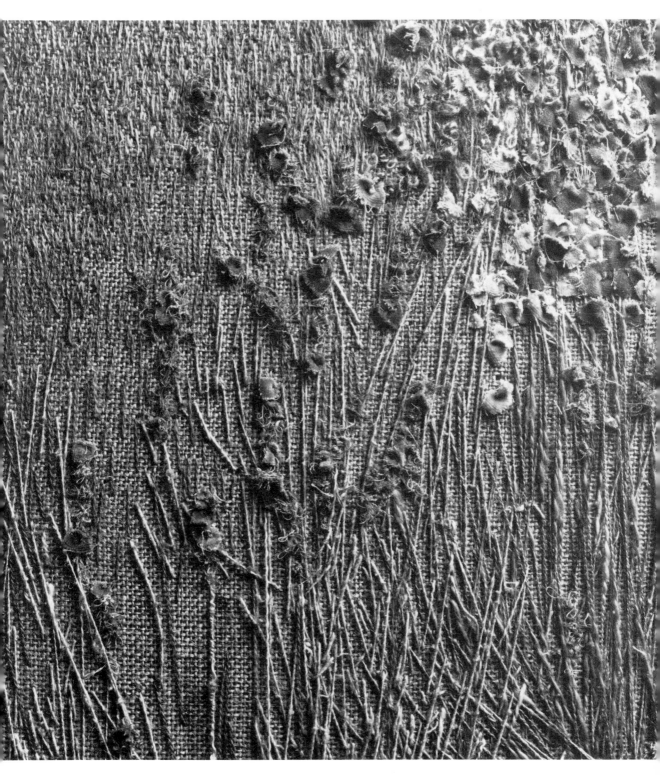

5 1978 – Dorothy Tucker. A detail of *Lavender*

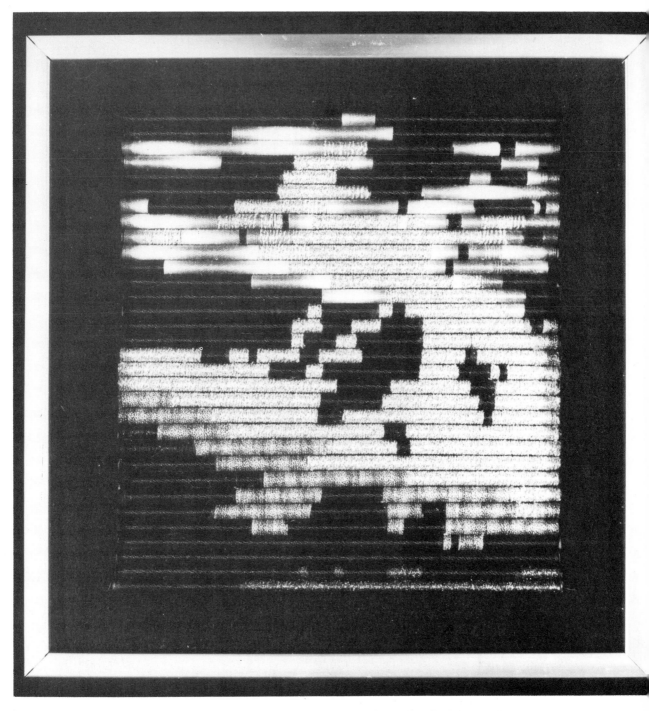

6 Left: 1978 – Polly Hope. *Africa*. A panel 5 ft 10 in. × 8ft
2½ in. (1.80 m × 2.50 m) in appliqué with padding to give a relief
effect

7 Above: 1978 – Alison Barrell, *Butterfly Wing*. Resin rods
bound in perle cotton and lurex threads. Based on the study
of a butterfly's wing

8 1978 – Elizabeth Ford. A hanging approximately 42 in. × 24 in. (140 cm × 51 cm) on a turquoise background with a dark red diamond and black satin border. The stitching is entirely on the Irish machine using a number of colours of thread. Appliqué in orange, dull orange, red, blue and lavender. *Photograph by Hawkley Studios*

9 1978 – Anne Butler Morrell. *Diamonds.* A panel 22 in. × 13 in. (56 cm × 33 cm), with fabric over card and canvas stitchery. *Propety of the Ministry of the Environment*

10 1978 – Heather Clarke-Martin. *Up the Garden Path*, 8 in. (20 cm) square. Hand embroidery in grey, cream and silver; denim and silk. Detached filling stitches and straight stitch fillings

11 1978 – Heather Clarke-Martin. *Belle Vue*, 8 in. (20 cm) square. Hand embroidery in grey, cream and silver. Denim, silk cut work

embroidery in grey, cream and silver.
12 Facing page: 1978–79 – Esther Grainger *Clonfert Doorway*. A panel $79\frac{1}{4}$ in. × $44\frac{1}{4}$ in. (201.5 cm × 112.5 cm). Collage in a variety of fabrics and colours, with some stitchery

13 1978 – Beryl Page. *Jardinière*, approximately 24 in. × 12 in. (61 cm × 30.5 cm). A collage of brightly coloured cotton fabrics with a pot of gold linen, all laid over black felt to give a strong outline. Details are couched

14 1978 – Moyra McNeill. *Graven Image.* **A panel approximately 40 in. × 28 in. (101.5 cm × 71 cm) started as an exercise in technical metal-thread shading. The body of the car is couched in black thread over silver, the wheels are in leather and suede, the clouds in net and domette spray dyed with the road in white plastic 'kid'.** *Owned by Mrs C Colman*

15 Above: 1978 – Ann Hunter, a student at Manchester Polytechnic. An ecclesiastical hanging based on the Trinity. Included are handwoven strips of fabric with hand and machine embroidery in silk and wool

16 Right: 1978 – Maria-Theresa Fernandes. *Vistas*. A detail, in various fabrics, dye, and hand and machine embroidery

17 1978 – Maria-Theresa Fernandes.
Doors to Freedom. **A series of episodes
in her life. A kind of patchwork 8½ ft ×
4 ft (2.59 m × 1.22 m) with dye and hand
and machine embroidery. The dye is
dark greyish with touches of greens,
ochre and other colours, and small areas
of sewn rags, with textures in wool and
cotton**

18 Right: 1978 – Maria-Theresa Fernandes. A detail of the hanging *Doors to Freedom*

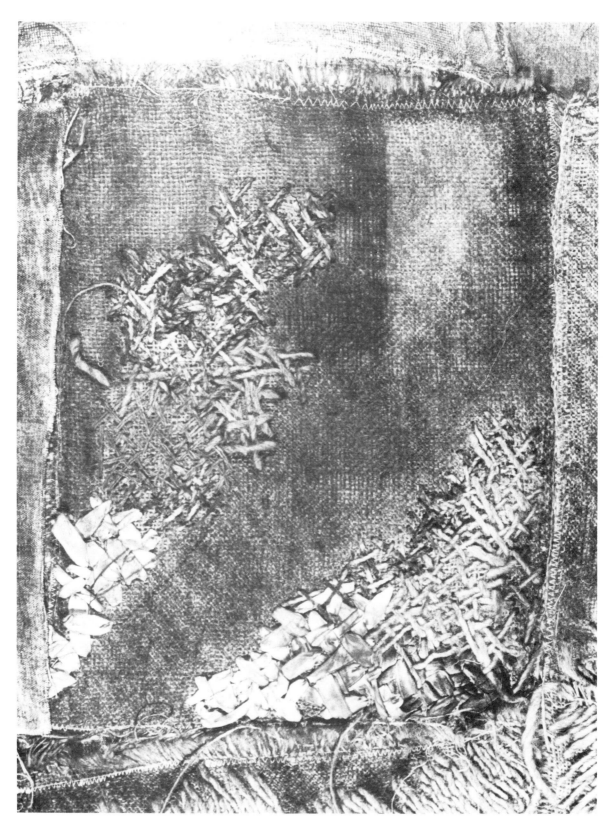

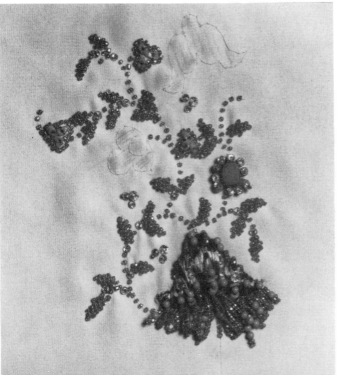

19 Above: 1978 – Suzanne Howitt, a student at Manchester Polytechnic. A panel of embroidery using the domestic machine, varying the tensions, with some fine hand work. On a background of cotton twill

20 Left: 1978 – Margaret Nicholson. *Bead Motif*, aproximately 8 in. (20 cm) square. A freely-worked motif in different types and colours of beads

21 1978 – Margaret Wade, a student at Bournville School of Art. *Textures***. In machine and hand embroidery and appliqué, carried out for the City and Guilds examinations**

22 1978 – Elizabeth Ashurst. *House on a Hill*, 8 in. (20 cm) square. Embroidered freely on canvas in reds, green, blues and pink

23 1978 – Elizabeth Ashurst. *House on Fire*, 15 in. (38 cm) square. Freely worked straight stitch in a variety of colours – blues, purple, pinks, red, orange

24 1978 – Eirian Short. *The Movil Foxes,* **34 in. × 28 in. (86 cm × 71 cm). Stitching in wool on flannel.** *Property of Mr and Mrs Llewhelyn George, Photograph by Denys Short*

25 1978 – Diana Thornton, a student at Goldsmiths' School of Art, *Reflections,* **a panel 23 in. × 21 in. (58 cm × 53 cm). Worked in machine embroidery, surrounded by four mirrors set at an angle to reflect the patterns. Colours include pinks, blue, dark blue and gold, with variations in tone which are enhanced by the direction of the stitching on the Irish machine.** *Photograph by Diana Thornton*

26 1978 – Diana Thornton, a student at Goldsmiths' School of Art. The costume is inspired by and designed for 'a Mustard Fairy'. It is embroidered entirely on the Irish machine, using shiny, coloured threads in pale salmon, turquoise, gold, dusty pink and brown. *Photograph by Diana Thornton*

27 1978 – Catherine Riley, a student at Manchester Polytechnic. A full-size figure in costume, entirely made of fabrics. The figure is in calico, with vilene punched with holes to simulate lace as a part of the costume

28 Above: 1978 – Herta Puls. *Graffiti*, 42½ in. × 37¾ in. (108 cm × 69 cm). The letters are hand quilted on three layers of fabric, the top layer in coarse calico with padding and a base of fine calico. Some letters are applied in poplin. Painting and spraying with dye emphasise the quilting

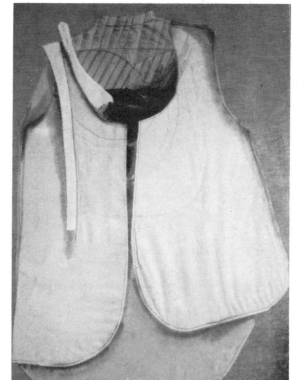

29 Right: 1978 – Audrey Brockbank. *Alpi Venezia*. A panel based on rain using striped fabric with sprayed and stained areas, small labels, one saying 'made in Italy'. Colours are mainly blues, greens, grey, yellow and brown

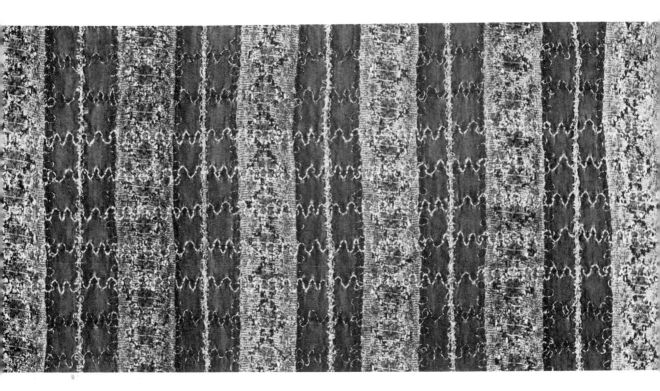

30 Above: 1978 – Ariana Ayazi, a student at Manchester Polytechnic. A constructed, hand-dyed fabric, using ribbons stitched on the domestic machine with automatic patterns

31 Left: 1978 – Kay Young, a student at Loughborough College of Art and Design. A panel based on Loughborough Fair, 22 in. × 16 in. (56 cm × 40.5 cm). Parts of horses, in hand and machine stitching, are shown as flat shapes, the aim being to keep a simple pattern with bright colours of reds, oranges, pinks and greens. Nets, with two layers of chiffon trapping sequins and lengths of thread; small pieces of fabric; lettering and other details are worked over these in hand and machine stitching

32 1978 – Patricia Foulds. *In Search of New Horizons.* **A small panel using goldwork and hand embroidery on a spray-dyed background**

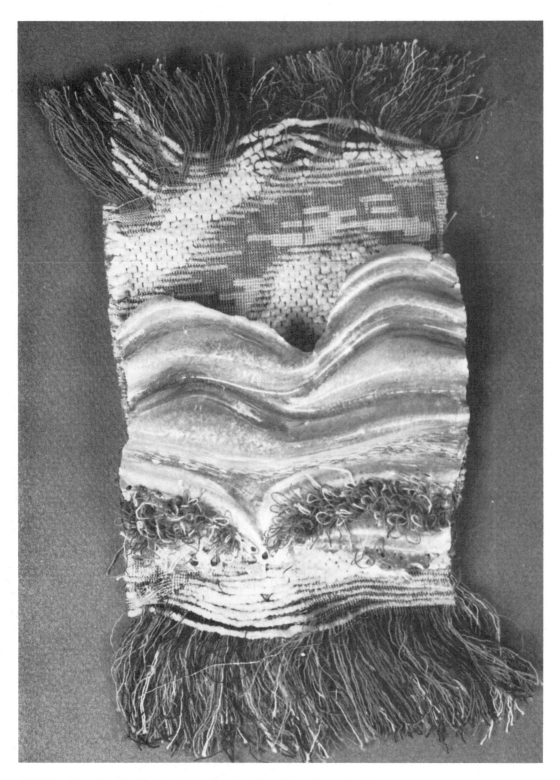

33 1978 – Alison Barrell. *Silver Landscape.* **Beaten sterling silver with punched holes attached to weaving, with the warp pulled through the holes**

34 1978 – Cath Cliff, a student at Manchester Polytechnic. A sculpture in calico, to create a tensile structure; with faggoting, other insertion stitches and knots

First Man On The Moon

35 Left: 1978 – Barbara Siedlecka. *Autumn*. A panel 20 in. × 15 in. (51 cm × 38 cm) commissioned by Jaeger Wools to show the complete range of their yarns. This work was to advertise the autumn wools and was completed within two weeks

36 Above: 1978 – Lorna Tressider. *Man on the Moon*. One panel of three, *Space Trio*, for Manchester Airways. Applied fabrics on a black and tan velvet background. The figure is in white and silver fabric with metal thread machine embroidery. USA flag

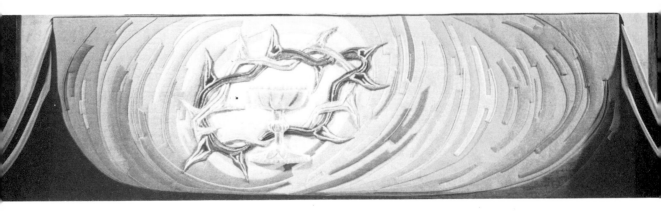

37 1978–82 – Jane Lemon. The 'Energy' frontal for the High Altar of Salisbury Cathedral, worked by the Sarum Group. This is designed for all seasons, the Sarum rite using red instead of green for general purposes. In appliqué from yellows to pinks, reds and blues; these colours signify a living faith and the energy required to live as a practising Christian. The crown of thorns is in gold kid, the chalice in *or nué* gold work, highly padded

38 1978–79 – Joy Clucas. *Christ*, 108 in. × 42 in. (274 cm × 106.5 cm). The background is in applied coloured nets. Applied fabrics in red, orange and brown for the gown, edged in satin stitch with a white halo and grey shadows. Free machine stitching for the face and hands. *St William's School, Market Weighton, Yorkshire*

39 1979–1980 – Netta Ewing. Mitre for His Grace Thomas Winning, Archbishop of Glasgow, commissioned by Mrs Janet Boyd Moss of Edinburgh. The mitre is worked in silks, stranded cotton, gold kid and jap gold on a 50-year old oyster-coloured watered silk. The celtic knot twists a ribbon of rainbow coloured stem stitching with a ribbon of gold kid, the stranded cotton unravelled at the bottom gives an effect of stylised wings. (Embroidery photographed before making up into mitre)

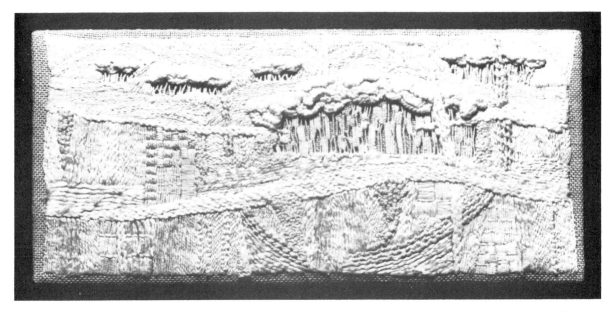

40 1978–79 – Constance Howard. *Landscape*, 11¾ in. × 5¼ in. (29.8 cm × 13 cm). **The fabric is covered with a variety of stitches and beads in cream and white threads, shiny and dull.** *Photograph by Paul Scott*

41 1978–79 – Frederick Glass. *Landscape in Kent – The Farm*. **Worked in canvas stitches. The design is based on the farmlands of Kent, using a number of colours**

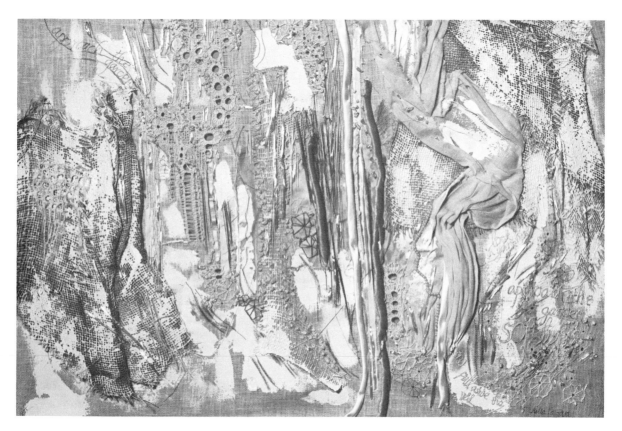

42 1979–80 – Julia Caprara. *Approach the Garden Softly,* **36 in. × 24 in. (91 cm × 61 cm). Cream and white fabrics are applied, with painted areas. The whole idea is drawn together with surface stitchery**

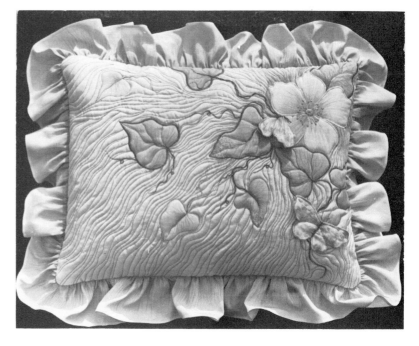

43 1979–80 – Sue Rangeley. Cushions with dyed and painted areas, quilting and machine embroidery, with semi-detached butterflies. Colours in delicate pinks, mauves and grey

44 Above: Late 1970s – Jan Messent. *Hanging Warrior*, 20 in. (51 cm) high. A three-dimensional head, the face in brown felt and leather, quilted on a base of rug canvas. Brown and gold woollen plaits make the hair and beard. The helmet is in brightly coloured log-cabin patchwork, surmounted by a silver kid dome. *Photograph by V A Campbell-Harding*

45 Above: Late 1970s – Linda Beard, a student at Liverpool Polytechnic. *Cat*, a panel in appliqué and hand stitchery

46 Right: 1979–80 – Lesley Miller. *Walk in the Park*. 13½ in. × 11½ in. (34 cm × 29 cm); inner panel 9 in. × 7 in. (23 cm × 18 cm) Hand embroidery in silk and cotton on silk, with silk padded forms

47 1979–80 – June Tiley. A patchwork, quilted jacket on black silk, with ribbon and fabric appliqué. *Exhibited in the 1980 Eisteddfod*

48 1979–80 – Back view of June Tiley's jacket

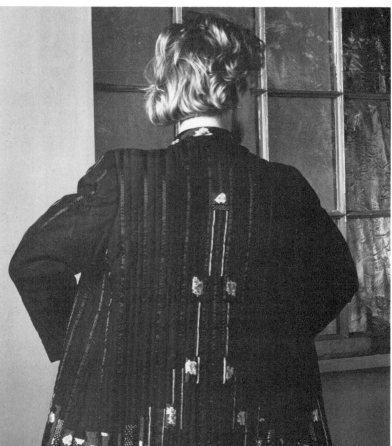

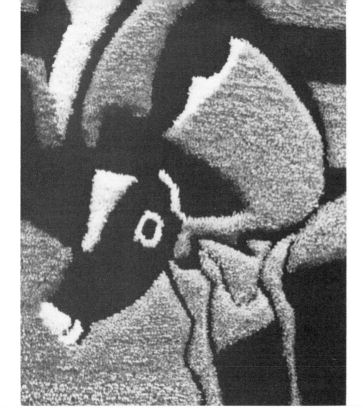

49 Above: 1975–80 – Diana Springall.
A detail of the Chester embroideries
Friesian Cows, designed by Diana
Springall and worked by about 300
ladies. The five canvas-work panels were
designed to commemorate the European
Heritage Year of 1975, and completed in
1980

50 Right: Late 1970s – Jan Messent.
Ostrich, approximately 11 in. (28 cm)
square. Worked on soft canvas in canvas
stitches and straight stitches; in wools,
cotton and glitter yarns in black, grey
and white. *Photograph by Norman
Weston*

79

51 Above left: 1979 – Marjorie Self. *Going Places*, 12 in. × 36 in. (30.5 cm × 91 cm). The background is a deep smokey-grey Harris tweed. The sheep are in straight stitches in thick wools in grey, blue and clover pink. Suede ears, with fluffy woollen fabric, make the faces. *Loaned by Mr and Mrs Ian Houghton. Photograph by Hawkley Studios*

53 Above: 1979–80 – Karyn Prowen. *Sheep*. A panel using natural-coloured knitting wools, sheep skin, leather and various fabrics. *Petit point* on canvas, rug hooking on rug canvas, teased wool to give a fluffy appearance, unravelled couched wool and padded areas, among the techniques used for this panel. *Photograph by Hawkley Studios*

52 Left: 1979 – Marjorie Self. *The Wool Gatherers*, 30 in. × 20 in. (76 cm × 51 cm). Worked on rug canvas with strips of fabric in a rug-hooking technique. The back sheep is in thick knitting wool. Faces are in suede and leather, stuck down; fleece is padded. The legs are crotcheted in black wool, stuffed and free-swinging. Colours are earth brown, reds, ochre, grey and green. The complete work is mounted on hardboard. *Photography by Hawkley Studios*

54(b) Detail of *Roundel*

54(a) Late 70s – Mary Maguire. *Roundel*, approximately 8 in. (20 cm) in diameter. A collection of junk sewn onto organdie, with carefully selected and arranged bits and pieces, including feathers, ribbons, metal papers, beads, sequins, diamanté, stitchery and small pieces of fabric

55 1978 – Jean Carter. *Sussex Meander*, **10 in. × 10¾ in. (25.4 cm × 27.3 cm). Hand and machine embroidery on slub-weave furnishing fabric in flecked lime green, with stitching in shaded green, mid-green and ochre in a variety of threads.** *Photograph by Richard Welsh*

56 1977–80 – *Bunyan's Dream*. A community project designed by Edward Bawden and worked by 19 women members of the Bedfordshire Music and Arts Club to commemorate the Silver Jubilee. The grid is symbolic of the prison bars and also hides the joins of the rectangles, each of which is 7 in. × 9 in. (18 cm × 23 cm) in size. It is worked in cross stitch, with the border in long-armed cross stitch. Christian's journey starts in the lower left-hand corner. When finished, the embroidered sections were assembled by the Royal School of Needlework. Colours include a scarlet path linking the episodes; brown, blue, grey, green, navy, white, and gold are also used. The embroidery is in the Cecil Higgins Art Gallery, Bedford. *Photograph by Hawkley Studios*

57 1977–80 – Details from *Bunyan's Dream*

58 1979–80 – Betty Myerscough. *Man in Tube*, 52 in. × 25½ in. (132 cm × 65 cm). **The idea was developed from a sketch made while travelling on the tube. A full-sized paper collage was made, the outline being traced on to iron-on vilene. The fabric shapes were cut and ironed on to the vilene and machine stitched. The figure is quilted and applied to a calico background with the newspaper worked separately, the photograph in free machine stitching, the newsprint using an automatic stitch. The letters have been cut from fabric ironed on to Bondaweb**

59 1980 – Betty Myerscough. *Eighties Girl*, 52 in. × 26 in. (132 cm × 66 cm). A combination of hand and machine embroidery. The figure and background are in appliqué and machine stitching. The parts of the scooter were made separately in silver kid and plastic and applied to the ground

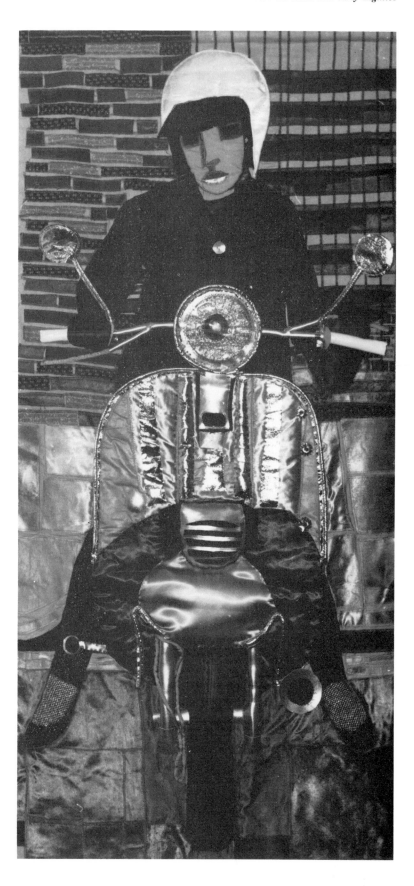

60 Above: 1979 – Barbara Siedlecka. The Canons' copes for Winchester Cathedral, designed by Barbara Siedlecka. The designs for the four copes are based on Gothic architecture, with vertical panels in velvets, the colours merging from crimson at the front of the garments to gold at the centre back. Throughout, the colours are in gold, orange, scarlet and crimson. Hoods are different for each cope with designs derived from Gothic vaulting. To differentiate the Dean's cope from those of the Canons, the velvet panels are reversed in order of colour with wider strips of lurex between each one, and it has a circular hood

61 Right: 1979 – Isabel Clover. A semi-circular Tabernacle stand, 42 in. high × 30 in. (107 cm × 76 cm). The design depicts a divided field of corn with the sun shining through, symbolic of God surrounded by the Faithful. Corn near the sun bright gold, away, dull brown/grey. Corn symbolic of bread and grapes of wine – the Eucharist. The background is aubergine/brown heavy furnishing fabric, the corn in padded cream and gold kid, with stalks in pleated and folded kid. Crotchet and bobbin lace are used on the ears of corn. Satin stitch, couching, french knots, beads and jewels, with wool and silk threads are employed. The sun is gold-orange. *Loaned by permission of the Catholic Church of Our Lady of Sorrows, Stowmarket, Suffolk. Photograph by Peter Clitheroe*

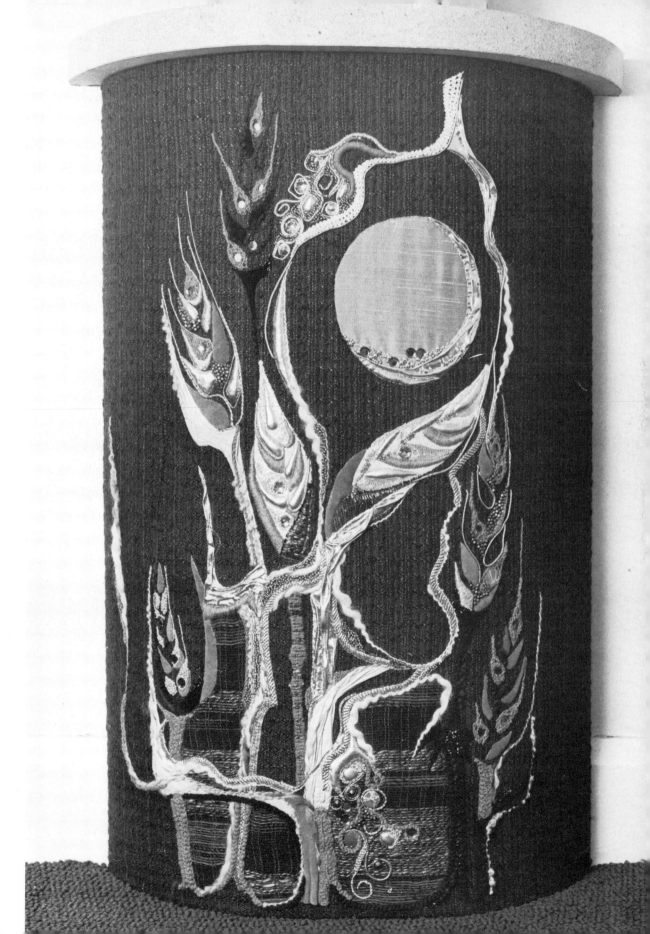

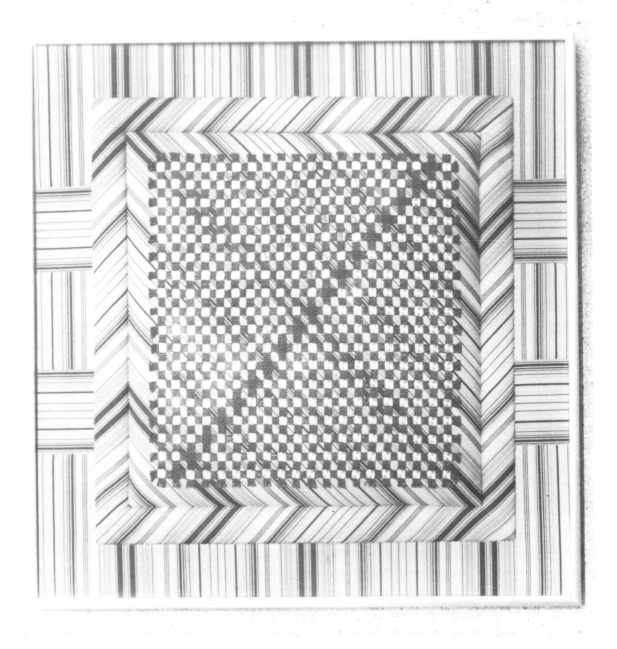

62 Above: 1979 – Irene Ord. *Criss Cross*, 18 in. (46 cm) square. Rayon drawn-thread fabric applied to a striped cotton ground. Squares of diffraction foil are stitched like sequins at intersecting points of the grid. Padded and applied striped cotton surround

63 Right: 1979 – Bridget Moss. A canopy for a four-poster bed, 51 in. × 70 in. (130 cm × 179 cm). The canopy is in layers of cotton, spray-dyed in pale colours over stencils. In yellows, oranges, pinks, red and green. Each panel is 25½ in. × 35 in. (65 cm × 89 cm) in size, made and quilted separately in runing stitch in deeper colours than the dye

64 1979 – Diana Thornton, a student at Goldsmiths' School of Art. A canvas-work panel 10 in. × 9½ in. (25.5 cm × 24 cm). A variety of colours of thread and stitches is used in the panel. *Photograph by Diana Thornton*

65 1979 – Verina Warren. *Landscape*. **A panel in a variety of greens and greeny-blues, in machine stitching, spray dyeing and painting, on fabric and card**

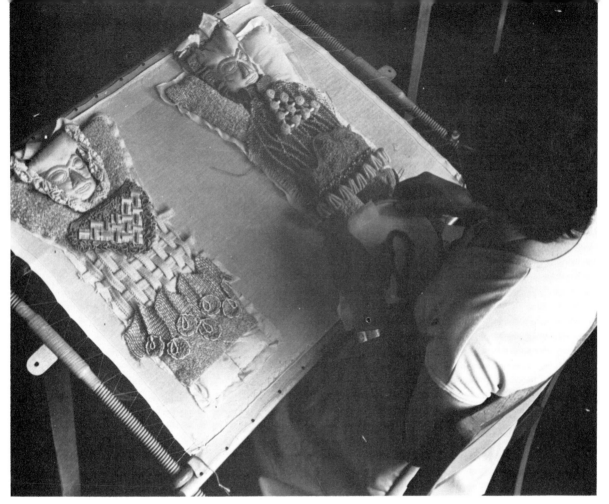

66 Above: 1979 – Tessa Franks, a student at Bournville School of Art. *Aztec Figures*. Raised and padded shapes, with hand embroidery and beads. Carried out for the City and Guilds examinations

67 Below: 1979 – Renate Meyer. Two life-sized stitched heads, *Grandfather and Grandmother*. Various fabrics stitched and stuffed, an idea which developed into the apples, symbolic of life from youth to old age (149 and 150)

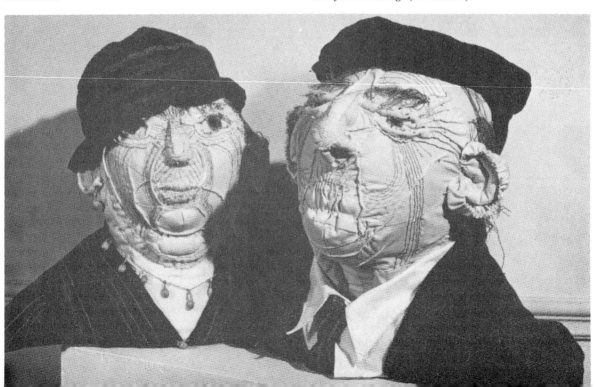

69 1979 – Catherine Riley. Three-dimensional, life size table and shoe, using stiffened fabric

68 1979 – Gisela Banbury. *Turkish Squares*, 28¼ in. × 15¾ in. (72 cm × 40 cm). A hanging inspired by a Turkish silk rug, in machine patchwork padded with foam rubber. Colours are gold, ambers and yellow-greens. The divisions between the blocks of patchwork represent the walkways between the piles of carpets in the warehouse where the rugs were seen

70 1979 – Joan Blencowe. A panel combining screen printing with embroidery. The photograph is a part of the Queen's House, Greenwich. The embroidery is in straight stitches and french knots in various colours.
Photograph by Hawkley Studios

71 1979 – Kirsty McFarlane. *Snow Goose.* **A collage panel approximately 30 in. × 24 in. (76 cm × 61 cm). The goose in relief in a variety of white and cream fabrics, the nest in various textures of fabric, in browns, greys, dirty greens, and other dark colours**

72 1979 – Julia Caprara. *Babiy Yar.* **A panel 72 in. × 42 in. (183 cm × 107 cm). 'And there is no garden at Babiy Yar.' The panel has crude stitchery, harsh lettering and broken shapes. It employs leather, hessian, torn fabrics and paint and is in natural colours of fawns, black, brown and white. The work symbolises 'Man's inhumanity to Man' and is in memory of the massacre of the Jews in Russia during World War II**

73 1979 – Valerie Riley. Blackwork houses, developed from an exercise on the technique. The two houses on the left are in blackwork, the one on the right is in canvas work. City and Guilds samplers

74 1979 – Jane Page. A small bag, approximately 5 in. (12.7 cm) in width in pink silk. The design based on nasturtiums is worked in silk in reds and greens

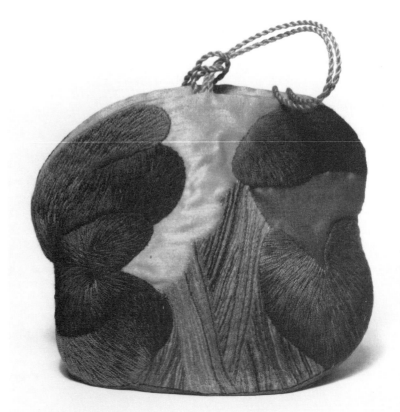

75 1979 – Jane Page. A purse approximately 4 in. (10 cm) in width. The fabric is entirely covered in gold thread, couched over a padded surface

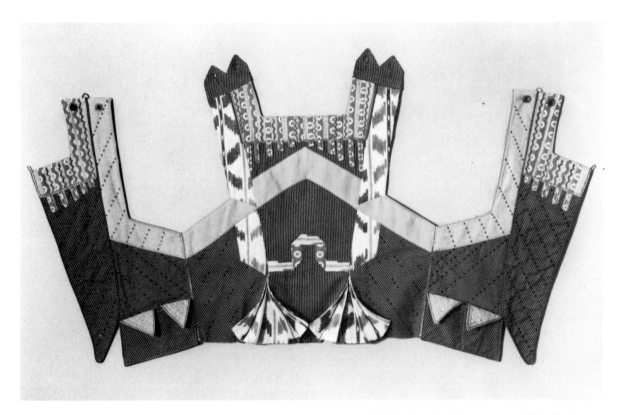

76 1979 – Lucy Goffin. A 'waistcoat' in Mexican hand-loom cotton, and ikat-dyed cotton. Constructed from a series of panels, piped and joined with linen faggoting. Appliqué, and hand embroidery using stem stitch, feather stitch, faggoting, herringbone, french knots and buttonhole stitch. Glass buttons and beads from the 1930s. Colours are brown, saffron and blues with royal blue and gold beads. *Photograph by Hawkley Studios*

77 1979 – Lucy Goffin. *Marriage Coat.* In silk *crêpe de chine* and silk shantung, in delicate creams and pinks. Hand embroidery using stem stitch, feather stitch, chain stitch and hand quilting with silk thread. Glass beads, appliqué, quilting and ribbon are used in the general texture and decoration of the piece. *Photograph by Hawkley Studios*

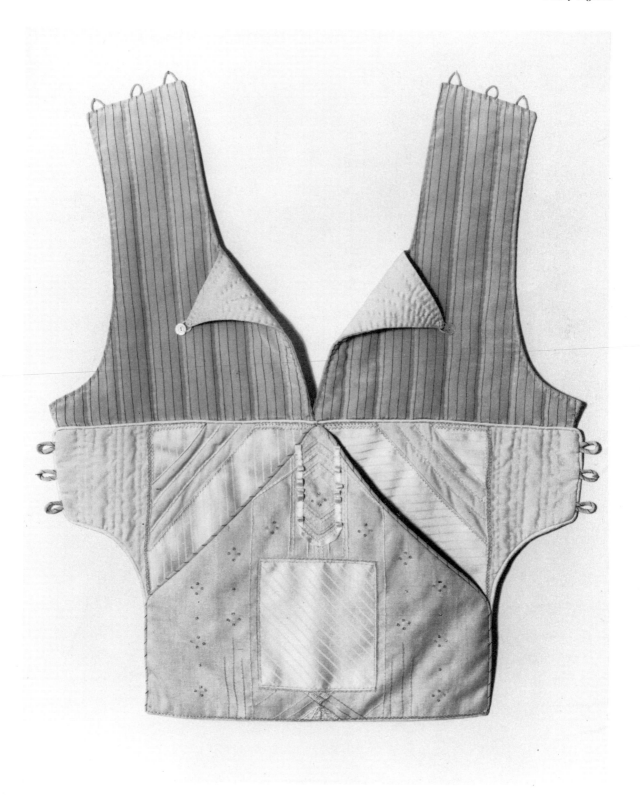

78 1979 – Polly Hope. A fantasy garment with foliage and flowers, stuffed birds and insects. The hem of the dress is padded. Colours are mainly blues and greens. *Photograph by Hawkley Studios*

79 1979 – Jane Happs. A dress in silk strips batiked in pinks and greens with some red. Cornely machine stitching worked on vanishing muslin in similar colours to those of the batik, gives an effect of insertion stitches

80 1979–80 – Jane Happs. A light cotton jacket with colours inspired by watercolours. Cotton on vanishing muslin, machine stitching with ribbon details; Cornely and Bernina machining. *Seen in 1982 at the Crafts Centre, 'One-off Wearables' exhibition*

81 Left: 1979 – Margaret Traherne. Five sail-shaped triangular flags 25 in. × 13 in. (63.5 cm × 33 cm) at the base and 36 in. (91 cm) wide. In black and white bunting. Hung from three points to interact with one another; the group can be viewed from below from any angle. *Displayed at the Tate Gallery, London*

82 Right: 1979 – Diana Springall. A panel 43 in. × 44 in. (109 cm × 112 cm) made entirely in relief in felt rouleaux. *Owned by Mr and Mrs F Joyce.* *Photograph by John Hunnex*

83 Right: 1979 – Eleri Mills. A painted and stitched panel 6 ft × 9 ft (1.90 m × 2.80 m) for the Central Toxicology Laboratory of ICI at Alderley Edge, Cheshire. Architects – Building Design Partnership

84 Above: 1980 – Eleri Mills. *Alderley Edge*. Panel 9 ft 2¼ in. × 11 ft 9¾ in. (2.8 m × 3.6 m). In dark greens and blue-greens, grey-green, greens, browns, yellows and golds. The panel is surrounded by a wide frame of fabric over board, painted with sky and mountains

85 Right: 1980 – Eleri Mills. Detail of *Alderley Edge* panel

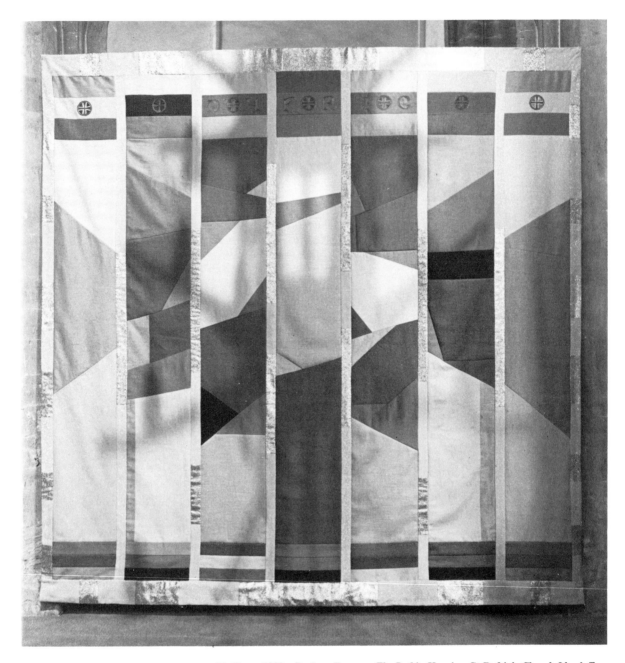

86 Above: 1980 – Barbara Dawson. *The Dyfrig Hanging*, St Dyfrig's Chapel, Llandaff Cathedral. In patchwork, in linen and man-made fibres, with some silk. The lettering and the crosses are in split stitch in floss silk. 'The idea of the hanging is to catch the attention with colour and shape, with reduced texture ... often over used in textiles.' The lettering is inspired by the manuscript of the Lichfield Gospels which once rested in the Cathedral. The angular, broken design symbolises old thoughts giving place to new. Colours are also symbolic

87 Right: 1980 – Isabel Clover. A chasuble in plum-red fabric, designed by Isabel Clover and worked by Susan Gurney. The design shows modern symbols of torture – barbed wire, drugs and guns (triggers). Appliqué in Thai silk and dull aubergine velvet, pewter kid, Russian braid, knotted gold elastic and beads. Stem stitch, french knots; gold thread and weaving wools – detail

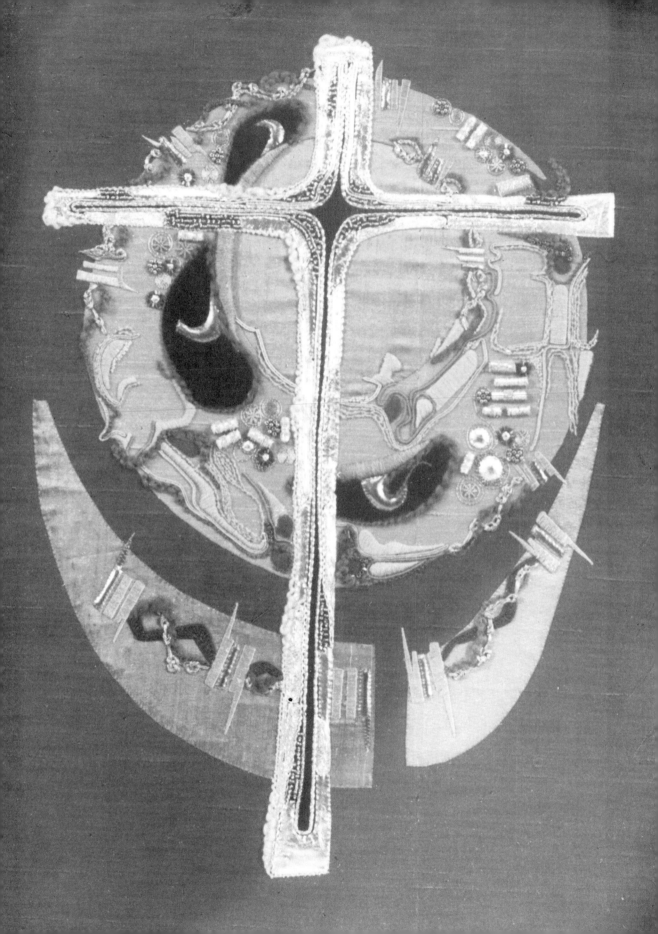

88 1980 – Kathleen Whyte. Pulpit fall, 'Stenton Church Fall', in Midlothian, Scotland. In memory of Dorothy Angus and her sister-in-law Margaret Angus. On the right side the blues and purples are for Dorothy. On the left side the yellows and yellow-orange are for Margaret; their characteristic colours. The design is built up of superimposed heart shapes. The centre is composed of a double heart motif in gold and silver overlapping, similar to a 'Luckenbooth' brooch. The background is in slightly quilted, natural silk

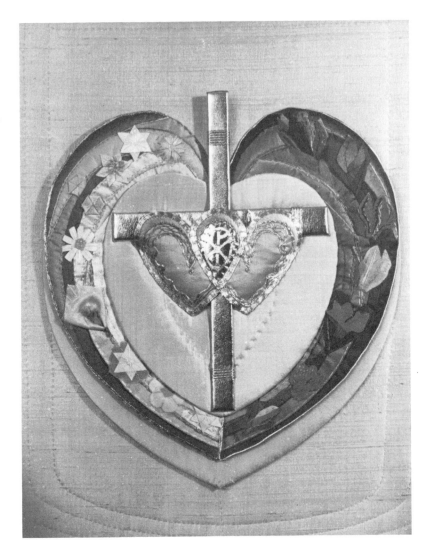

89 1980 – Beryl Dean. The cope and mitre for the Archbishop of Canterbury completes the set of copes commissioned in 1974, for the Dean and Chapter, to be worn at the enthronement. The main fabric of the cope is dull, dark gold lamé, with front and back panels in cream wool. Appliqué in olive greens, lime green and gold, in transparent and opaque fabrics similar to those for the Canons' copes, are used for the pattern. Symbolism is based on the wide influences emanating from Canterbury: the earth represented by mountains and fire; water by the sea, rivers and a waterfall; the air by thermal currents. Shapes represent Man's habitation seen from the air – roads, houses and factories. On the front panels and the hood the large cross of Canterbury is applied, with padding on the hood. Gold cords, braids and silk threads are used for the embroidery. *Photograph by Hawkley Studios*

111

90 1980 – Jan Beaney. *Secret Meeting.* A panel from the 'Welsh Slate' series. Dyes on calico in tans, browns, greyish browns and yellows. Straight stitches are worked in silk thread. *Owned by Elizabeth Benn. Photograph by Dudley Moss*

91 Right: 1980 – Jan Beaney. *Thrift Cliff*, 16 in. × 26 in. (40.5 cm × 66 cm). Hand and machine appliqué in silks and rayon fabrics applied to calico. Wool and cotton threads worked in straight stitches, knots and eyelets. *Photograph by Roger Cuthbert*

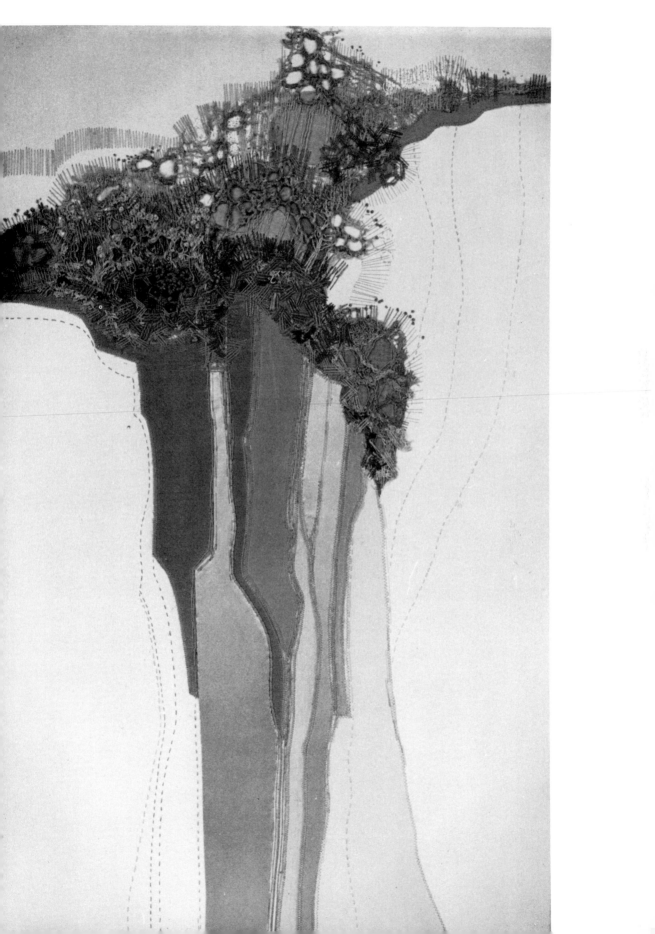

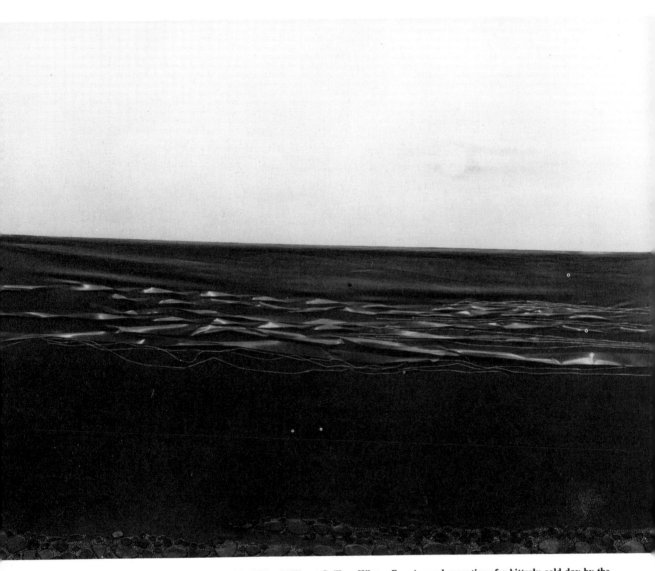

92 1980 – Millicent Spiller. *Winter Sea.* **A panel evocative of a bitterly cold day by the sea. Polythene strips are twisted to catch the light and are sewn down on to a grey glazed cotton. The silver lines are threads removed from carpet backing. Pebbles are in leather.** *Photograph by Hawkley Studios*

93 1980 – Jennifer Hex. *Night Sky*, **14 in. × 18 in. (35.5 cm × 45.5 cm). An original method of darning using silk threads on linen**

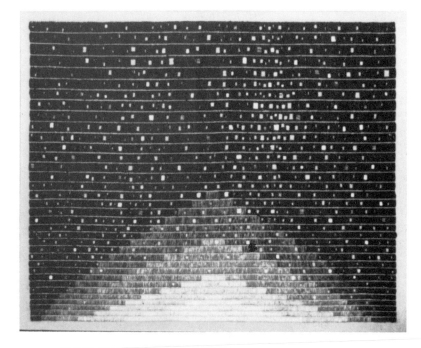

94 1980 – Jennifer Hex. *Pebbles in the burn*

95 1980 – Jennifer Hex. Detail of *Pebbles in the burn*

115

96 Left: 1980 – Jan Beaney. *White Tree*. A panel 47 in. × 34 in. (119 cm × 86.5 cm), from a drawing done at Clevedon. Applied fabrics in net, domette, hessian and satin, with some painting, on a hessian ground. Stitches include straight, french knots and couching worked in a variety of yarns. *Photograph by Dudley Moss*

97 Right: 1980 – Janet Ledsham. *Friday Afternoon*, approximately 38 in. × 22 in. (97 cm × 56 cm). In layers of organdie; in black with small areas of colour in the shadows, in pinks, greens and grey running stitches

98 1980 – Gentillia Balcombe. A panel 20 in. (51 cm) square worked in a craft class for the physically handicapped, taught by Dorothy Tucker, at a day centre in London. Gentillia Balcome has difficulty in manipulation owing to rheumatoid arthritis. She made her own design. The panel is worked in straight stitches and couching, the colours including dark browns and reds, tan, bright green, grey-black, cream, pink and orange.
Photograph by Hawkley Studios

100 1980 – Janet Russell, a student at Bournville School of Art. *Landscape*. A blackwork panel for the City and Guilds examinations

99 1980 – Nancy Kimmins. *Winter*. A patchwork hanging using a variety of plain and patterned fabrics in limited colours

101 1980 – Julia Caprara. A wedding dress commissioned by David Butler. All white fabrics are used, but in many contrasting textures. The background is an openweave curtain net. It is darned, embroidered and interwoven with narrow satin ribbon, shiny crochet threads, fine mohair, pearl and glass beads. Strips of fabric, lace, net and silk threads in white matt and shiny textures

102 1980 – Julia Caprara. A detail of the wedding dress

103 Left: 1980 – Beryl Page. *The Omega Dress*, 27 in. × 22 in. (69 cm × 56 cm). Screen printed on a white ground in purple, with the dress in shades of tan and pink. The background is painted in pale blue and green. Single-thread embroidery of straight stitch and fly stitch. Beads and sequins give sparkle

105 Right: 1980 – Mary Ward. *Refraction*. A panel 36 in. × 48 in. (91 cm × 122 cm) using tapestry wools in blues, purples and browns on a black ground, working in blanket stitch. The aim is to give an illusion of depth with the use of the colour and direction of stitch (View horizontally)

104 Below: 1980 – Jennifer Shonk. *Teatime I*. A panel 24 in. × 33 in. (61 cm × 84 cm). In relief, with draped sleeves and padded, separate biscuits. Materials include lace, satin and cotton

106 1980–1 – Janet Ledsham. *Alton Field*, 12 in. × 8 in. (30.5 cm × 20 cm). Organza over a cotton square, the central area heavily stitched in contrasting bands

107 1980–1 – Janet Ledsham. *Magneroarty*, **6 ft × 4 ft (1.83 m × 1.22 m). A detail of an embroidery worked on a linen ship's cloth, using knotting and long, straight stitches which are then cut**

109 Early 1980s – Margaret Kaye. *Cock and Butterflies*, 21 in. (53.5 cm) square. The background is red wool with cotton, silk, towelling, linen, and painted jersey, printed velvet and indigo discharged cotton applied

108 Left: 1979–81 – Hannah Frew Paterson. *The Cardross Panels*, 12 ft × 7 ft (3.66 m × 2.13 m). Commissioned for the screen behind the Communion Table in Cardross Parish Church, Dumbartonshire. The gift of Elizabeth C Hendry in memory of her sister Lorna Hendry. The design is based on the hill, giving a setting for the cross, with each panel depicting life from its development to fulfilment. The day panel on the left shows a view of Cardross and in the lower part the beginnings of plants, then flowers, fruits and trees with biblical and symbolic significance, and a garden of wild flowers. The night panel on the right shows another view of Cardross with mineral resources under the earth below, and above, fossils of animals and fish life during the centuries. The central panel contains the cross with a golden circle edged with a rainbow. The lower part of the panel contains patterns developed from parts of the body and its structure, the discs show the human embryo and its growth to a baby. The family unit above the motto shows twelve figures, the number of the apostles, and the symbol of the entire Church. (Abridged from the description by the Reverend Andrew J Scobie.)

The panels are worked on cotton in machine and hand embroidery and are mounted individually on heavy linen stretched over boards. Many colours are employed – blues and greys for the sky; browns, ochres, various greens and tans for the earth, with details in many different colours

110 Above: 1979–81 – Belinda Montague. *The New Forest Embroidery*. The first panel. Historic events are shown in the centre part commencing with William I who established the Forest around 1079 AD. Relevant coats of arms and seals are superimposed on the foliage of the trees

111 Below: 1979–81 – Belinda Montague. *The New Forest Embroidery*. A detail from the second panel depicting the exercise of common rights in the Forest. Canvaswork tree trunks and foreground contrast against the machine embroidered landscape. The overall size is 25 ft × 2 ft (7.62 m × 0.61 m). The hangings are executed in appliqué with surface stitching and canvas embroidery in a variety of greens, reddish and golden browns, and depict the legendary element of the Forest's history, including local flora and fauna. The last episode in the third panel shows the Queen planting a commemorative tree on 12 April 1979. (Information supplied by the designer and from the booklet *The New Forest Embroidery*, 1981, The New Forest Association/M Russell.)

112 Left: 1976–81 – Esther Grainger. A hanging 5 ft 4¼ in. × 2ft × 11½ in. (163 cm × 91 cm). An idea based on St Pierre-sous-Vézelay, using nets, transparent fabrics, tweeds and other textures, emphasised with stitchery

113 Above: 1976–81 – Esther Grainger. A detail of St Pierre-sous-Vézelay

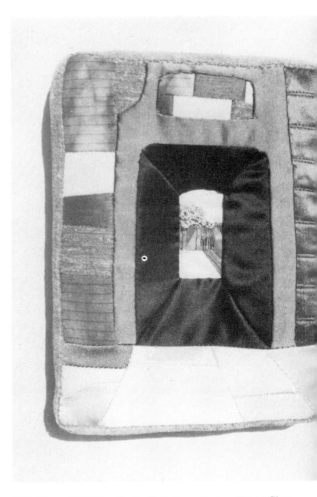

115 Above: 1980–81 – Kirsty McFarlane. *Custom House Close*. Unframed, 8 in. × 6 in. × 2 in. (20 cm × 15 cm × 5 cm). Pieced silk padding with some hand and machine stitching. The inner frame is black satin, the outer one dyed fabric in ochre, pinkish brown, greyish brown and cream

114 Above: 1980–81 – Janet Ledsham. *Windows in a Greek Village. Kardamina I.* Layers of linen, *Vilene* and wadding, quilted in silk threads. Size 24 in. × 16 in. (61 cm × 40.5 cm)

116 Right: 1980–81 – Christine Risley. A plastic box approximately 9 in. (23 cm) square with layers of fabrics arranged as a sandwich within the box. Machine stitching is in red, blue and yellow. *Photograph by Hawkley Studios*

117 1981 – Jane Happs. A triangular hanging. The pale colours are inspired by watercolour paintings. Worked over vanishing muslin on the Cornely machine in braid and cord embroidery, with some moss and chain stitch. Ripstock nylon used to create the transparent 'butterfly areas'. Small quilted sections occur throughout the work. Calico, silk and fine cotton are also incorporated. *Exhibited at the British Crafts Centre 'Stitchery' Show 1982 and at the British Festival of Arts and Crafts, New Jersey, USA*

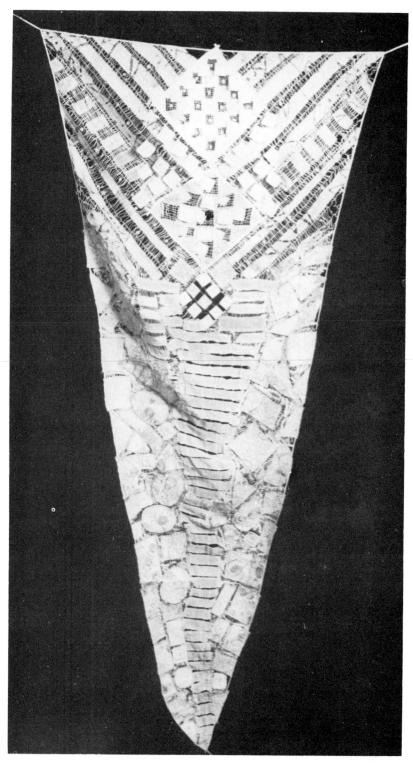

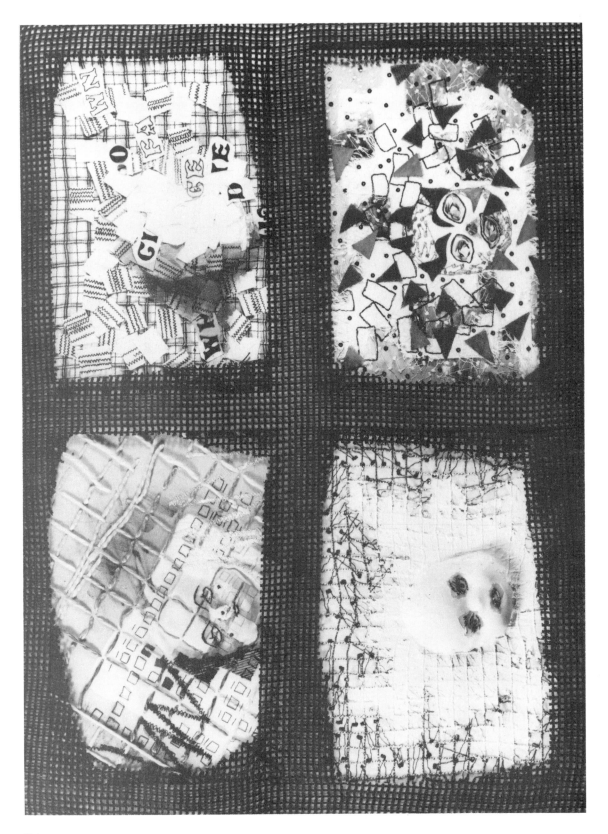

119 Above: 1980–81 – Esther Grainger. *Mosque at Cordoba.* A panel in collage in a variety of fabrics and colours, with some stitching. See colour plate 5 for complete panel

118 Left: 1980–81 – Geraldine Bone. *Decay,* 21¼ in. × 15½ in. (54 cm. × 39 cm). In black, white and grey. The frame, part of the design, is in coarse black net over white cotton. Doll faces are in relief, painted white. Black sequins, lurex threads and others are worked in hand and machine stitching. *Photography by Hawkley Studios* (View horizontally)

120 Left: 1981 – Isabel Dibden. A quilt, 49½ in. (125.5 cm) square. Log-cabin patchwork in silk and cotton fabrics, mainly in bright red, blue, orange, and pink with some green, machine stitched. *Embroiderers' Guild Collection. Photograph by Hawkley Studios*

123 Above: 1981 – Caroline Pitcher, a student at Manchester Polytechnic. A sample 16 in. × 22 in. (40.5 cm × 56 cm) overall size, worked on Japanese rag paper. Striped silk fabric interwoven through paper and straight machining on a painted surface. *Embroiderers' Guild Collection. Photograph by Hawkley Studios*

121 Far left: 1981 – Barbara Siedlecka. *Peloponnese I – Nafplion*, 30 in. (76 cm) square. In appliqué of thick suedes and fabrics, with embroidery in various yarns, texture in hooked rags and rubberised horse hair. The aim is to give a bleached, sunny atmosphere. *Photograph by Hawkley Studios*

122 Left: 1981 – Patricia Foulds. *Crumbling World*, 11½ in. × 9½ in. (29 cm × 24 cm). Quilted silk with crayon, ink and machine embroidery mounted on unprimed canvas

137

124 Left: 1981 – Jennifer Chippendale, the London College of Fashion. A 'sheep' panel using various fabrics and threads

125 (a) Above: 1981 – Pamela Harrison, the London College of Fashion. Detail of an altar frontal showing sheep, using various fabrics and threads

125 (b) Right: 1981 – Pamela Harrison. Enlarged detail of sheeps' head

**126 and 127 1981 – Wendy Hawkin.
Two examples from a series of four.**
Increasing Images, **approximately 8½ in.
(22 cm) square. A dark grey printed
background with light shapes masked
out. The centre is handmade paper,
printed in black-grey images. Lines of
white thread break up the dark shapes,
with black threads breaking up the white
shapes.** *Photograph by Hawkley
Studios*

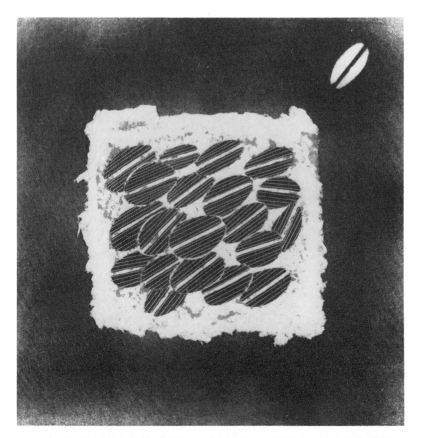

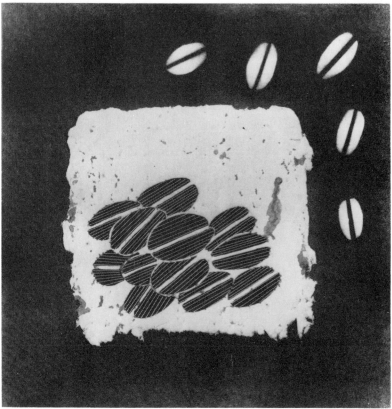

128 1981 – Anne Butler Morrell. A panel with a felt top fabric, 38½ in. × 33 in. (98 cm × 84 cm). The ovals are worked in stem stitch in mohair and silk threads

129 1981 – Dorothy Tucker. Sleeveless jacket in dark green velvet with appliqué of tulips in brilliant coloured silks in pinks, orange, reds, yellows, greens and other related colours. *Photograph by Hawkley Studios*

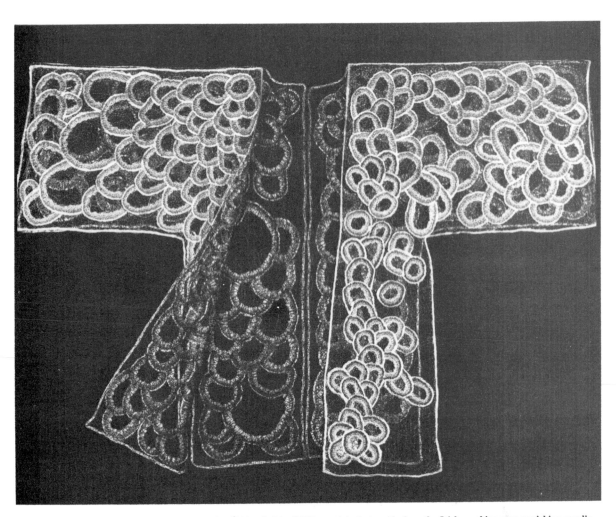

130 1981 – Robin Giddings. A jacket worked on the Irish machine over vanishing muslin which is removed by heat or acetone after completion of the stitchery. Couched silver threads and floss silk are used for the garment

**131 Right: 1981 – Jane Page. Stole of
Thai silk in brilliant pink, apricot and
orange stripes, some of which have been
re-cut to give wider areas of one colour.
The embroidery is in jap gold and twist,
with blue, red and pale apricot silk used
for the stem stitch.** *Photograph by
Hawkley Studios*

**132 Far right: 1981 – Carole McRae, a
student at Manchester Polytechnic.** *Jelly
Bags*. **A hanging 9 ft 11 in. (3 m) high.
Various weights of white cotton fabrics
are used**

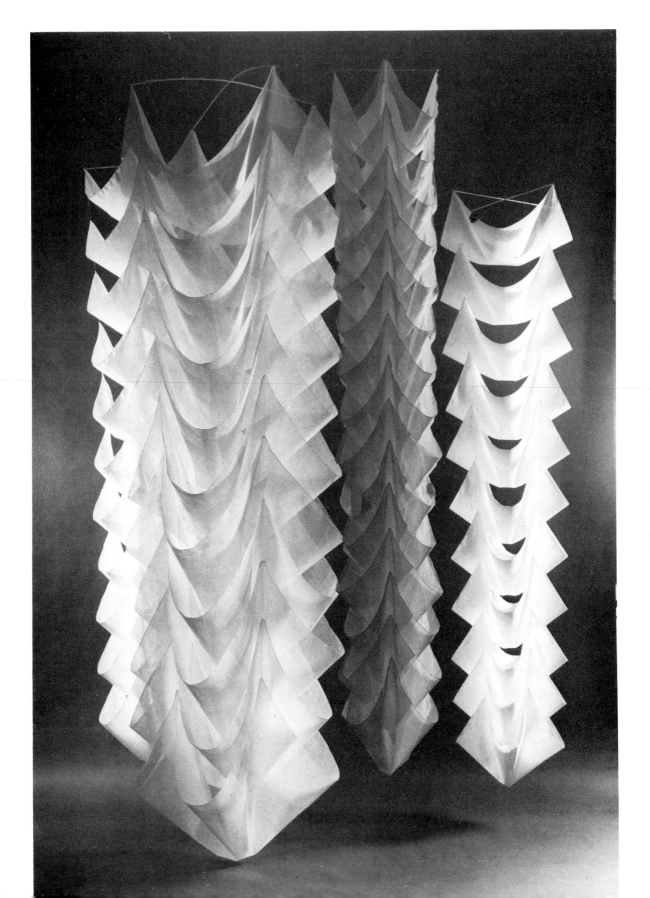

134 1981 – Kathleeen Whyte. *Silver Thimble*. Made for the 'Argent' exhibition to mark the twenty-fifth anniversary of the Glasgow School of Art Embroidery Group exhibitions

133 1981 – Alexa Wilson, a student at Glasgow School of Art. A structure on wire netting in wire and sisal, using paper, fabric, wire mesh and sisal. The example was made in sections, baked in an oven, then assembled

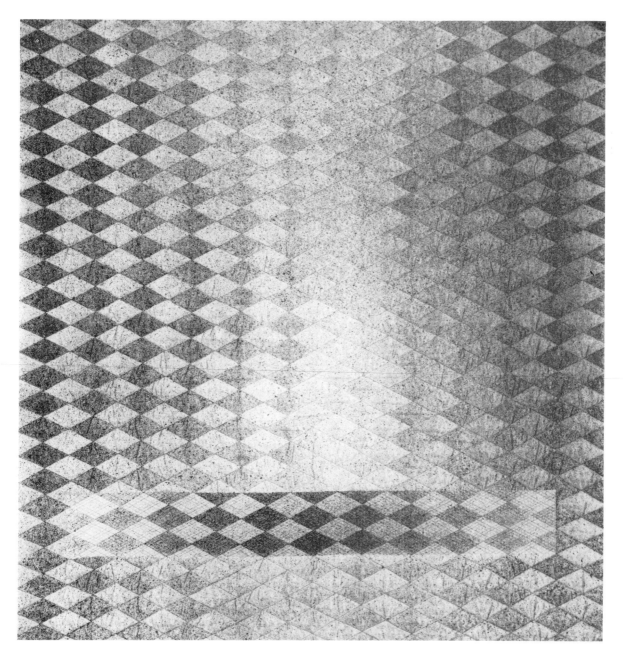

135 1981 – Diana Harrison. *Hanging Quilt*, approximately 72 in. (183 cm) square. Spray dyeing in overlays of colour, machine quilted

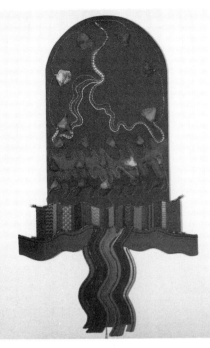

136 Left: 1981 – Pauline Hann. A panel *Neon*, 58¼ in. × 31½ in. (148 cm × 80 cm). The background is electric blue dupion, with twisting electric cable, dotted with tiny flashing coloured bulbs, covered with silk fringes in pinks, purples, blues, emerald green. Surface stitchery, satin cords, canvas work appliqué, wrapping and cording are among techniques employed

137 Below: 1981 – Pauline Hann. A detail of *Neon*

138 1981 – Moyra McNeill. *Battle Array*. **A panel 39½ in. × 25 in. (100 cm × 64 cm) in silver and shades of blue, on calico. Couching in metal thread; sprayed dye, appliqué and surface stitchery**

139 Left: 1981 – Cherry Crawford, a student at the Windsor and Maidenhead Adult Centre. *Cornfield.* Most fabrics are moygashals, all in different yellows, with a variety of threads for the stitching among which are silks, crewel wools, perle cotton and sylko. Stitches include cretan, wave, bullion knots and french knots, among others. *Photograph by Dudley Moss*

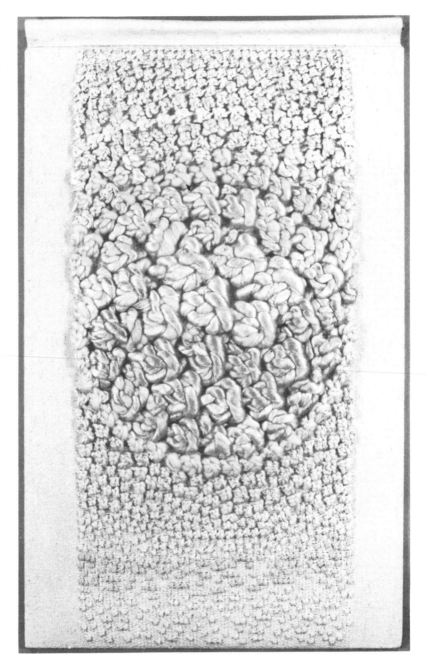

140 1981 – Hannah Frew Paterson. *Growing Round*, $31\frac{1}{2}$ in. wide × $45\frac{1}{4}$. high (80 cm × 115 cm). A large scale white and natural coloured silk stitchery, using one stitch in different thicknesses of handspun silk and wool, on a background of heavy, plain white woollen fabric with some background threads withdrawn

142 Above: 1981 – Janet Ledsham. *Field*. A panel 8 in. × 7 in. × $\frac{1}{4}$ in. (20 cm × 18 cm × 7 mm) stitched in gossamer and silk twist through layers of cotton and foam, cut into sections and re-applied on to a second ground

141 Left: 1981–82 – Vicky Lugg. *Garden*. A panel in pale grey, greens, mauves and greyish colours. The flowers have detached petals; twisted and padded fabrics and fabrics over card are also a part of the work. Stitches include knots and loops. *Photograph by Hawkley Studios*

143 1981 – Eirian Short. *The Clump* **approximately 18 in. (46 cm) square. The fabric is covered completely with stitches in stem worked in several layers, in greens, browns, fawn, blues and grey-blue crewel wools.** *Photograph by Denys Short*

144 1981 – Kate Hobson-Wells.
Ayrshire – White Space, 36 in. × 33 in.
(91 cm × 84 cm). A painted and
embroidered panel, mainly in straight
stitch

145 1981 – Doris Anwyl. *The seasons
seen through a chestnut tree.* A four-fold
screen designed by Doris Anwyl and
worked by members of the East Kent
Branch of the Embroiderers' Guild under
her direction. Shown in the Chapter
House of Canterbury Cathedral, summer
1981, at an exhibition 'Old and New'
staged by the East Kent Branch for the
Asthma Council, to whom the screen was
presented. Each panel is worked on a
different coloured ground, with flowers,
fruit, etc, appropriate to each season.
Plain and patterned cotton, lace, velvet
and nets with a variety of stitches are
used for the work. The branches are
finger cords in different thicknesses

**146 1981 – Sue Read, a student at the
Windsor and Maidenhead Adult Centre.
Hippo floor cushion approximately
30 in. (76 cm) high, made for a blind
child. The background is fine, grey
polyester cotton. Quilting and ruched
effects have been obtained on the
machine. Ears are in velvet with sylko
for whiskers. Eyes are in leather and the
base is stuffed to make a firm seat. The
aim was to give as effective a variety of
tactile surfaces as possible.** *Photograph
by Dudley Moss*

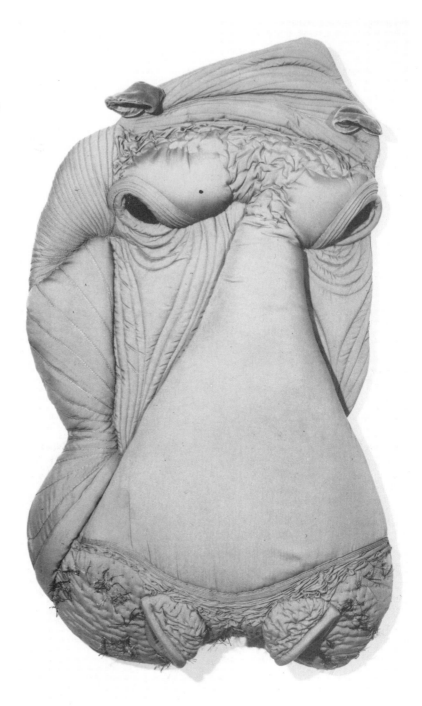

147 Right: 1982 – Sadie Allen. *The Bull*, **30 in. × 36 in. (76 cm × 91 cm). Based on a
champion in a Shrewsbury show called Eifion Jumbo. In browns and cream fabrics in
hand stitching, including couching and whipped running. The embroidery hangs in the
butcher's shop at Chatsworth House**

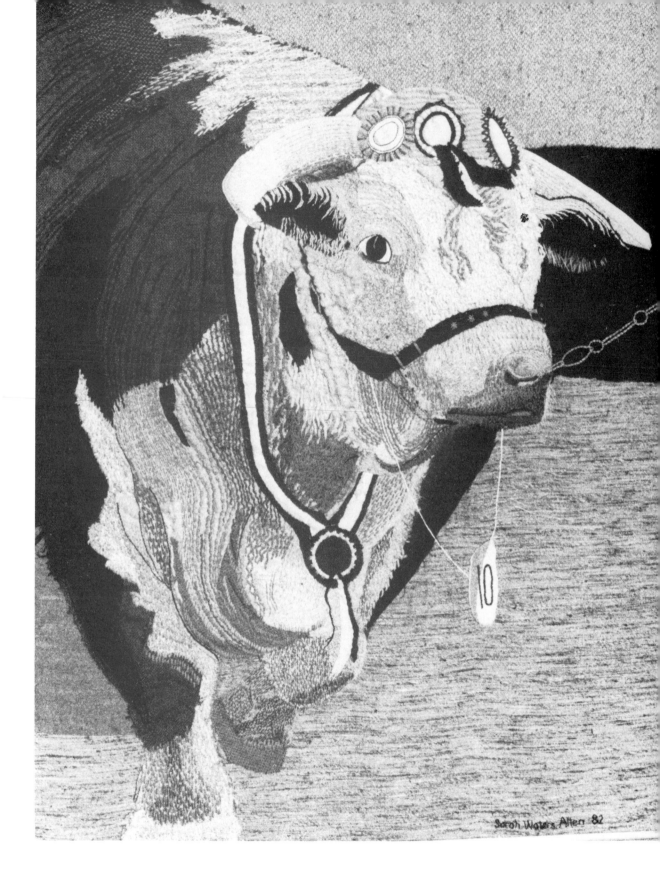

Sarah Waters Allen '82

157

**148 1981 – Patricia Roberts, the London College of Fashion. 'A bunch of strawberries'
in reds and greens, using velvets and satins**

149 1981 – Renate Meyer. Full-sized apple, originally one of 50. Ripe youth to old age – peeled after marriage, then bruised, knocked about, mouldy etc. Various materials are used for the apples, with dye, stitching and stuffing. Red skin, lined with cream fabric, cream apple

150 1981 – Renate Meyer. Mouldy apple – wrinkled greenish brown skin, with stitched ridges and mould

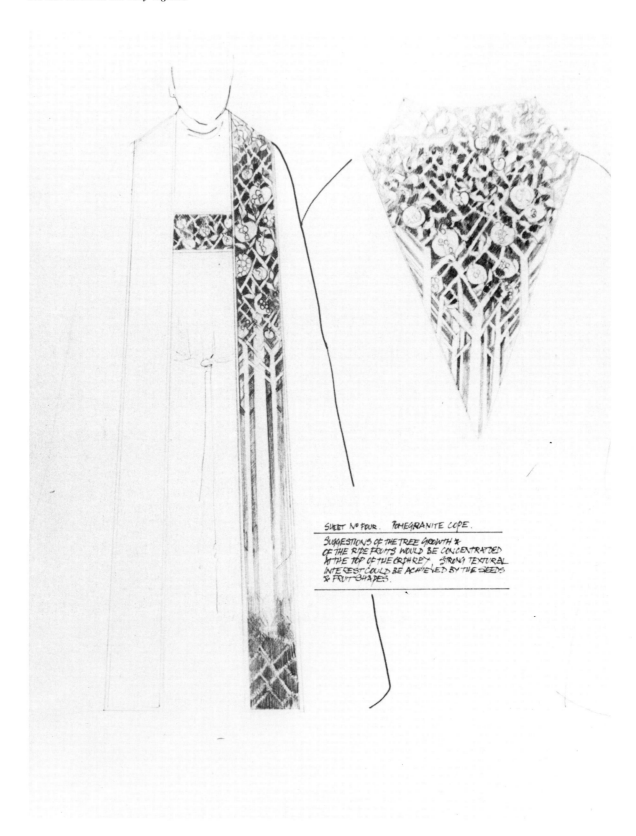

SHEET Nº FOUR. POMEGRANITE COPE.

SUGGESTIONS OF THE TREE GROWTH &
OF THE RIPE FRUITS WOULD BE CONCENTRATED
AT THE TOP OF THE ORPHREY. STRONG TEXTURAL
INTEREST COULD BE ACHIEVED BY THE SEEDS
& FRUIT SHAPES.

151 Left: 1979–82 – Judy Barry and Beryl Patten. A design for the Pomegranate cope for Chester Cathedral showing the orphrey, morse and hood

152 1979–82 – Judy Barry and Beryl Patten. Hood of the Pomegranite cope

153 1979–82 – Judy Barry and Beryl Patten. The Chester Copes. A set of five copes for Chester Cathedral, from left to right:

red –Corn, the 'Chester' cope
magenta –Pomegranate cope
purple –Vine cope
blue –Thorn cope
mauve –Olive cope

All the copes are made from Welsh flannel. Each one is decorated with different symbols; the Chester cope has corn as decoration and is in red, while the pomegranate cope in a subtle magenta echoes the growth of a tree and is embroidered in deep magenta, purples and pinks, bright reds and royal blues. The vine on a purple background is embroidered in dark purples to the palest mauves and pinks; the Olive cope is in a greyish mauve, with embroidery in mauves, silvery greys and greys to blue. Gold and silver brightens the subtle colour of this cope. The Thorn cope is in silvers, blues and mauves on an intense blue ground. Orphreys consisting of tall tree trunks merge into the decoration of the hoods, which are detachable. This gives an alternate use of the copes which may be arranged in any combinations of the five colours. All embroidery is by machine, carried out on separate pieces of fabric, worked simultaneously to give continuity to the group. (1983 – Information supplied by Beryl Patten and Judy Barry in the annual report of the Friends of Chester Cathedral.)

1 1979 — Margaret Traherne. Two brilliantly coloured banners hung from the flagstaffs flanking the entrance to the Tate Gallery. These were made in honour of the opening of the completed Tate Gallery building in May 1979

2 1982 — Susan Kennewell. A panel worked on canvas, 24 in. × 18 in. (61 cm × 46 cm). Hand painting, appliqué, hand and machine stitching

3 Late 70s-early 80s — Ione Dorrington. A cope for the church of St Peter-le-Poer, Muswell Hill. Appliqué of Thai silks

4 1980 — Judy Barry and Beryl Patten. Passiontide altar panels and cope for Manchester Cathedral

5 1980-81 — Esther Grainger. *Mosque at Cordoba*. A panel 41 in. × 47½ in. (104 cm × 120 cm) in collage in a variety of fabrics and colours, with some stitching

6 1981 — Beryl Dean. *Head of Christ*. An icon 8 in. × 5½ in. (20 cm × 14 cm) worked in the or nué technique. Neutral and flesh colours are stitched over Japanese gold

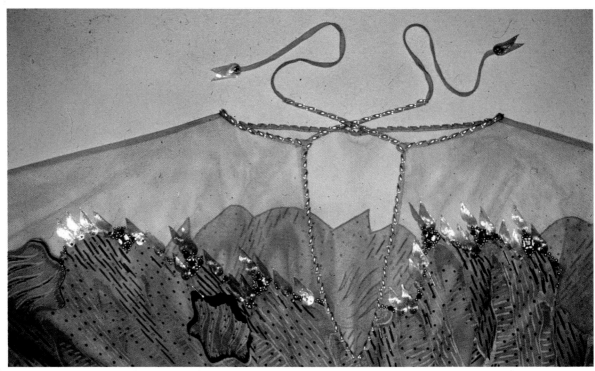

7 1982 — Zandra Rhodes. Detail of chiffon dress with diamanté and metallic beads. The bodice is smocked. *From her Indian collection*

8 1983 — Renate Meyer. One of a set entitled *Pile of Stones* in a variety of fabrics. Patchwork, spray dyeing, stitching, all stuffed

9 1982-83 — Audrey Walker. *There's a Rainbow Round my Shoulder*, approximately 54 in. (137 cm) square. Worked on and round a 1920s' partly embroidered tablecloth with a flower design. The idea has been extended into a wide border of hand and machine stitching, gathered fabrics, applied flowers cut from cretonne, a variety of embroidered textures, with areas sprayed and painted with dye. *Photograph by Hawkley Studios*

10 1983 — Ann Spring. A panel 31 in. (79 cm) square on coarse natural silk. The central panel is in pleated and folded silk, with a batik surround. *Photograph by Hawkley Studios*

11 1982-83 — Rosalind Floyd. *1000 Hours*, a detail of the panel approximately 48 in. (122 cm) square. The panel is on a fabric with a hand-printed line pattern of squares. The illustration shows the top central portion, the complete work being 15 squares in depth and 16 horizontally, with plain fabric stripes between them in yellow, green, blue and red. The stitchery is in perle cotton, the overlaying of colours and couching with different colours of thread, producing a variety of effects. *Photograph by Hawkley Studios*

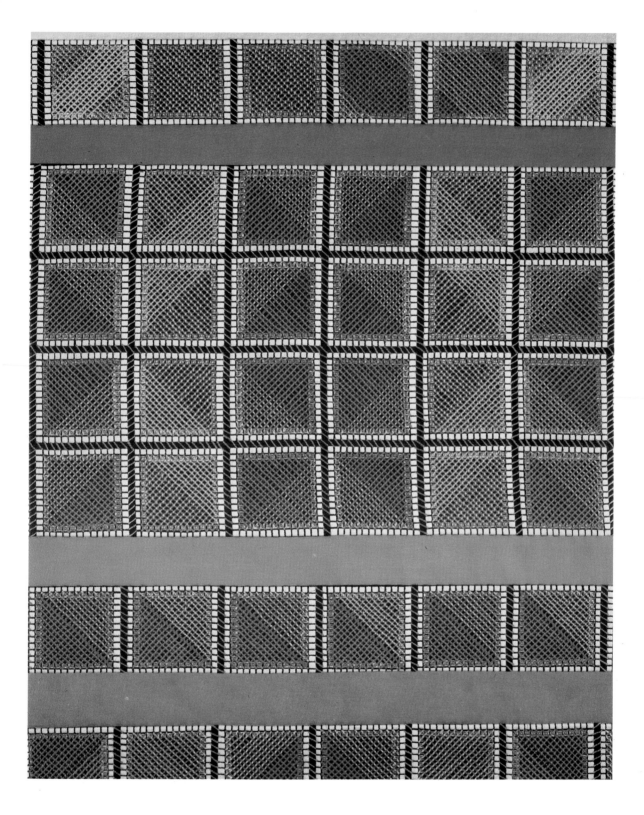

12 1984 — Richard Box. *Primroses*, 3 ft 6 in. × 2 ft 6 in. (106.7 cm × 76 cm). Carried out in hand and machine stitching on an old brocade curtain with an interesting texture. A number of different materials are used and some flowers have been worked separately and attached to leave petals free

154 1981–82 – Pat Russell. A banner for Wells Cathedral. *Thine is the Glory* **in yellows, oranges and red fabrics, machine stitched.** *Photograph by Hawkley Studios*

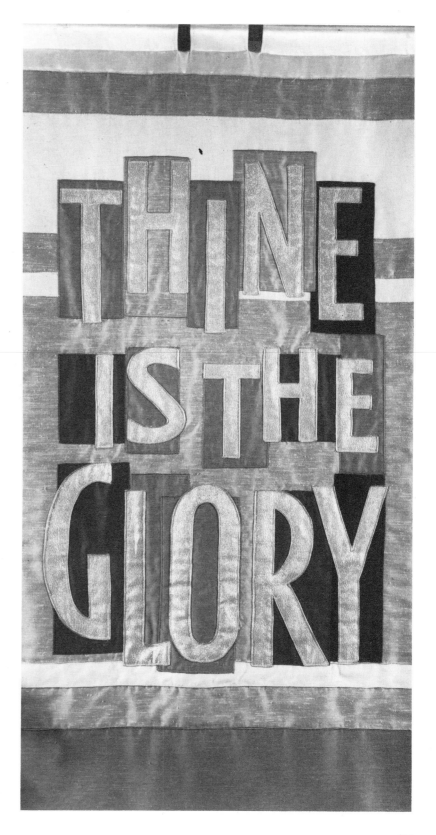

155 Above: 1981-82 – Margaret Perkins. A 'cape' coat of cream Welsh wool, worked in darning stitches in a variety of coloured threads including crimson, brown, black, pinks, greens and yellows. The design was based on many drawings of the embroiderer's garden. *Photograph by Hawkley Studios*

156 Left: 1982 – Lynda Wix, a student attending adult part-time classes with Anna Wilson. *Tramp.* A variety of fabrics is used including velvet, tweed and felt. Colours are mainly browns, fawns, cream, greyish browns and ochres. *Photograph by G Macgregor*

157 Right: 1981–82 – Diana Springall. Detail from *Kells.* A low-relief panel 36 in. × 24 in. (91 cm × 61 cm) in furnishing fabrics. *Designed for the home of Doctor and Mrs Coen. Photograph by John Hunnex*

158 1981–82 – Irene Ord. *Overlapping Squares,* **32 in. (81 cm) square. The ground is natural Honan silk, with machine cable stitching in ten tertiary colours. The gold lurex shapes are applied by hand**

159 1981–82 – Audrey Walker. *A Little Bowl of Cherries*, 17½ in. × 19½ in. (44.5 cm × 49.5 cm). Worked on a corner of an early twentieth-century afternoon tea-cloth in white linen and crocheted lace. The bowl is shaded in greys, fawn, pinks and greens in straight stitches. The cherries are in a variety of reds, from blue-red to orange-red, in straight stitches. Crosses are in straight stitch behind red lettering. Stems are in long stem stitch. Stranded cotton and perle cotton threads are used for the embroidery. *Photograph by Hawkley Studios*

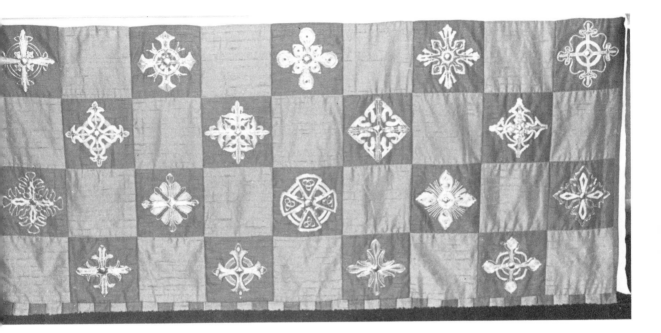

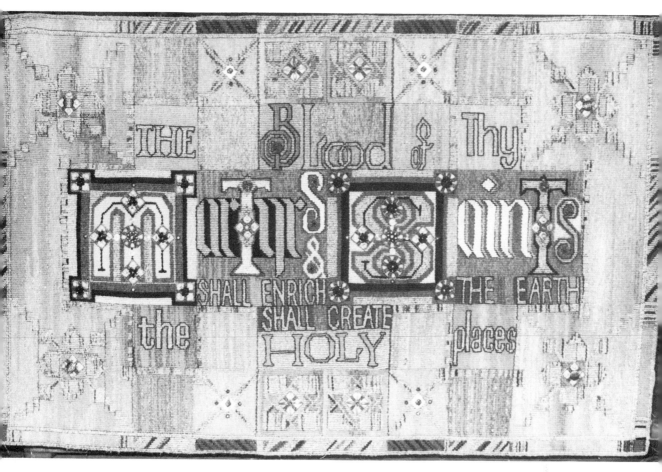

160 Above left: 1982 – Communal work. Altar frontal for St Pol's Church, St Paul, Cornwall. The frontal was produced by part-time students at Penzance School of Art, under the supervision of Ruth Tudor. Ten students participated, each designing and working one or more squares. The background is in two colours of red and pink dupion, the embroidery in couched gold thread and sylko perle cotton. The centres of the designs are in padded gold kid. The whole idea was inspired by the Victorian floor tiles in the chancel of the church. The fringe is attached separately and consists of 2 in. (5 cm) squares of dupion

162 Above: Completed 1982. Joyce Conwy Evans. Frontal for Canterbury Cathedral, Chapel of the Martyrs and Saints of Our Time, 6 ft 3 in. × 3 ft 3 in. (1.91 m × 99 cm). Tapestry woven in wool and metal threads in tones of amber, gold and silver. Embroidered by Elizabeth Geddes in gold thread and jewels. Weaving by the Edinburgh Tapestry Co. The quotation reads 'The blood of the martyrs and saints shall enrich the earth, shall create the Holy place'. From TS Eliot's *Murder in the Cathedral*. The intention is that the quotation should appear in the design through the decoration, as a part of it, and that one should dwell long enough to consider its content

161 Left: 1982 – Detail from altar frontal for St Pol

163 1982 – Pat Russell. A banner for the Queen Mother's birthday. It is 12 ft × 5 ft (3.66 m × 1.52 m) in golds, yellows, tan and greenish turquoise fabrics

164 1982 – Pat Russell. The Slater cope for Lichfield Cathedral. Tree of Life with appliqué of lettering, 'I will give you to eat of the tree of life', in latin. Various fabrics and textures, with blues, greens and other colours on a white ground

165 1982 – Judy Barry and Beryl Patten. Three hangings for St Paul's Chaplincy HMS Raleigh, Royal Navy Initial Traning Establishment, Tor Point, Cornwall. Based on the theme of Trinity, the travels of St Paul and aspects of the countryside near Tor Point. In various blues, pinkish mauves, golds, fawn, cream, brown and orange. *Photograph by the area photographic unit, HMS Drake, Plymouth*

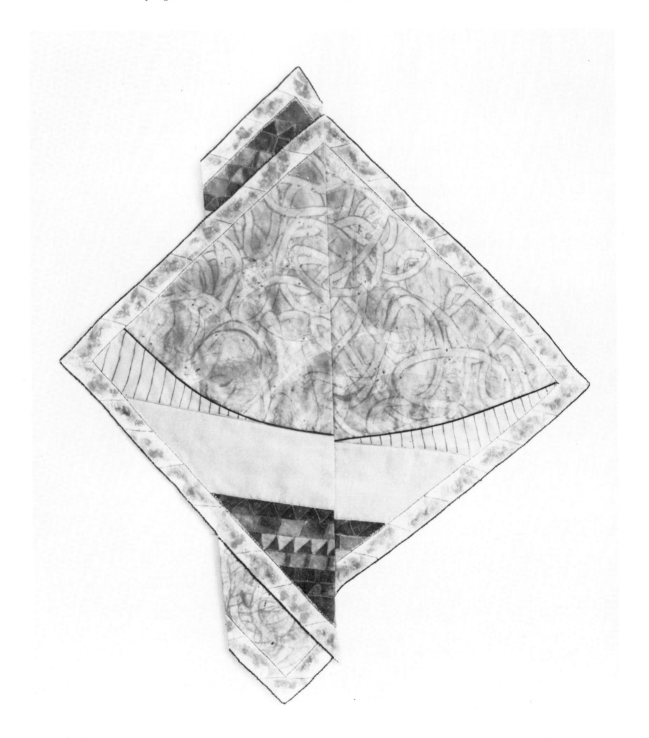

166 1982 – Stephanie Tuckwell. *Serpentine*. A panel, 27 in. × 30 in. (68.5 cm × 76 cm), in silk collage, sprayed, monoprinted and painted, with machine embroidery

167 1982 – Stephanie Tuckwell. *Field Day*. A panel, 38 in. × 40 in. (96.5 cm × 101.5 cm), in silk collage, sprayed, painted and machine embroidered

168 1982 – Pauline Burbidge. *Cubic Maze.* **A wall hanging 33 in. (84 cm) square made in Honan silk in vivid colours of black and primaries – red, blue and yellow.** *Photograph by John Coles*

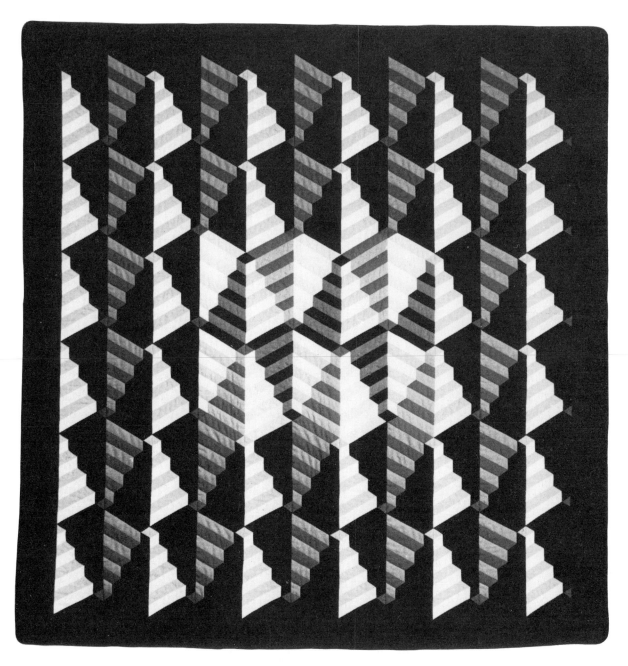

169 1982 – Pauline Burbidge. *The Final Pyramid.* **A cotton wall hanging 44 in. × 42 in. (112 cm × 106.5 cm) with some hand dyed fabrics. Black outer area with four tones of grey. The central panel changes to vibrant reds and blues.** *Photograph by John Coles*

170 (a) 1982 – Valerie Taylor, a student at Trent Polytechnic. A panel approximately 65 in. × 43½ in. (165 cm × 110 cm). The ground is calico covered with cross stitching worked on the Schiffli multiple needle machine. Variations of pattern and density of stitching and colour are achieved through adjustment of needle and pattern spacing. Red, yellow and blue primary colours

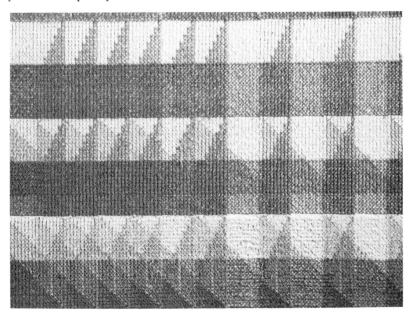

170 (b) 1982 – Valerie Taylor. Detail from panel

171 1982 – Mary Youles. Photographs taken in Venice of various details, also drawings from which the samples are worked using some dye and stitchery. *Photograph by Hawkley Studios*

172 Above: 1982 – Julia Walker. *Fan-pipes*, 27 in. (68.5 cm) square. Quilted on unbleached calico, with plain squares and squares constructed in the grandmother's fan patchwork technique. *Photograph by Brian McNeill*

173 Right: 1982 – Kay Lynch. *Pearly Queen and Granddaughter*. A panel entirely in machine stitching with a patterned fabric ground in various colours of blues, pinks and greens, and a stitched wallpaper in blue with a green pattern. The child wears a white dress, using some automatic machine patterns; the adult's dress is red with white spots and the hat is also red. *Photograph by Hawkley Studios*

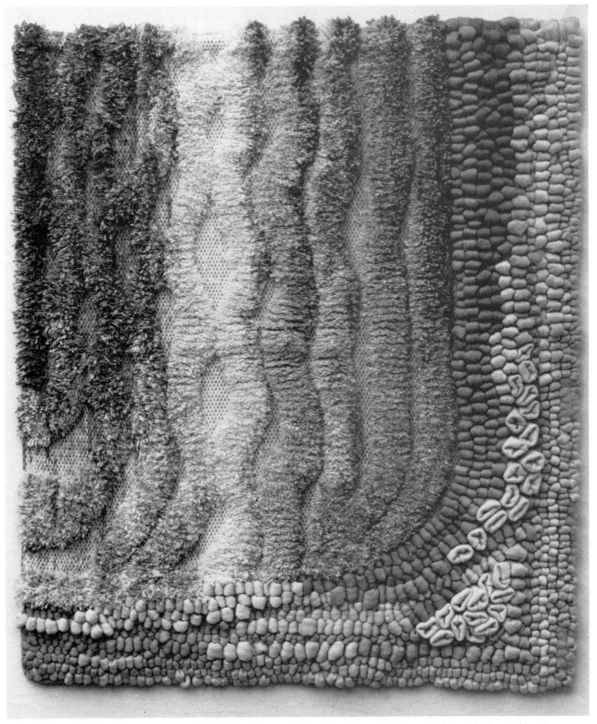

174 1982 – Margaret Gaby. *Sea Shore*, 4 ft 5 in. × 3 ft 3 in. (134.5 cm × 99 cm). Worked in wool on canvas; flat stitches and cut loops using many hand spun and dyed yarns. Machine knitted fabrics compose the closely packed loops at the bottom right of the photograph. The idea resulted from photographs and sketches in Brittany

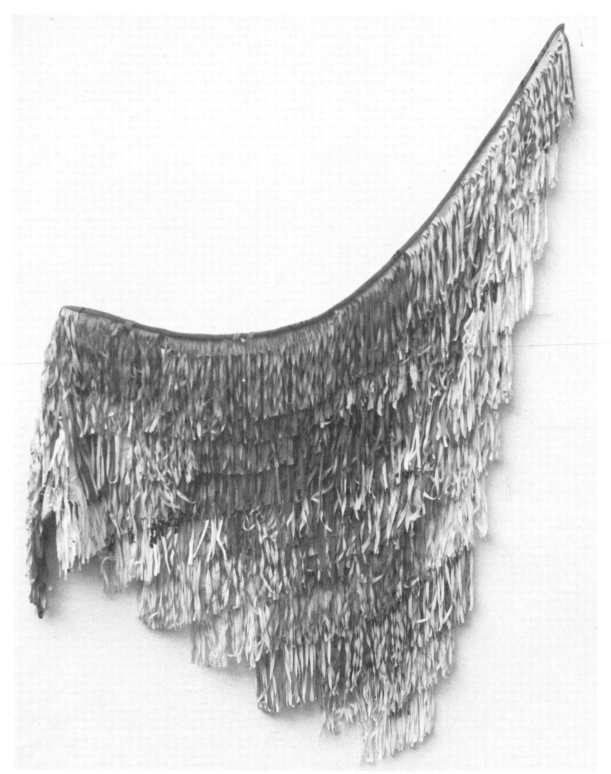

175 1982 – Mary Fogg, a member of the Beckenham Textile Studio. 'Shawl', an experiment using reject materials – cheap nylon, polyester knits, worn clothing thrown out of Oxfam. The fabrics do not fray and are light and springy. The idea is inspired by the Pacific peoples' feather cloaks. A subtlety of colour is obtained by overlapping fabrics of different types. *Photograph by Brian McNeill*

176 1982 – Jean Davey Winter. *Memory Symbol II*, **12 in. (30.5 cm) square. Plaster cast from etching plates, collage, handmade paper and fabrics; set into plaster and worked over with graphite and stitchery**

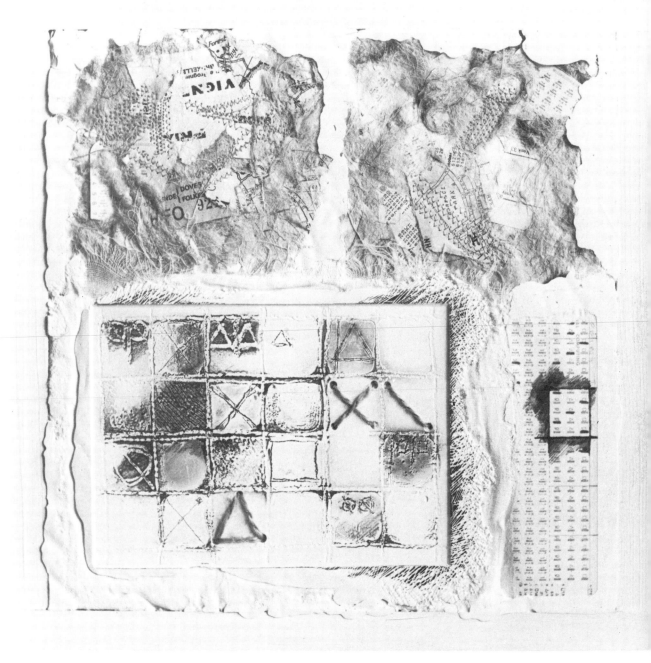

177 1982 – Jean Davey Winter. *Memory Symbol IV*, 12 in. (30.5 cm) square. Plaster cast from etching plates, collage, handmade paper and fabrics; set into plaster and worked over with graphite and stitchery

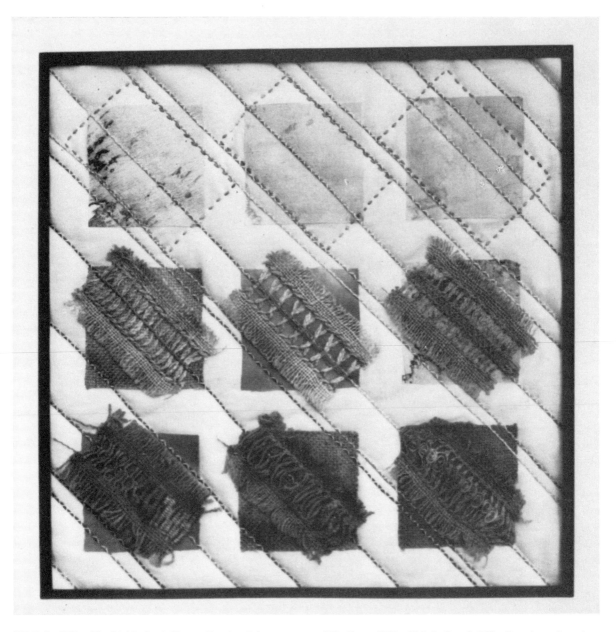

178 Left: 1982 – *The Maidenhead Charter Hanging*, 7 ft ×
11 ft (2.13 m × 3.35 m). A community project, designed by Jan
Beaney and Jean Littlejohn. Made to commemorate the 400th
anniversary of the Charter, the hanging was worked by 64
women and six men. The focal point of the hanging is the bridge
and the Guards' bridge in the centre panel. The flowers are in
pinks, purples, reds and mauves, symbolic of the parks and
gardens in Maidenhead. The roundabout system is shown by
three hand quilted roundels which depict St Mary's Church, the
original seal of the first Charter of Maidenhead and the clock
tower. The tulips are worked as a block of machine stitching.
The trees, grasses, leaves and other foliage are in hand
embroidery. *Photograph by Dudley Moss*

179 Above: 1982 – Valerie Campbell-Harding. A panel on shot
silk, based on moiré patterns and water movement. Dyed areas
with appliqué of drawn thread patterns

180 Right: 1982 – Sue Rangeley. *Garden Quilt*, 7 ft 6 in. × 8ft 6 in. (2.9 m × 2.59 m). Hollyhocks, delphiniums and butterflies adorn the quilt. Hand embroidery, beading with quilting in ripples to petal shapes. Airbrush colour

181 Below left: 1982 – Sue Rangeley. A detail showing the centre panel of the quilt

182 Below right: 1982 – Zandra Rhodes. A detail of a chiffon dress with embroidered bodice. From her Indian Collection

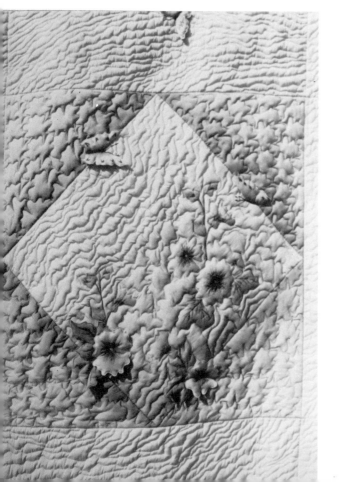

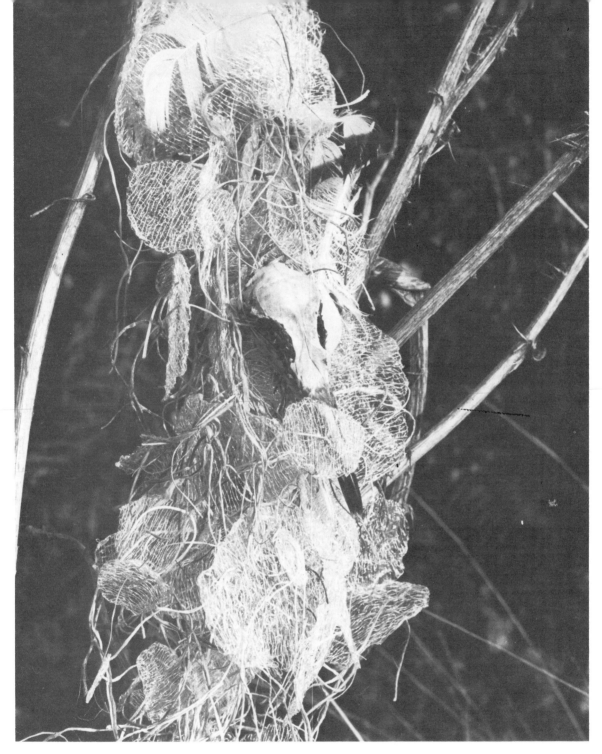

183 1982 – Janet Ledsham. *Ice Bird*, **24 in. × 6 in. (61 cm × 15 cm). Three dimensional. Heated cellulose film stitched with silver thread, interwoven with waxed threads incorporating a seagull skull**

184 Left: 1982 – Rozanne Hawksley. *Absolvo te in nomine Patris*. Experimental work, 45 in. × 36 in. (114 cm × 91 cm). 'I absolve you (your sins) in the name of the Father'. Pale leather gloves, except one, mounted on wood. The hand of the Church is in silk and the handmade lace on a black lacquered cross, mounted on wood. *Photograph by Brian Hawksley*

185 Above: 1982 – Rozanne Hawksley. *Pale Armistice – in death only are we united*. Experimental work; collage. A wreath of kid gloves and artificial flowers. The flowers are plastic and fabric, the leaves and buds are bleached bones. *Photograph by Brian Hawksley*

186 1982 – Gay Swift. A small panel, 6½ in. × 7 in. (16 cm × 18 cm), in hand and machine stitching. Padded pink silk, jubilee spotted white cotton voile, rouleaux of silk ribbon, minute cerise silk buttons, faience flowers, wired bead decoration, moonstones and small bells. The spots are red and raised in a tie-dye technique

187 1982 – Anne Butler Morrell. *Opposing Diagonals.* A panel with the upper fabric in felt, machine and hand stitched, in mohair in stem stitch. The ovals are in mohair and silks in stem stitch. Mainly worked in pinks

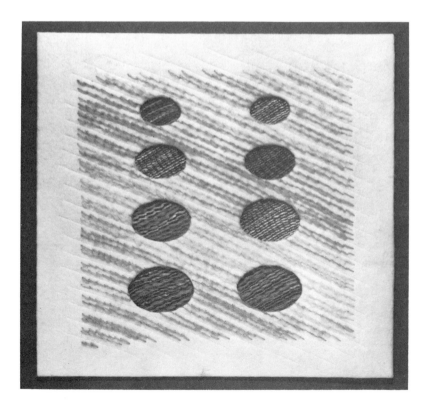

188 1982 – Enid Mason. *Patchwork Landscape*, **14 in. (35.5 cm) square. Fabric over card, in a variety of fabrics in dark turquoise, grey-browns, dark blue, pinkish orange, yellow and dull greens.** *Owned by the Horncastle Residential College*

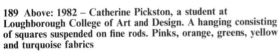

189 Above: 1982 – Catherine Pickston, a student at Loughborough College of Art and Design. A hanging consisting of squares suspended on fine rods. Pinks, orange, greens, yellow and turquoise fabrics

190 Above right: 1982 – Valerie Campbell-Harding. A cushion cover in striped ticking, with fabric manipulated to give a variety of pattern; machine stitching

191 Right: 1982 – Margaret Kaye. Collage with stitching for emphasis; fabrics frayed and twisted, loosely attached to the background. Brilliant colours include red, pink and blue with some patterned fabric

192 1982 – Moira Broadbent. *Parquet.*
Hand embroidery in silk threads in pink
and green with a little grey

194 1982 – Daryl Pascall. A collar and fan executed by a Loughborough student, using black and coloured organzas with machine stitching

193 1982 – Susan Aiken. A sample in couching and seeding using a mixture of wools, silks and cotton threads, developed from pastel drawings

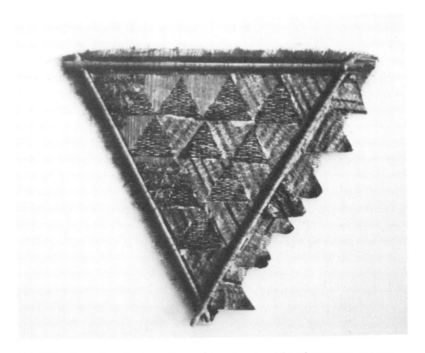

195 1982 – Karen Spurgin. A panel on metal mesh, using strips of newspaper, sewn on to this background in triangles, embroidered on cotton thread. Spaces between are embroidery in linen thread. The frame is dowling. Triangular, each side 12 in. (30.5 cm) long

196 Above: 1982 – Pauline Hann. Back view of a black Thai silk kimono jacket with appliqué, canvas work, surface stitchery and satin cords. In pinks, greys, creams, ivory, rusts and browns

197 Below: 1982 – Pauline Hann. A detail of the jacket

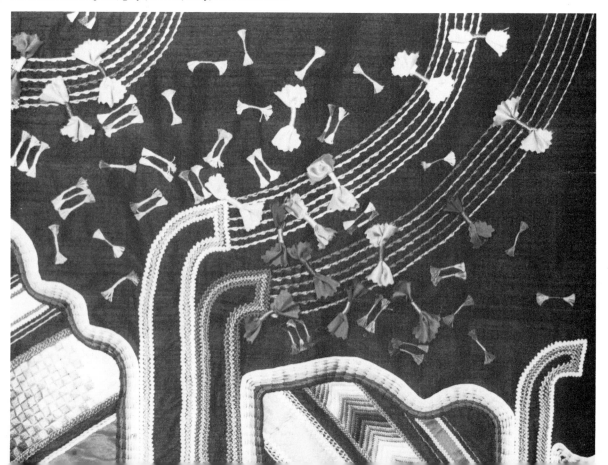

198 Right: 1982 – Valerie Holmes, a student at Manchester Polytechnic. A small panel 3 in. × 3½ in. (8 cm × 9 cm) in ceramic with hand knitted cotton crushed into the clay through holes. *Embroiderers' Guild Collection. Photograph by Hawkley Studios*

199 Below: 1982 – Moyra McNeill. *Twilight.* **An embroidered panel, 11¾ in. × 15¾ in. (30 cm × 40 cm), in black, red and blue, on white, even-weave linen with net appliqué and spraying**

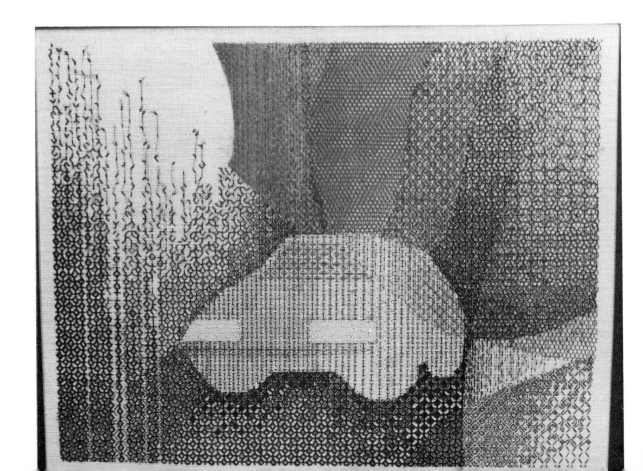

200 1982 – Dorothy Walker. A sampler, 4½ in. × 9 in. (11.5 cm × 23 cm), machine stitched on acetate, mainly in emerald green, pink, white and grey coloured silks. *Embroiderers' Guild Collection. Photograph by Hawkley Studios*

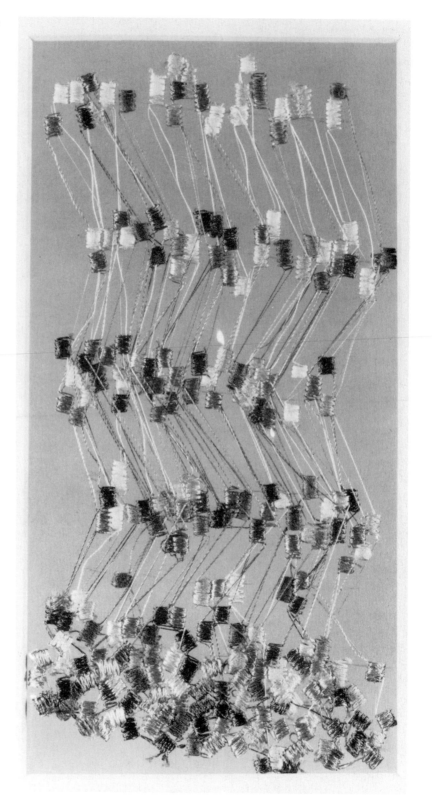

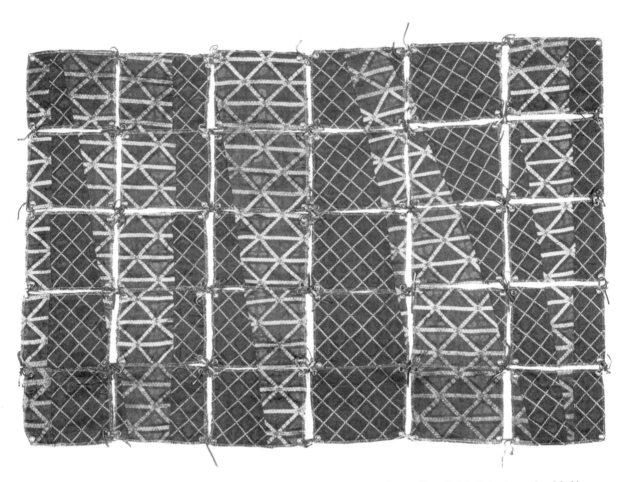

201 Above: 1982 – Joanna Smith, a student at Trent Polytechnic. A sample of fashion fabric 27½ in. × 17¾ in. (70 cm × 45 cm). Dyed and printed silk and organdie, machine stitched together, with the top layer partly cut away to show the printed silk. The resulting fabric is cut into strips, rejoined and cut again into rectangles. These are overlocked in metallic thread. The rectangles are tied together with gold leather, through the eyelets. Colours are deep tones of blue, green and gold

202 Right: 1982 – Joanna Smith. A detail of the fashion fabric. Each tied section measures approximately 4½ in. × 3½ in. (11 cm × 9 cm)

203 1982 – Bridget Moss. *Mutations.* **A small panel in white stitches in varied weights of thread on a brown ground**

204 1982 – Nancy Kimmins. *Persian Garden,* **12 in. × 8 in. (30.5 cm × 20 cm). Embroidery on a lurex ground with laidwork patterns and beading**

205 1982 – Margaret Swales. *Roots.*
39½ in. × 59 in. (100 cm × 150 cm)
Machine embroidery and trapunto
quilting on a cream silk ground

206 1982 – Amanda Clayton, a student at Birmingham Polytechnic. Lace techniques carried out in calico, using rouleaux as yarn

207 1982 – Amanda Clayton. Detail of a single bed cover

208 1982 – Diana Thornton. *Sitting with the Fireplace,* **29 in. × 23 in. (73.5 cm × 58 cm). The fireplace and pot were drawn on white cotton material then filled in completely with stitching on the Irish machine. Tones are emphasised with different shades of cotton and synthetic threads. The direction in which the stitching is worked also emphasises light and shade**

209 1982–83 – Eirian Short. *Spring at Castell Bach*. Detail of a panel approximately 48 in. × 30 in. (122 cm × 76 cm). The fabric is completely worked over in straight stitches, french knots, stem and other stitches, in wools in bright blue for the sky, red earth and various greys for the rocks. The foreground is in different greens with yellow blossoms

210 1982–83 – Mary Cozens-Walker. *The Topiary Garden*, 84 in. × 53 in. × 22 in. deep (213 cm × 135 cm × 56 cm). A private place, a garden-room standing on a raised lawn with a red brick supporting wall. The idea is based on stylised plans for seventeenth-century formal gardens. The lawn is dyed towelling, painted, padded and stitched. The perimeter bushes are on a wooden base, with wadding and calico over chicken wire. Yew trees have textures of wood shavings and sawdust applied and painted as have other bushes. Chicken wire peacocks. The tufting machine makes the grass on the edge of the lawn; mosses are in velvets

211 Above: 1982–83 – Maureen Helsdon. *Trattoria*, **45 in. (114 cm) square. A detail of a larger panel of torn fabrics, reassembled with bags containing garlic, cloves and herbs to introduce three dimensions and smell to the senses. Machine embroidery. Colours are fawn, browns, greyish fawns and some red**

212 Right: 1982–83 – Wendy Yeomans. *Two Punks on a Bench*. **Three-dimensional figures in which many materials are used for the clothes which are in blue denim, blue fishnet for stockings for the girl, bright pink for the boy, the same colour making the girl's shoes. Appliqué of plain and patterned pieces of fabric make the decoration, with hand and machine stitching.** *Photograph by Hawkley Studios*

213 Left: 1982–83 – Linda Gomm. A hanging approximately 48 in. × 24 in. (122 cm × 61 cm) using white dyed silks in stripes of blue, orange, mauve and pink, draped over a rigid panel with coloured, dyed and stitched stripes. *Shown at the '62 Group exhibition in Bath in 1983. Photograph by Hawkley Studios*

214 Above: 1980–83 – Wendy Lees. *Spring into Summer*. A wall hanging 17½ ft × 6 ft (5.33 m × 1.83 m). On a calico background with a screen printed geometric design. Applied units of log-cabin patchwork, ranging from 2 in. (2.5 cm) to 36 in. (91 cm) in width, in silks and dupion fabrics. Colours are pale yellows and soft pinks against a turquoise sky, changing to intense pinks, reds and oranges, ending with the chrysanthemum and michaelmas daisy colours of late summer. *See* Embroidery, *Volume 34, Number 4, Winter 1983. Photograph by Peter Lees*

215 Right: 1980–83 – Wendy Lees. *Autumn into Winter*. A wall hanging in Elvin Hall, University of London, 17½ ft × 6 ft (5.33 m × 1.83 m). On a calico background, with a screen printed geometric design. Appliqué in log-cabin patchwork units in seven sizes, from 2 in. (2.5 cm) to 36 in. (91 cm) across, in silks and dupion fabrics. Colours range from corn colours of the harvest to greys and mauves and to the holly of December. *Photograph by Peter Lees*

216 Far left: 1982–83 – Ruth Tudor.
Titania. A fantastic figure 36 in. (91 cm)
high in greenish greys, bluish greys and
a variety of dull and paler greens.
Chiffons and net, velvet and dupion
furnishing fabrics are used. Couched fuse
wire stiffens the wings and leaves, and
an armature of bamboo canes supports
the figure. The face is hand embroidery,
the rest of the embroidery is by machine

217 Left: 1982–83 – Ruth Tudor. Back
view of *Titania*

218 Right: 1982–83 – Ruth Tudor. *Lady
with a Dog*, 54 in. (137 cm) high. Based
on the 'dummy board figures' of the
seventeenth century of paintings of
members of a family or servants,
sometimes with pets. (Information from
a National Trust leaflet.) Worked in a
variety of fabrics including wool, cotton,
silk and lace – some of these are old and
faded – in dark browns, purples, greys
and black. The aim was to try and get
the quality of a heavily varnished
painting. The face, hands and rose are
hand worked, the rest machine
embroidery

219 Left: 1982–83 – Susan Kennewell. *Rug*, a hanging. Appliqué of small pieces of fabric in brilliant bands of strips of colour, giving a variety of textures. Colours include reds, yellows, blues, purple, orange, pink and green. Mainly machine stitching. *Photograph by Hawkley Studios*

220 Right: 1982–83 – Karen Borland, a student at Glasgow School of Art. A panel in balsa wood, with silk, net, wire and handmade paper and using silk thread and polythene

221 Below: 1982–83 – Beverley Clark. *Snake Piece*, approximately 6 ft (1.83 m) in width. Manipulated, gathered and pleated fabric with a pattern, screen printed in browns, ochre and greys. Some pleated areas are twisted, some areas are tightly pleated, some are more open. *Shown at the '62 Group exhibition in Bath in 1983*

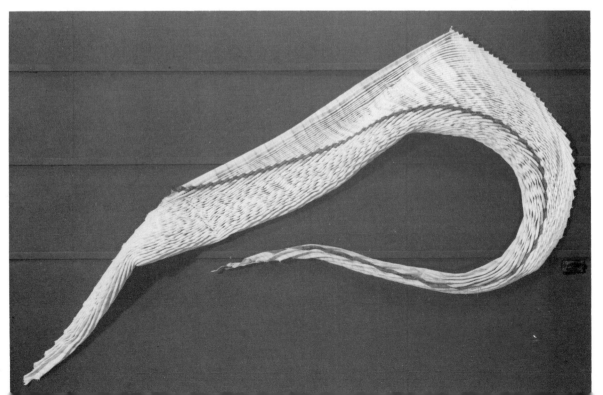

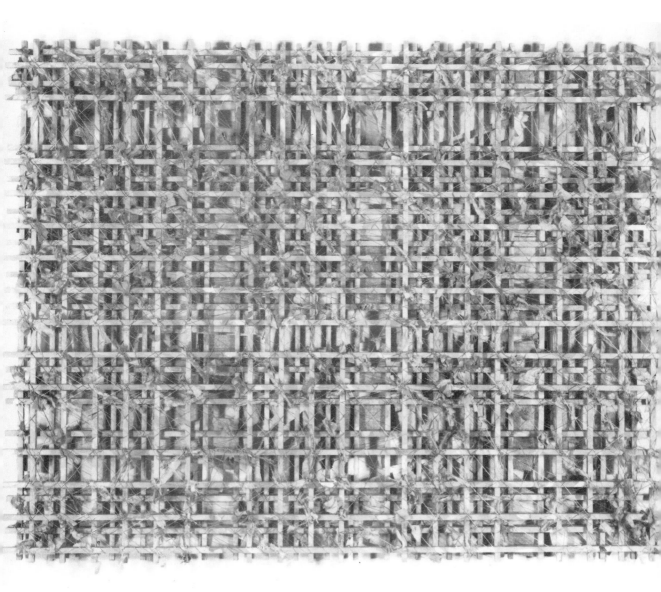

222 Above: 1982–83 – Michael Brennand-Wood. *Untitled II*. A three-dimensional
structure approximately 53 in. × 41 in. (134.5 cm × 104 cm). A wooden grid structure is
arranged in several layers interspersed with various textures of dyed thread and rags in
cottons, silks and other fabrics. Colours are light rather than dark, giving a sunny effect.
These are in greens, pinks, yellows, golds, apricot, with some light red. *Photograph by
Hawkley Studios*

223 Right: 1982–83 – Christine Risley. A panel approximately 34 in. × 24 in. (86.5 cm ×
61 cm). Machine embroidery on white organza, using sequin silver waste, silver fabric
and thread, with some pale colours. Worked in separate areas on the Irish machine, the
pieces being reassembled into design after working. *Photograph by Hawkley Studios*

224 1983 – Carrie Robertson Wright. *Out of the Blue*, 13½ in. × 14½ in. (34.5 cm × 37 cm). The background is blue Thai silk. Canvas stitchery, silk wrapping, spray dye and fringed chiffon are combined. Based on landscape

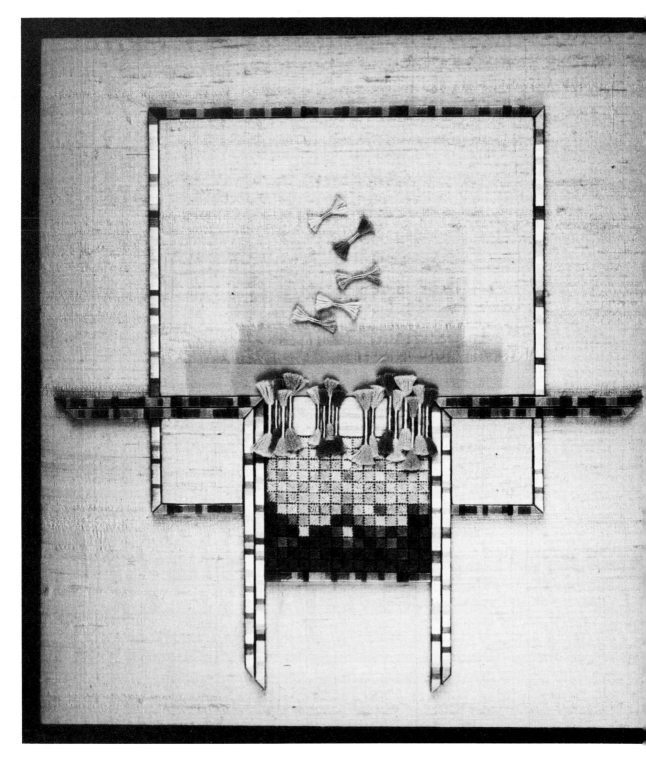

225 1983 – Carrie Robertson Wright. *Weather Effects*, 13 in. × 14½ in. (34.5 cm × 37 cm). Background of pure Thai silk. Machine and hand stitchery, wrapping in silk and lurex threads. Based on fields and fences

226 1983 – Julia Caprara. *Colour Sound – Heaven and Earth Unite.* A panel approximately 54 in. × 27 in. (137 cm × 69 cm) with a border in hooked rags. Within this is a narrow border of hand stitching – running with loops and some machining. The centre of the panel is in manipulated fabrics, spotted muslins and fine textures, folded and hand and machine stitched, with more appliqué stitched in loops, straight and other stitching. Colours are mauves, cream, pink, green, pale blue-green, with dyed areas. *Photograph by Hawkley Studios*

227 1983 – Julia Caprara. A panel, *Colour Sound – Joy*

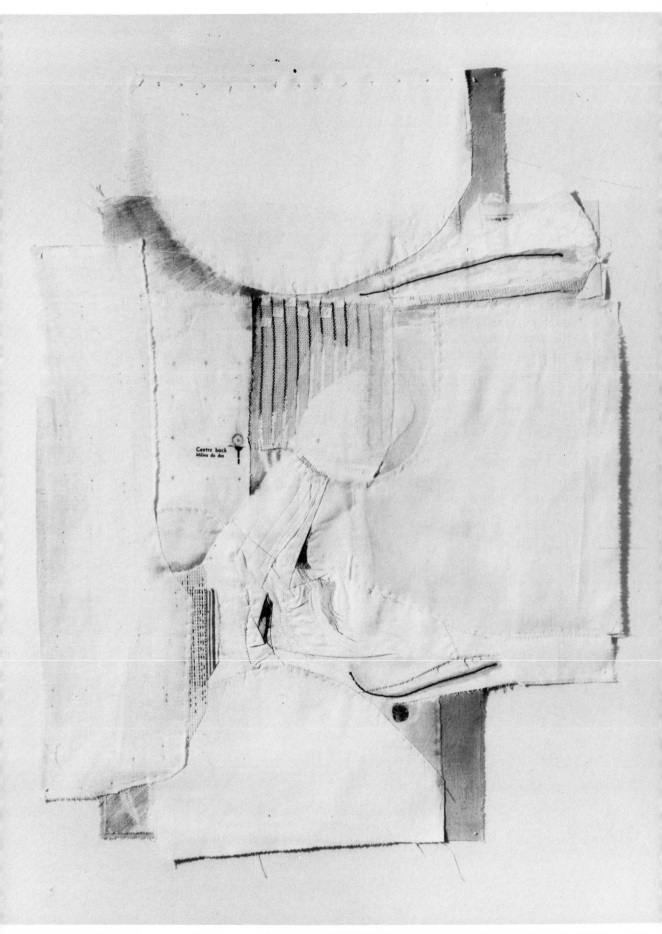

Centre back
Milieu du dos

229 & 230 Above: 1983 – Lorna Weston, a student at Manchester Polytechnic in her final year's study for the BA Honours degree. Lingerie worked on the Schiffli machine

228 Left: 1983 – Audrey Brockbank. *Week End.* A panel in collage with stitching by hand and machine. Pieces of a garment have been reassembled, with some paper pattern shapes for the collage, which is mainly white on a creamish ground, with some dye and touches of yellow, pink and grey. *Shown at the '62 Group exhibition in Bath in 1983. Photograph by Hawkley Studios*

231 Left: 1983 – Jody Smith, a student on the Manchester Polytechnic MA course. A dress in dyed organdie, consisting of two layers of fabric stitched on the Schiffli machine, hand cut and beaded

232 Below: 1983 – Jody Smith. A detail of the organdie dress

233 Right: 1983 – Jody Smith, a student on the Manchester Polytechnic MA course. The sample made while working for a Swiss firm in Switzerland. It is in cork fabric with imitation suede

234 Left: 1983 – Jody Smith, a student on the Manchester Polytechnic MA course. A sample of silk tulle threaded with ribbon; made while working for a Swiss firm in Switzerland

235 Above: 1983 – Daphne Nicholson. A panel approximately 20 in. × 12 in. (51 cm × 30.5 cm) in red and black threads showing different patterns in blackwork techniques

236 Right: 1983 – Sheila Miller. A panel on grey corduroy in the *or nué* technique worked in silks and metal threads. The design is based on a ballet of dancing figures. *Photograph by Hawkley Studios*

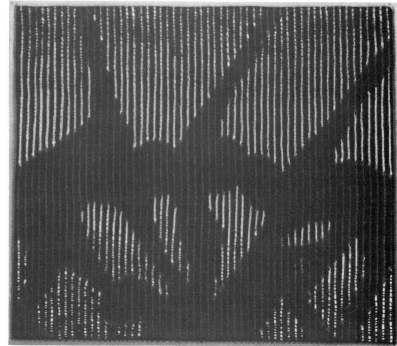

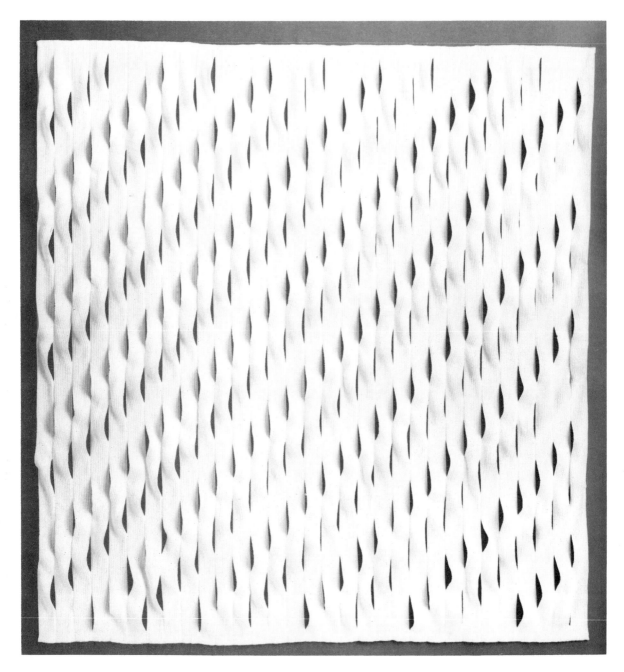

237 1983 – Phyllis Ross. *Flight*. **A hanging 6 ft 5 in. × 6 ft 8 in. (1.96 m × 2.04 m). In strips of Italian quilting in white silk, which are joined at intervals to produce a pattern of slits**

238 1983 – Margaret Rivers. A sleeveless jacket in cream jap silk, machine quilted, with a design based on rubbings from an old box of paints. The waistcoat is reversible to calico. The jacket fastens on the shoulders and at the sides. *Photograph by Hawkley Studios*

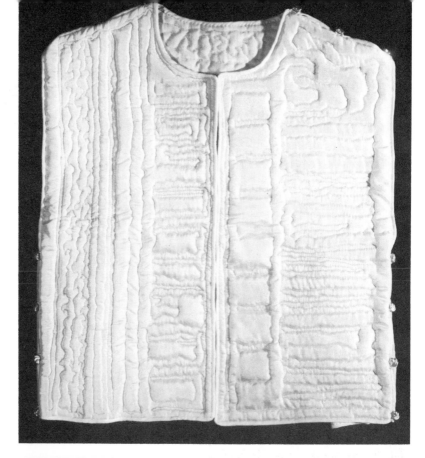

239 1983 – Margaret Rivers. A sleeveless jacket in silk strips and lace, applied to a viyella background and further embellished with tucks, pleats, insertion stitches and surface stitchery. The jacket fastens on the shoulders and at the sides. *Photograph by Hawkley Studios*

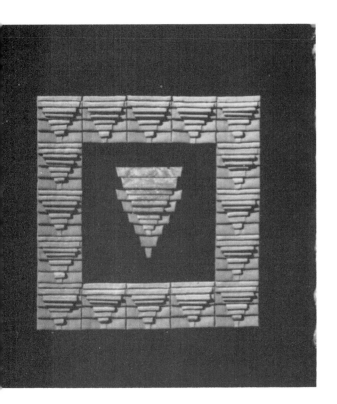

240 1983 – Anne Spring. A panel approximately 30 in. (76 cm) square. Pleated grey silk and black fabric. *Photograph by Hawkley Studios*

241 1983 – Lilla Speir. Patchwork quilt in dull reds, green, cream, and fawn; plain with patterned fabrics containing orange and black

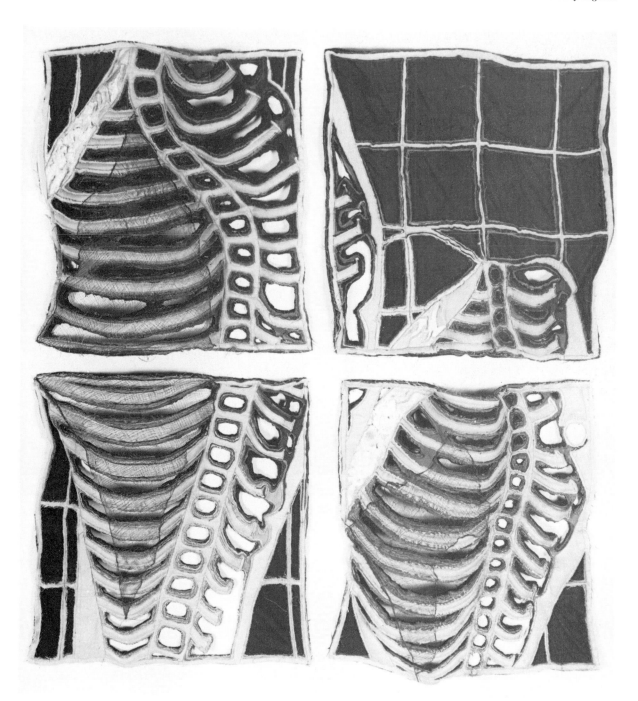

**242 1983 – Amanda Smith, a student at Loughborough College of Art and Design.
'Meat' panel in cut work and machine embroidery using a variety of fabrics, including
wool, cotton and synthetics; in reds, cream and small pieces of various colours**

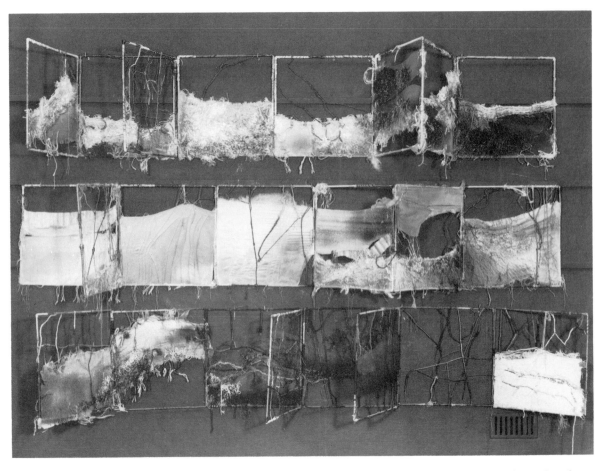

243 1983 – Maria-Theresa Fernandes. *Winter II USA.* **Construction of a number of 12 in. (30.5 cm) square metal frames arranged to make a composition. A variety of dyed fabrics is used, stretched in the frames, with wrapped cords, tufting and looping, hand and machine stitching. Colours include yellows, golds, browns to purplish reds, cream and greyish blues and a little blue-green.** *Photograph by Hawkley Studios*

244 1983 – Jennifer Shonk. *It seems such a long time ago*, **36 in. × 39 in. (91 cm × 99 cm). Mixed media – drawing, machine cut-work and quilting, stitchery, appliqué, hand embroidery, dye. Colours are mainly blues, white, browns, pale pink, yellow and green**

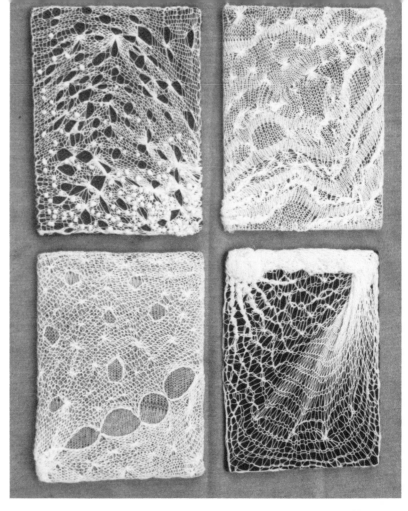

245 1983 – Pamela Pavitt. Samples of machine knitting, embellished with machine embroidery. Each piece about 7 in. × 9 in. (18 cm × 23 cm)

246 1983 – Pamela Pavitt. Sample of machine knitting, embellished with machine embroidery, about 7 in. (18 cm) in diameter

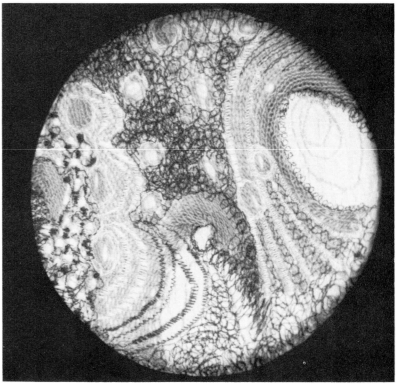

247 1983 – Pamela Rooke. *Midnight Surf*, 10 in. × 12 in. (25.5 cm × 30.5 cm), on a blue furnishing dupion, using both sides, with mainly blues and greens. Stitches include stem, back and running, french knots and beads. The enamelled copper has holes through which straight stitches and beads are sewn

248 1983 – Anne Butler Morrell. A panel 22 in. × 20 in. (56 cm × 51 cm) in hand stitching

249 1983 – Eleri Mills. *In My Craft or Sullen Art*, 48 in. × 83½ in. (1.22 m × 2.12 m). **Dye and stitchery in various threads. Browns, blues, fawns, black and cream threads with straight stitches and herringbone.** *Commissioned by John Graytten*

250 1983 – Eleri Mills. Detail of *In My Craft or Sullen Art*

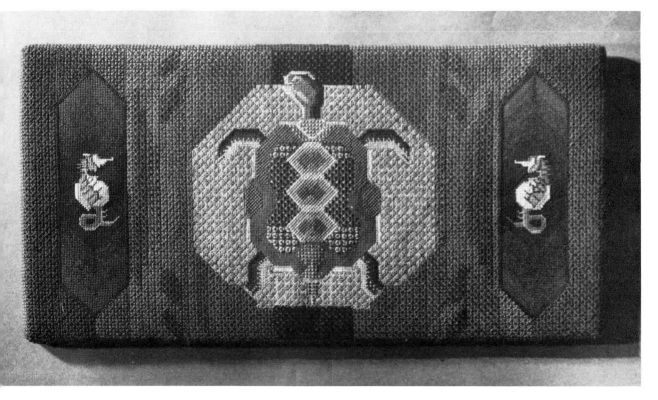

251 1983 – Sylvia Green, designer. A set of three sanctuary kneelers in canvas stitchery for St Michael's Church, Highgate. The theme is *The Creation. Photographs by John Gay*

(a) Above: Embroidered by Katherine Hetherington in various canvas stitches. The terrapin represents reptile creation

(b) Above right: Embroidered by Margaret Hill in various canvas stitches. The bee represents insect creation

(c) Below right: Embroidered by Rosemary Davis. The bird representing bird creation

252 1983 – Isabel Dibden. *Papaver.* A patchwork wall hanging, 56½ in. × 72½ in. (143.5 cm × 184 cm), in machine embroidery, showing flowers in outline on a geometric background. Silks, wools, cottons and satin fabrics are incorporated in the hanging

253 1983 – Veronica Togneri. *Heraldic.* A patchwork panel in a variety of colours

254 1983 – Sylvia Green. A pennant designed by Sylvia Green, embroidered by Mary Brooks. Appliqué in tones of lime green in silk and silk organza on a soft green ground. Made for the 'Cathedral in the Forest', Newland. Photograph by *Dean Forest Studios*

255 Left: 1983 – Jean Davey Winter. *Traces of Uncertainty – Homage to Heisenburg*. A panel with stripes of coloured pattern printed on *Vilene* in blue, yellow-green, pinkish fawn and others. Handmade paper background and applied paper; machine stitching. *Photograph by Hawkley Studios*

256 1983 – Sian Martin. *Secrets I*. A panel 25 in. × 17 in. (63.5 cm × 43 cm). A panel in cotton ticking and black silk. The idea is based on one of a series of drawings of crumpled and folded, striped paper. *Secrets I* developed when drawing the folded back corner of a piece of striped paper that appeared as if something interesting was hidden behind the fold. Small pieces of gold peep out from behind the folded edge of fabric

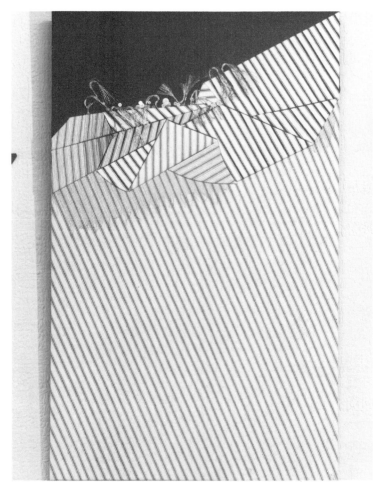

257 1983 – Jean Davey Winter. *Ephemeral Form*, approximately 36 in. × 42 in. (91 cm × 107 cm). Handmade paper, print, hand and machine stitching. *Photograph by Cynthia Bradford*

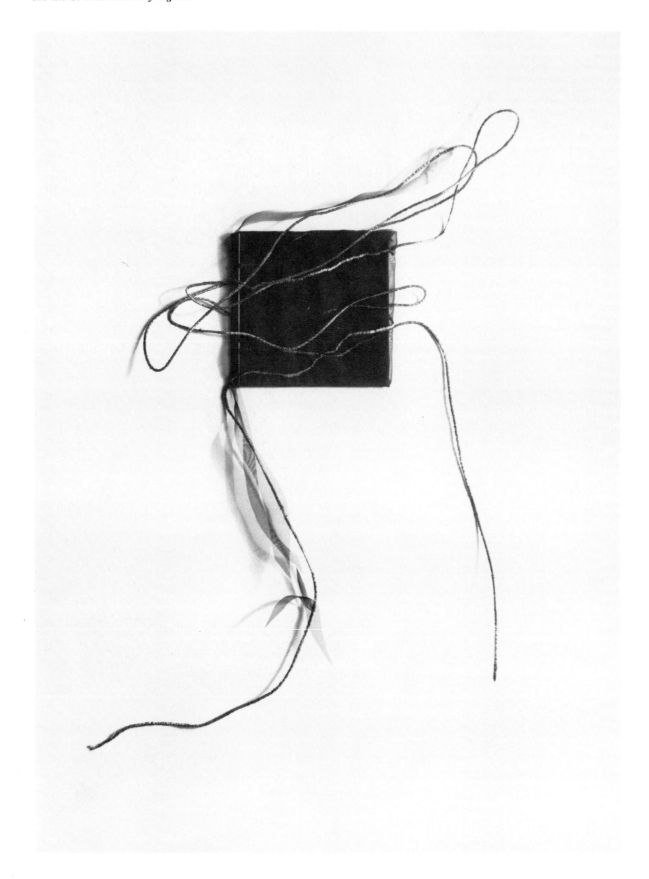

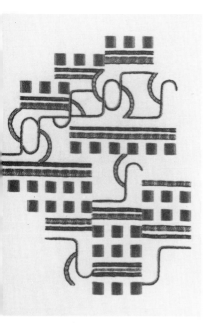

258 Left: 1983 – Anne Bingham.
Leaping Square, 20 in. × 12 in.
(51 cm × 30.5 cm). Two layers of black
organdie stretched over a square mirror,
giving a moiré effect. Machine stitched
satin lines in brightly coloured
variegated thread in reds, blue, green,
orange and yellow on the organdie and
over the wire to give three-dimensional
lines running out from the square

259 Above: 1983 – Molly Picken.
Abstract of a child's toy train, worked in
satin stitch and couching in various
greens; mainly in perle cottons.
Photograph by Hawkley Studios

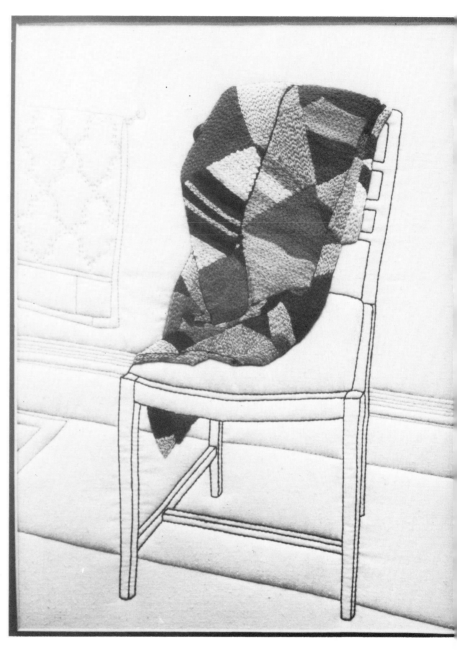

260 1983 – Valerie Tulloch. A patchwork blanket in brilliantly coloured chain stitch.
The outlines, in brown, are worked over padding to give a three-dimensional effect.
Owned by Mr and Mrs D Philpot. Photograph by GK Photographic Ltd

261 Left: 1983 – Muriel Best. *Mexicalia.* A variety of colours and threads including perle and stranded cottons, worked mainly in straight stitches and seeding. *Photograph by Hawkley Studios*

262 Right: 1983 – Joan Blencowe. *Time Glimpse.* A 19 in. (48 cm) square. Life arising from graptolites, through strata to the present-day landscape, seen through a gap in net curtains. An original screen print in cotton, with straight stitches and french knots in cotton and silk threads; hand embroidery. *Photograph by Hawkley Studios*

263 Below: 1983 – Barbara Siedlecka. *Rhodos.* An experiment using a photograph of a collage in stitchery and fabric, combined with a small embroidery of a man, on a paper background. *Photograph by Hawkley Studios*

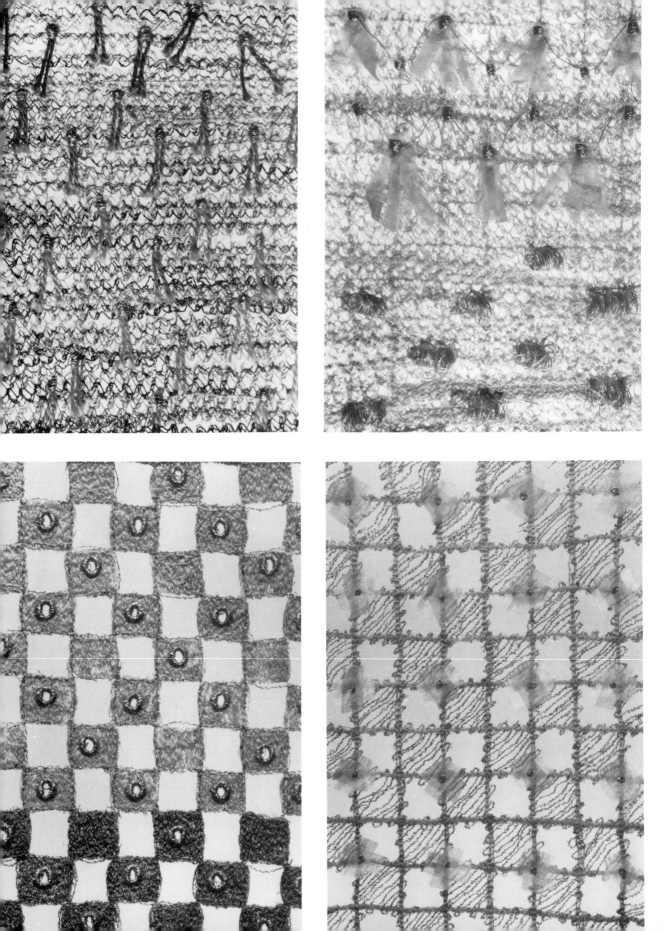

264 Opposite: 1983 – Dorothy Walker. Four samples of
embroidery worked on the domestic sewing machine.
Photograph by Hawkley Studios

(a) A grid with zigzag stitching over straight stitching, in blue,
pink and yellow threads and tassels in dark to pale pink, with
gold tops. Worked on vanishing muslin

(b) A grid of zigzag stitching over straight stitching, in cream to
pale apricot. Pink fabric tassels with gold tops. Raised loops
made with the basting foot in gold and apricot. Worked on
vanishing muslin

(c) On a grid of straight stitches alternate squares are filled
with straight stitches with eyelets in gold thread. Threads from
cream to pale pink to pinkish orange. On vanishing muslin

(d) Zigzag over straight stitch with alternate squares in gold
thread. Frayed pink silk squares with gold dots. Pale to darker
pink grid. On vanishing muslin

265 Above: 1983 – Elspeth Crawford. *Summer Garden*. A panel
28 in. × 24 in. (71 cm × 61 cm) on a grey-blue cotton
background with cotton and velvet applied, in brilliant colours.
Sequins are applied throughout the panel which is machine
stitched. The idea is developed from an aerial view of garden
allotments. *Owned by Graham Stewart*

266 Left: 1983 – Pauline Hann. *On the Crest of a Wave II*, 36 in. × 22 in. (91 cm × 56 cm). Pale yellow Thai silk with cut work, appliqué, surface stitchery, wrapping and silk tufts. In yellows, golds, purples and lilacs

267 Above: 1983 – Pauline Hann. Detail of *On the Crest of a Wave II*

268 1983 – Barbara Hatts. Mirror
frame, *C & B Enjoy Camping*,
approximately 18 in. (45.5 cm) square.
A variety of canvas stitches and colours
depicting holidays of the embroiderer

269 1983 – Beryl Page. *Poppy Field*,
21 in. × 23 in. (53 cm × 58 cm).
Canvaswork frame in long and short
stitches in cream, purple and burgundy
anchor soft cotton. Centre panel:
sprayed silk background, field gold
deepening to brown, corn embroidered in
fly stitch

270 1983 – Maragaret Hall. *Moon Lady*. The ground is black satin with blue slubs. Eyelet holes, hand worked into this, reveal behind pearlised foil abalone shells caught between two layers of fabric; with the top layer pulled back to show the shells. The lady is quilted into trapunto padding, with silk thread couching on top. The hair is in twisted silk and the arch is blue and couched. The ground outside the arch is quilted. The frame is in *papier mâché* with layers of foil and cellophane, painted with black enamel – diameter 12 in. (30 cm)

271 1983 – Constance Howard. A panel approximately 33 in. × 27 in. (84 cm × 69 cm). Embroidered on a geometric patterned, Swiss woollen fabric in red, orange, green mauve and beige. The pattern has been stitched over to change the original print. The embroidery is mounted on a black and white printed cotton, also stitched. Colours mainly bright blue, red, orange, and beige with some metal thread. Stitches, mainly couching and cretan with herringbone over the stripes. *Photograph by Hawkley Studios*

272 Right: 1984 – Constance Howard. A hanging, one of a pair, 18 ft × 12 ft (5.4 m × 3.6 m) commissioned by the Friends of the Northampton Museums. The brief was that the hanging should contain buildings well known in Northamptonshire, to be enclosed within a border of letting, with flowers and birds of the area, also the coat of arms of Northamptonshire. I omitted the birds and flowers and substituted artefacts from the Museum, such as Roman pots and the Desborough mirror. The first hanging, showing costume and shoes, was completed in 1973 but owing to pressure of work, this one was not finished until May 1984. Most of the embroidery, both hand and machine, was carried out by Karen Spurgin over two years. I had commenced this hanging in 1973, with Kay Cosserat (Macklin) working the major part of the coat of arms. I than abandoned it until 1982.

The background is of patches of blue and green dyed Welsh flannel on a backing of calico, the stitching being taken through the two layers of fabric. The buildings are mainly in woollen fabrics in greys, browns and mixtures of these, but any fabrics of a suitable texture have been used. Details such as windows and doors were attached to the buildings by machine before they were applied – hand embroidery was worked afterwards onto the background, which is in eight parts, these being sewn together before applying the buildings to the central areas. *Reproduced by permission of Northampton Museums and Art Gallery*

273 Above left: 1983 – Diana Dolman, a student at the London College of Fashion. Blackwork panel 8 in. (20 cm) square based on drawings of balconies, window boxes and pot plants. Black silk on white evenweave linen. For Part 1 City and Guilds examination

274 Above right: 1984 – Sara Woods, a student at the London College of Fashion. The project is about appliqué and reverse apliqué. The mounting board contains drawing. The plain shapes are in appliqué, leather and felt. The samples with spots and stripes are in the molar technique – cutting fabric away from the top to reveal the layer below. City and Guilds Part 1 sampler

275 Facing page: 1983 – Lilian Temple, a student at the London College of Fashion. A panel 4 ft (121 cm) square, based on a series of ideas stemming from her deeply felt concern about the oppression and suffering of women in society. Lillian Temple felt that the idea should be expressed in a medium chiefly used by and explored by women, and that it should evoke the emotional and political aspects of our lives as well.

The scene is from the period of the Beirut massacre. It portrays not only the universal nature of sons as victims of war, but that she too is a victim, unable to influence events. For Part 1 City and Guilds examination

276 Right: 1983 – Lilian Temple. Detail of above

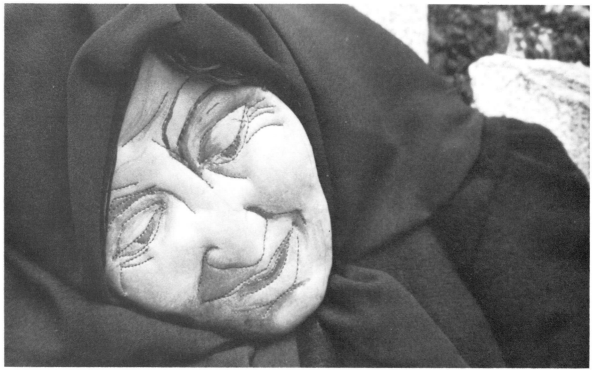

278 1982–84 – Yvonne Morton. Cloth necklaces with wrapped wire or cords, twisted, and knotted, some beading. *Photograph by Hawkley Studio*

Left: Tan suede, dull blue buttonhole in perle thread, tan lurex fabric. Blue and tan wrapping in perle cotton and silk

Right: Canvas stitchery and fish skin in tan and pale grey-blue; wrapped cords and wire, steel grey beads

Below: Cream and gold kid, gold thread, beads and sequins; wrapped cream cords in silk threads

   Average size of lockets about $2\frac{1}{2}$ in. × $1\frac{3}{4}$ in. (6.5 cm × 4.5 cm)

277 Left: 1981–84 – Jane Denyer. Detail from *Fantasy*. A hanging using dyes and hand stitching in wools, silks and cottons on cotton fabric. Brilliantly coloured small areas are worked in satin, stem, chain and buttonhole stitches, with running and scattered straight stitches interspersed. Dye is painted or splashed on to the background fabric. *Photograph by Hawkley Studios*. See also front of book jacket

279 1983–84 – Beryl Dean. Hanging, 8 ft × 21 ft (2.4 m × 6.4 m) for the east end of
Chelmsford Cathedral. Patchwork crosses in brilliant colours. Work carried out with the
help of former students

280 1983–84 – Sister Kathleen. A pulpit fall based on mediaeval drawings of the four evangelists

281 Left: 1983–84 – *The Croydon Charter* centenary panel, 10 ft × 6 ft (3.05 m × 1.83 m). Designed by Moyra McNeill, the panel has been worked by 50 members of the Croydon Branch of the Embroiderers' Guild. The design incorporates local buildings, worked individually, and landmarks in the area. Techniques include patchwork, canvas work, ribbon appliqué, machine embroidery on acetate (vanishing muslin) and hand stitchery. *Embroidery, Volume 35, Number 4, Winter 1984. Reproduced by permission of* The Croydon Advertiser

282 1983–84 – Edith John. *Tasmanian Waterfall.* In looped and plain couching in white thread. Trees are in needleweaving and lacy buttonhole. The rocks are in a variation of triple herringbone, in slate blues. The background is faintly striped fabric in dark blue. ***Photograph by Des Byrne***

283 1984 – Rosemary Macmillan Campbell. *Windblown.* A seascape, 15¾ in. × 16 in. (40 cm × 40.5 cm), in two layers, the lower layer of the sky in machine embroidery, the sea smocked and sprayed then unsmocked, cut and twisted, couched with metal thread and sequin waste. The top layer is painted organdie, burned in parts to reveal the lower layer. Shadow work and surface stitching for birds and grass

284 1984 – Rosemary Macmillan Campbell. *Starting Up.* A landscape, 15¾ in. × 16 in. (40 cm × 40.5 cm), made in two layers, the lower one in painted silk, hand quilted and machine embroidered. The top layer is painted organdie, with shadow work and surface stitchery; burning reveals machine stitching on the lower layer. Colours are greenish blues and greenish yellows, darker blue-greens, grey-greens and brownish greens, on white silk

285 1984 – Rosemary Macmillan Campbell. Detail of *Starting Up.*

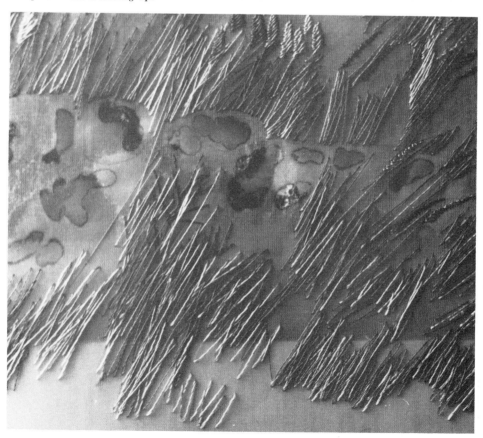

286 1984 – Linda Taylor. A drawing in Carn d'Ache pencil on cartridge paper, a preliminary preparation for design for machine embroidery. She is recently working from drawings of washing on washing lines, which fascinate her

287 1984 – Anne Bingham. *Papilio*, **7 in. × 5 in. (17.8 cm × 12.7 cm). Blocks of satin stitch in silk threads in a variety of colours, mainly including blues and greens with yellow and pink, with 'free' gold work, on a shaped base**

288 Right: 1984 – Stephanie Tuckwell. *Lipilli*, **10¼ in. × 13½ in. (26 cm × 34 cm). Silk, paper, plaster and threads**

289 Facing page: 1984 – Patricia Sanders, a student at Goldsmiths' School of Art. Jacket in handmade paper, net and silk patterend fabrics and ribbons, with finely hand sewn appliqué in silk on net. The shaping of the body of the jacket is obtained with seams laced together with ribbons

290 Above: 1984 – Dorothy Reglar. Embroidered leather jacket, with punched hole decoration and appliqué

291 Right: 1984 – Victoria Brown, a student at Goldsmiths' School of Art. Handmade felt coat, in blues and pinks. The coat is covered in silk organza, through which small holes are pierced to show the coloured felt. The coat is quilted by machine throughout. The buttons are made from whorls of felt strips

292 and 293 1984 – Ann Rutherford.
Little Precious. An embroidered oval
box approximately 6½ in. (16.5 cm) in
the wider dimension, for Part 1 of the
City and Guilds examination in
embroidery. The box contains a baby
wearing a bonnet lying in a cradle. The
lid of the box is shaped inside, machine
quilted, and decorated with faces. The
figures peering into the box are in relief
and depict a family and friends. Many
materials and colours are utilised.
Photographs by Hawkley Studios

294 1984 – Paddy Ramsay. *Dreamed Garden – et in arcadia ego*, 30¾ in. × 24½ in. (78 cm × 62 cm). **One of a series. Machine embroidery using quilting techniques on velvets and satins. The** colours are greens and vibrant pinks. The frame is made and hand-painted by Paddy Ramsay. *Property of William Dodd.* *Photograph by Keith Pattison*

295 1984 – Hannah Frew Paterson. *The Cup.* A pulpit fall, 23½ in. wide × 33 in. high (59 cm × 84 cm), for Wellington Church, Glasgow. The background is in strips of multi-coloured silks applied to a gold fabric ground. At the lower edges are 20 shaded gold pillars with detached multi-coloured wrapped strips below, fastened by a triangular metal base. The fall is surmounted by a half-circle covered with gold leathers and wrapped gold threads enclosing a smaller circle worked similarly to signify the cup

296 1985 – Kathleen Whyte. Pulpit fall 21 in. × 30 in. (53 cm × 76 cm) dedicated to St Baldred who lived on the Bass Rock in the Forth. A pastoral scene and a river with the Lamb as a central focal point. In Prestonkirk, Midlothian

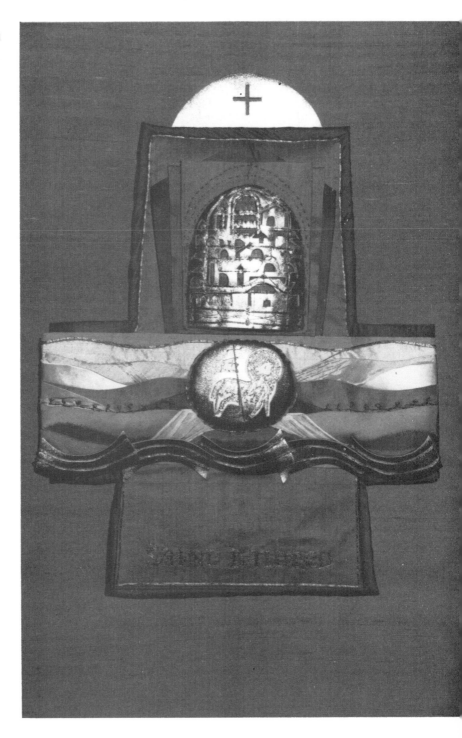

298 1977–85 – *The Wisborough Tapestry*, 13 ft × 4 ft (3.9 m × 1.2 m). Worked in tent stitch on canvas and carried out by the villagers of Wisborough Green. The design, in three panels, shows the West, Central and Eastern parts of the Village, with roundels depicting the listed buildings of architectural interest, the history and industry of Wisborough Green past and present, and its main activities. The Tapestry was worked in separate frames, the strips of canvas afterwards being rejoined by the Women's Home Industries.

It was unveiled in the Parish Church of St Peter ad Vincula, Wisborough Green on Sunday 24 March 1985

297 Left: 1985 – Dorothy Sim. A hanging designed by Dorothy Sim for the fiftieth anniversary of Prestwick Airport. Worked with the help of nine other people; three on the main hanging, three on the gold work and three on the quilting. These were members of embroiderers' guilds or the Quilters' Guild.

The brief was dictated, and included the Isle of Arran, an aeroplane, a runway and the transatlantic nature of the airport.

The hanging is in strip patchwork, appliqué and machine embroidery with gold lettering on a separate hanging behind the pictorial patchwork

299 1985 – Constance Howard. *Turn About I.* Panel 10½ in. (27 cm) square. Wrapped card using perle cotton in Cream, yellow, dull pink, with a bright blue streak. *Photograph by Hawley Studios*

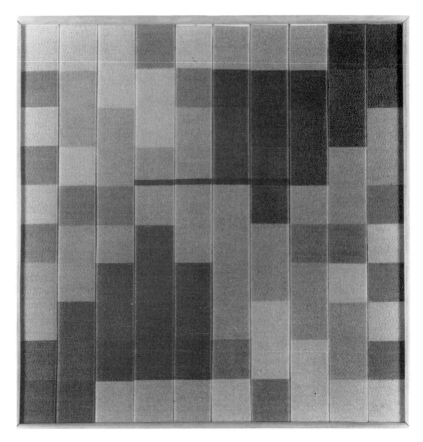

300 1985 – Constance Howard. *Turn About II.* Panel 10½ in. (27 cm) square. Wrapped card using perle cotton in blue, grey, white and shell pink. *Photograph by Hawkley Studios*

274

301 1985 – Zandra Rhodes. A chiffon dress richly embroidered with a variety of beads, including bugles, pearls and sequins. Machine embroidery gives area of texture.
Photograph by London Daily Mail

Biographies

Abbreviations

ADF = Art and Design Fellowship. Manchester Polytechnic

ARCA = Associate of the Royal College of Art

ATC = Art Teachers' Certificate

ATD = Art Teachers' Diploma

C & G = City and Guilds of London Institute Examinations

CNAA = Council for National Academic Awards

DA = Diploma in Design (Scotland)

Dip AD = Diploma in Art and Design. This was a shortened form of NDAD known by students as Dip AD until 1975 when it became a BA Honours degree course

FRSA = Fellow of the Royal Society of Arts

FSDC = Fellow of the Society of Designer Craftsmen

FSIAD = Fellow of the Society of Industrial Artists and Designers

ILEA = Inner London Education Authority

NDAD = National Diploma in Art and Design

NDD = National Diploma in Design

HDD = Higher Diploma in Design

MPAA = Mid-Pennine Arts Association

NWAA = North West Art Association

As space is very limited, information given in the biographies in *Twentieth-Century Embroidery 1940–1963*, is not repeated here but, where applicable, additions are given to those already published

Susan Aiken (née Irwin) DA ATC 1951–

1968–72	Training at Belfast College of Art – embroidery
1972–73	Brighton College of Art, Teacher Training Department
Teaching 1973–74	Assistant art teacher – Dundonald Girls' High School
1974–76	Lecturer II – Art and Design Centre, Belfast, Ulster Polytechnic
1976 to date	Full-time Senior Lecturer, embroidery, Ulster Polytechnic/University of Ulster
1978–81	Freelance lecturing Embroiderers' Guild; Ulster Folk Museum; St Mary's Training College; Department of Extra Mural Studies, Queen's University, Belfast and various schools in N Ireland
Exhibitions 1975	Tom Caldwell Gallery, Belfast; Boston Society of Arts and Crafts, USA

1976	Joint show – Octagon Gallery, Belfast
Commissions 1976	Pulpit fall – Banbridge Presbyterian Church, Co Down
1984/85	Dossal – St Patrick's Church of Ireland, Coleraine, Co Londonderry
	Private commissions in USA and Canada – embroidered panels and quilts

Eugenie Alexander NDD ATC 1919–

1979	Arts Council shop, Longacre, London – Theatre figures (see back cover of *Twentieth-Century Embroidery 1964–1977*)
1982	Edwin Pollard Gallery, Wimbledon

Sadie Allen NDD 1930–

	Training at Cardiff College of Art – NDD in book illustration
Teaching 1950–67	In various schools and colleges
1967–77	Senior Lecturer in Art and Education at Newcastle upon Tyne Polytechnic; evening classes, Women's Institute
1982 to date	Speaker for Winsor & Newton within Border area; private teaching – people from Border area – also organises holiday tuition Member of Society of Designer Craftsmen; Red Rose Guild Guild of Lakeland Craftsmen; Blue Coat Centre, Liverpool
Exhibitions	Pictures for Schools; Crafts Centre of Great Britain; Whitworth Art Gallery, Manchester; Abbot Hall, Kendal
1978	Joint shows with Colin Allen – Nashville, Tennessee
1981	Nashville and Memphis USA
1982	Huntsville, Alabama and others Work purchased by public and private clients
Commissions	Memorial hanging, Dacre Church, Cumbria; panel for restroom, Carlisle Civil Centre; panel depicting Women's Institutes Movement in Cumbria – to commemorate the W I Jubilee Year
Publication	*Creative Embroidery Collage*, Bell and Hyman 1978

Dorothy Allsopp ARCA ATD 1911–

Late 70s	Honorary member of C & G
1978	Chairman of the Examinations Subject Committee for Creative Studies for C & G

Doris Anwyl FSDC 1912–

	Continuing projects organised for the East Kent Embroiderers' Guild
Teaching 1981	Disabled at Tenterden Day Centre
Commissions 1980	Laudian altar frontal – St Mildred's, Tenterden, Kent, in collaboration with a weaver
1981	Four-fold screen, *The seasons as seen through a chestnut tree* (see figure 145)

Joan Archer (née Hughes) NDD DA ATC 1931–

1985	Assesor for C & G examinations in embroidery
Exhibitions	Continues to organise and exhibit in biennial exhibitions
1985	'Textiles and Stitchery' – Manchester Business School

Gisela Banbury 1939–

1960	Came to England from Germany; married
1974–78	Training at Beckenham and Penge Adult Education Centre
1979	C & G Advanced Level in embroidery
Teaching	Adult Education Centres of Ashford, Beckenham, Tunbridge Wells; Courses on ecclesiastical embroidery at the Royal School of Church Music, Canterbury. Specialist in patchwork
Exhibitions	Rochester Cathedral, Derby Cathedral (ecclesiastical embroidery); art galleries in London and the Home Counties (secular work)
Commissions 1978	Altar frontal and pulpit fall – St James's, Iddesleigh, Devon
1979	Pulpit fall and burse for the same church; a set of chasubles and stoles (with Angela Dewar) – Lyndhurst Parish Church, Hampshire
1980	Burse and veil and altar frontal for the same church
1981	Pulpit fall, altar frontal and two almsbags (with Angela Dewar) – Parish Church of Sullingham, Sussex
1982	Designed and prepared altar frontal for Stonegate Parish Church, Wadhurst
1982–83	Altar frontal in two colours – Plaxtol, Kent
Publication	*Embroidery For Fashion* with Angela Dewar, Batsford 1984

Alison Barrell NDD ATC 1939–

1978	Retired from the Beckenham Textile Studio. Took up restoration of antique furniture

Judy Barry NDD ATC 1941–

1959–62	Training at Hammersmith College of Art and Building – NDD in embroidery
1962–63	London University – ATC
Teaching 1963 to date	Senior Lecturer in the School of Embroidery, Department of Textile/Fashion, Manchester Polytechnic
Career 1973 to date	In partnership with Beryl Patten, designing and carrying out ecclesiastical commissions
Commissions include	
1973	Festal chasuble – Bolton Parish Church, Bolton, Lancashire
1975	Dossal curtains, inset altar panels (multi-seasonal) – St Andrew's, Edge Lane, Droylsden, Manchester
1977	Red Laudian frontal and chasuble – All Saints Church, Elton, Bury, Lancashire
1978	Cope and set of three detachable altar panels for Advent scheme – Manchester Cathedral High Altar
1978–79	Twelve hangings – Yeshurun Hebrew Congregation Synagogue, Gatley
1982	Five copes for the Dean and Canons of Chester Cathedral
1982	Three hangings – Royal Naval Establishment, Tor Point, Cornwall
1983	Mothers' Union Deanery banner
1984	Festal cope – Stand Parish Church, Whitefield, Manchester
1984	Festal scheme – High Altar, Church of All Saints, Bury, Lancashire
1984	New building, consecrated November 1984, Parish Church of St John the Baptist, Barlaston, Stoke-on-Trent; interchangeable panels for the High Altar, with liturgical colours added or removed, according to season; also multi-seasonal scheme for Lady Chapel and festal vestments for both altars

Jan Beaney NDD ATC 1938–

1955–58	West Sussex College of Art – painting NDD and lithography
1958–59	Hornsey College of Art – ATC
1961–63	Hornsey College of Art – evening classes. C & G Parts I & II
Teaching 1959–64	Eliots Green Grammar School – art and embroidery
1964–68	Lecturer in art department – Whitelands College of Education
1967–76	Part-time lecturer for ILEA classes for the Embroiderers' Guild; and courses for Berkshire teachers
1976 to date	Windsor and Maidenhead College of Adult Education, C & G, embroidery courses for Berkshire County Council, branches of the Embroiderers' Guild
Professional work	Member of the '62 Group in 1963. Chairman 1971–73
	Work exhibited in 'Contemporary Hangings', Pictures for Welsh Schools, Embroiderers' Guild, Crafts Council, '62 Group
1980	BBC Television programme 'Embroidery' in ten parts, each part introduced and demonstrated by her, with guest speakers
1981	Appointed examiner – C & G embroidery
1982	Joint designer (with Jean Littlejohn) of *Maidenhead Hanging*
1985	A series of short programmes on Pebble Mill
Publications	*The Young Embroiderer*, Kaye and Ward 1966; *Fun with Collage*, Kaye and Ward 1971 (Puffin 1976); *Fun with Embroidery*, Kaye and Ward 1976; *Buildings in Picture Collage and Design*, Pelham 1976; *Landscapes in Picture Collage and Design*, Pelham 1976; *Texture and Surface Pattern*, Pelham 1978; *Embroidery Approaches*, Pelham 1978; *Stitches: new approaches*, Batsford 1985; articles written for *The Flying Needle* (US), *Embroidery, Junior Education, Pins & Needles, Radio Times* Works purchased by Reading Museum Service, Derby Museum Service, Somerset Education Authority, Embroiderers' Guild, public and private buyers in Great Britain and in Germany, Australia and Canada

Anne Bingham NDD ATD 1936–

1956–58	Birmingham College of Art (now City of Birmingham Polytechnic) – NDD in hand and machine embroidery, special level
1958–59	ATD
Teaching 1959–61	King Edward VI Girls' Grammar School, Louth, Lincolnshire
1962–72	Combined Post with Birmingham Education Committee: quarter of the time 1st year degree students and C & G students in the embroidery department at Birmingham College of Art, the rest of the time teaching embroidery full time Bournville School of Art – specialist ecclesiastical and ceremonial embroidery (in 1970 Princess Margaret's personal guide standard completed at Bournville)
1971 to date 1972 to date	Visiting assessor for C & G courses for five colleges in the Midlands; full-time lecturer in charge of textile department at Bournville School of Art
Exhibitions	Exhibited in London and Midlands galleries and at art festivals
Commissions	Ecclesiastical commissions include: Altar frontal – Caverswall Church, Staffordshire; panel depicting St Monica – Edgbaston Old Church, Birmingham; Mothers' Union banner – Rubevey Church, Birmingham; designed chasubles and kneelers – St Nicholas, Warwick

Richard Box NDD ATC 1943–

1960–62	Training at Hastings School of Art
1962–65	Goldsmiths' School of Art – painting
1964	ATC course

1979	London University – diploma in history of art
Teaching 1964–68	Comprehensive School teaching
1968 to date	Lecturer in art – Avery Hill College of Education; Weekend schools and short courses in art and design
Exhibitions 1966 onwards	Work exhibited with the '62 Group and 'Contemporary Hangings'
1974 onwards	Mixed exhibitions
1976 onwards	Work shown in England and abroad including London galleries and Blackheath Art Gallery; Dusseldorf; Studio B, Sidcup
	Work bought by education authorities and private collectors
	One-person shows:
1980	Woodland Art Gallery, Blackheath
1981	Bakehouse Gallery, Blackheath
1984	Stitch Design
Other work 1980	A slot in the BBC film *Embroidery* with Jan Beaney
1984	One of twelve embroiderers selected for *Twelve British Embroiderers* by Diana Springall

Michael Brennand-Wood MA 1952–

1969–72	Training at Bolton College of Art
1972–75	Manchester Polytechnic – BA Hons degree in textiles
1975–76	Birmingham Polytechnic – MA in textiles
Teaching 1979 to date	Part-time lecturer at Goldsmiths' School of Art
Exhibitions 1975 & 76	In many galleries including: Peterloo Gallery, Manchester
1978	Third Exhibition of Miniature Textiles, Crafts Centre of Great Britain and foreign tour
1979	'Thread Collages' – Crafts Council Gallery and UK tour; Fitzwilliam Museum, Cambridge; Prescote Gallery, nr Banbury
1980	Warwick Gallery, London; Exempla Exhibition, Munich; World Crafts Council Conference, Vienna; Art Latitude, New York – one of four exhibitors; Fourth International Exhibition of Miniature Textiles and foreign tour; one-person show; Gardner Centre Gallery, University of Sussex; one-person show – John Hansard Gallery, University of Southampton
1981	British Council/Crafts Council – British Ceramics and Textiles, Knokke-Heist, Belgium
1982	One-person show – Sunderland Arts Centre, Tyne and Wear; 'The Makers' Eye' – Crafts Council, London; Aspects Gallery, London; 'Fabric and Form' – British Council/Crafts Council Gallery, London and foreign tour
1983	Goldsmiths' College Gallery
Awards and Fellowships	
1977	Birmingham Polytechnic
1978	Crafts Council Grant, London
1980	Medal, Exempla Exhibition, Munich
1982	'The Makers' Eye' – contributor and selector
1982	'Fabric and Form' – contributor, selector and organiser for the Crafts Council; Work in a number of public and private collections in England, Europe, USA, Australia, Japan and the Far East
Commissions 1975–76	Law Courts, Ilkestone County Council
1976–77	John Siddeley, International Limited, London
1980–82	Cheshire County Council

Audrey Brockbank BEd Hons 1938–

	Trained as a dancer
1956	Royal Opera Ballet – dancer
1957–63	Royal Ballet – dancer
1967–71	Training at Whitelands College – four-year course in education and art for BEd Hons
1980–82	Post-graduate course, Goldsmiths' School of Art
Teaching and career 1973–75	Lecturer at Whitelands College, Putney, London
1975 to date	Unicorn School, Kew, London
1975	Member of the '62 Group
1980	On committee of the Young Embroiderers' Society, Embroiderers' Guild
Exhibitions	With various groups including:
1982	'Superstitchers' – Oxford Gallery
1985	'Material Evidence' – Camden Arts Centre, London
	Works sold to public and private collectors in Great Britain

Pauline Burbidge Dip AD 1950–

1968–69	London College of Fashion
1969–72	St Martin's School of Art – Dip AD in fashion/textiles
Career 1972–73	Designed clothes for a small London company
1973–74	Designed and made clothes in business partnership
1976	Began making patchwork quilts, also freelance dress-pattern making
1978	'New Craftsman's Grant' from Crafts Council
1979–81	Began to make a living from her own work, making and exhibiting quilts, carrying out commissions
1981	Grant from East Midland Arts enabled her to experiment with new ideas
Award 1982	John Ruskin Craft Award – administered by Crafts Council
Teaching 1979 onwards	Occasional workshops
Exhibitions	Among these:
1979	Strawberry Fayre, Stockbridge, Hants; Camden Adult Education Institute, London; Contemporary Patchwork Quilts, Cirencester; Foyle's Art Gallery, London Workshops
1980	'New Faces' – British Crafts Centre, London; Strawberry Fayre; Patchwork at Doddington Hall, Lincoln; Crafts Fair, Chelsea
	Patchwork – The Quilters' Guild, Seven Dials, London
1981	Strawberry Fayre; Jews Court, London; Crafts Fair, Chelsea; John Mackintosh Hall, Gibraltar
1982	Cannon Hill Arts Centre, Birmingham; 'The Makers' Eye' – Crafts Council, London; '100% Pure Silk' – Rufford Craft Centre, Nottinghamshire; Lazarus Stones, Ohio, USA – work and demonstrations
1982–83	'Quilting, Patchwork and Appliqué' – Minories, Colchester, touring show, one-person shows
1983	'New Patchwork Quilts' – Midland Group, Nottingham; 'New Quilts' – Lady Lodge Art Centre, Peterborough
1985	Crafts centre of Great Britain, London
Publication	*Making Patchwork for Pleasure and Profit*, John Gifford 1981

Anne Butler Morrell NDD ATC 1939–

1958–61	Goldsmiths' School of Art – embroidery
1961–62	Goldsmiths' Schoot of Art – ATC
Teaching and career 1963–68	Lecturer in embroidery at Goldsmiths' School of Art
1968 to date	Lecturer in charge of embroidery and Principal Lecturer at Manchester Polytechnic; Textiles/Fashion, course leader. Co-ordinating Tutor – MA course; courses conducted in Great Britain and the USA
	Member of Crafts Advisory Panel, special projects committee (3 years)
1978 to date	CNAA Textile/Fashion Board – Special Adviser. Latest visits to Goldsmiths' College; Bath College of Further Education
1978	Panel member of North West Arts Craft Panel. Organised a NWA textile exhibition which travelled around the North West in 1984
1978–85	Vice Chairman of the Embroiderers' Guild, Hampton Court, London; Chairman of Leaflet Committee and member of Collections Committee
1979–80	Index Selection Committee, Crafts Council
Award 1984	Won Passold Research Award to look into origins of hand embroidery stitches in sewing, woven fabrics and basketry.
Exhibitions	Work exhibited in group shows in Great Britain and abroad
1971	Work accepted for the Lausanne Biennale
1971–72	Two travelling exhibitions with Janet Graham in USA and Australia
1981	September – Howarth Art Gallery, Accrington; October/November – 'Stitchery', BCC London, touring Scotland 1982
1983	Harris Museum and Manchester Royal Exchange craft shop
1984–85	Work exhibited in Japan
Commissions	For ecclesiastical and secular embroideries
	Work purchased by public and private collectors
Publications	*Teaching Children Embroidery*, Studio Vista 1964; *Simple Stitches*, Batsford 1968; *Embroidery in the Primary School*, Batsford 1969; *Pattern and Embroidery* (with David Green), Batsford 1970; *Practice of Collage* (with Brian French), Mills and Boon 1975; *Machine Stitches*, Batsford 1976; *The Encyclopaedia of Stitches*, Batsford 1979; second edition 1982, paperback 1983; *Using Simple Embroidery Stitches*, Batsford paperback 1985
1984	Inclusion in a book by Diana Springall for Japan, *Twelve British Embroiderers*
1971 to date	Articles written for magazines including 'Embroidery in Art and Craft Education', *Embroidery* magazine
1982	Article on Constance Howard in *Crafts* No 55, March/April
1983	Leaflet, *Stitchery*, E G Enterprises for the Embroiderers' Guild

Rosemary Macmillan Campbell DA 1943

	Training at Duncan of Jordanstone College of Art, Dundee
1963–67	DA in printed textiles and embroidery
1967–70	Designer with Nairn Floor Coverings, Kirkcaldy
Teaching 1972–76	Teaching art and design in primary, secondary and special schools, in Fife and Lothian region
1981–	Telford College – teaching a C & G class
Exhibitions	Group shows:
1980	Joint exhibition – Dalkeith Arts Centre
1981	With Embryo at Bonar Hall, Dundee
1981	New Solent Gallery, Edinburgh
1982	Edinburgh Festival Fringe, Embryo

1982	New Scottish Embroidery Group, City Art Centre, Edinburgh
1982	Festival exhibition, Embryo. Awarded travel prize by Coats for *Spring Shadow*
1982	'Through the Eye of a Needle' New Scottish Embroidery Group – City Art Centre, Edinburgh
1983	Embryo exhibitions – Fair Maid's House, Perth
1983	Embryo, Bonar Hall, Dundee
	Member of the Embroiderers' Guild
	Work in the collection of the Royal Scottish Museum and in private collections
1985	'Stitchin' time' Embryo, The Orangery, Holland Park, London

Valerie Campbell-Harding 1932–

1965–75	Training at Chippenham Technical College. C & G Parts I and II
1981–82	Loughborough College of Art and Nottingham University adult education department
Teaching	Part-time courses in adult education for guilds, colleges of education, colleges of art and summer schools
1983 to date	Chippenham Technical College, Newbury College of Further Education, Urchfont Manor, Devizes
Exhibitions	Embroiderers' Guild: Commonwealth Institute; Foyle's Art Gallery; South Hill Park Arts Centre, Bracknell, Berkshire; Ideal Home Exhibition; Newbury Festival, 'Art in Action', Waterperry House, Wheatley, Oxon; Salisbury and Loughborough Colleges of Art
Publications	*Textures in Embroidery* 1977, Batsford, paperback 1985; *Faces and Figures*, Batsford 1980; *Patchwork* 1 & 2 Search Press 1982; *Every Kind of Patchwork*, Pan 1983; *Strip Patchwork* Batsford 1983

Julia Caprara NDD ATC 1939–

1955–61	Training at Hornsey College of Art – NDD, main subject stained glass, wood-engraving additional
1960–61	London University – ATC
Teaching 1961–64	Art specialist at Henrietta Barnett School, Hampstead, London
1964–68	Head of Art Department at Henrietta Barnett School
1973–85	Part time – West Lodge Middle School, Harrow
1975 to date	Tutor in creative embroidery and design – Central Institute, Longford Street, London
1973–75	Freelance tutor on courses for the C & G embroidery course at Harrow
1970s	Other courses in textiles and creativity
1982–83	Stitch Design – an embroidery workshop in London started with Barbara Marriott
Career 1970	Member of the '62 Group exhibiting regularly
1974	Member of the Society of Designer Craftsmen
1981–85	Chairman of the '62 Group
Exhibitions 1966 & 70	Pictures for Schools and 'Contemporary Hangings'
1975	One-person show 'Stitch and Textile Assemblages' – Commonwealth Institute
1984	Work in '62 Group exhibition in Japan
Work 1979	Panel *There is no Garden at Babiy Yar* now in 'Ghetto Fighters' House' Israel
1982	Peace Mandala – about the Hyde Park Bomb
1985	Panel to commemorate Dresden 1945

Commissions 1976–78	Collection designed and embroidered for David Butler – *couture* evening and day wear. Work exhibited at London Fashion Fair, and international fashion fairs in Paris, Japan and New York
1979	Slot in BBC series *Embroidery* with Jan Beaney
1984–85	Embroiderered jackets for Japan
1985	Two wall panels 5 ft × 4 ft (152 cm × 122 cm) for a house in Hungerford
	Work purchased by public and private clients including National Museum of Wales; work in collections in Great Britain, Canada, Japan, Australia, USA and other places
Publications	Articles in magazines

Jean M F Carter (née Oliver) NDD ATD 1930–

1950–55	Training at Tunbridge Wells School of Art – NDD in fabric printing and embroidery. C & G
1955–56	Regional College of Art, Manchester – ATD
Teaching 1956–59	Hastings School of Art, Eastbourne School of Art
1959–84	Part-time courses and classes
1960–66	Examiner (embroidery) Union of Lancashire and Cheshire Institute
1961–68	Lecturer/senior lecturer Battersea College of Education
1968–80	Lecturer/senior lecturer Eastbourne College of Education; East Sussex College of Higher Education/Brighton Polytechnic
Exhibitions	Among these:
1957	Victoria and Albert Museum, London
1960s	Pictures for Schools; Paris Salon; Embroiderers' Guild
1966–76	'Contemporary Hangings' and 'Contemporary Pictures in Fabric and Thread' (travelling exhibitions)
1962–78	'62 Group
1973	Towner Art Gallery, Eastbourne
1978	One-person show 'The Gentle Downs' – Eastbourne
1983	Tokyo and Kyoto, Japan
Commissions 1959–84	Commissions for secular and ecclesiastical embroideries
1957–84	Work purchased by private collectors in Great Britain and abroad
Publications	Articles for *Embroidery* 1959–70; articles for *Creative Needlecraft* 1968–78; *Creative Play with Fabrics and Threads*, Batsford 1968

Heather Clarke-Martin Dip AD ATD 1949–

1968–71	Training at Loughborough College of Art and Design – Dip AD embroidery
1972–73	Cardiff School of Education – ATD
Teaching 1973–78	Five years teaching in secondary school and further education college; Barry Summer School; various day schools and Embroiderers' Guild branches
Career 1979–81	Papua New Guinea – Business Development Officer, assisting local people to run small businesses. Set up a regional sewing training scheme with local women Member of the '62 Group since 1971 and exhibiting with them to date
Exhibitions 1975	Three-person shows – Bristol Art Centre; five-person show – Warwick Gallery, London and other galleries including Southampton, St Helier (Jersey)
1978	one-person show – Bradford-on-Avon
Commissions 1978	Altar frontal for St Peter's Church, Lawford, Rugby Commissions for private clients

Joan Cleaver BA NDD 1927

1982   Retired from Birmingham Polytechnic

Publication   *Appliqué*, Search Press 1978

Isabel Clover NDD ATC 1941–

1978   A set of stoles 'Creation'

1980   White dossal – Kesgrave, Ipswich

1981   White burse, veil and stole – Kesgrave, Ipswich

1982   Red vestments, designed and supervised – North Cadbury, Somerset

1982–83   New Advent dossal and Christmas dossal – Kesgrave, Ipswich

1984   Frontal – Stoke-by-Clair, Suffolk; frontal – Leiston, Suffolk

Exhibitions 1982   Retrospective including students' work. Sponsored show, Ipswich Arts Festival

1983   Long Melford

Joy Clucas (née Dobbs) NDD ATC 1931–

Teaching 1977, 78, 79 and 84   Visits to the USA

1979 to 80   Visits to Canada

1984   Visit to Australia

Exhibitions 1978   Minories, Colchester; Textile Museum, Washington DC

1981   Oakwood Art Centre

1982   The Old Granary, Bishops Waltham, Hants

Commissions 1979   St William's School, Yorkshire

1983 & 85   Suffolk Craft Society sponsored exhibition

Joyce Conwy Evans NDD Des RCA 1929–

Training at Bromley College of Art – NDD 1st Class Hons in hand and machine embroidery; C & G 1st Class Hons hand embroidery

1954–57   Royal College of Art. Royal Scholar – Interior Design 1st Class Hons, Des RCA. Silver medal and travelling scholarship

Work   With Sir Hugh Casson for a number of years. Freelance designer also during this time

1975   Set up her own studio

Commissions 1968   Altar frontal embroidered by Elizabeth Geddes – King's College Chapel, Cambridge

1970   Set of vestments – King's College Chapel

1967   Ceremonial robes – Royal College of Art

1975   Two stool seats – Mississippi steamboat, USA

1981   Altar frontal embroidered by Elizabeth Geddes – Canterbury Cathedral

Elspeth Crawford (née Younger) DA 1936–

Exhibitions 1975–76   Modern Embroidery Group, Glasgow School of Art

1983   One-person show – Cornerstone Gallery, Dunblane

1983–84   Christmas show – Scottish Gallery

Jean Davey Winter NDD 1942–

1960–63   Training at Birmingham College of Art – printed textiles NDD. Royal Society of Arts Industrial Art Bursaries in Furnishing Textiles and Laminated Plastics

Teaching	Part-time lecturer at Buckingham College of Higher Education, High Wycombe, BA and Foundation courses – printmaking and textiles
Exhibitions	One-person shows:
1973 & 79	Peter Dingley Gallery, Stratford-upon-Avon
1979 & 83	Ingrid Presse Gallery, Wiesbaden, Germany
	Major group exhibitions:
1981	'Stitchery' – British Crafts Centre
1982	'British Needlework' – National Museum of Modern Art, Kyoto and Tokyo, Japan
1983	'Impressions and Imprints' – Museum of Modern Art, Oxford; 'Out of Print' – Southill Park touring show; 'Paper Round' – British Crafts Centre
1984	'Paper Trails' – Bluecoat Gallery, Liverpool; '62 Group shows Oxford Printmakers Co-operative Exhibits regularly with the Fibre Art group Work in various private and public collections including the Museum of Modern Art, Kyoto, and Leicestershire collection
1984	Selected for Crafts Council Index

Barbara Dawson NDD 1922–

1982	Retired from teaching
Commissions 1974–81	Manchester Cathedral and Truro Cathedral – vestments
1979–80	Hanging – Llandaff Cathedral; Downing and Jesus Colleges, Cambridge; Mountain Ash, other Welsh commissions, and Truro Cathedral
Exhibitions 1981	Master Craftsmen – Victoria and Albert Museum, London
1983	Guildford Art Gallery; Goldsmiths' College Gallery, London; Anatole Orient Gallery, London; International Exhibition of Ecclesiastical Embroidery
1984	Clarendon Park, Wiltshire
Publication	*Metal Thread Embroidery*, Batsford paperback 1982

Beryl Dean MBE ARCA FSDC 1911–

Commissions 1980	Cope and mitre – Archbishop of Canterbury
1982	Vestments, pulpit fall, pennants – The Cathedral of the Forest, Newland, Gloucester – project with students
1982	Head of Christ – icon
1983	Large wall hanging and kneelers – Chelmsford Cathedral; frontals, dossals, vestments, etc – churches in New York, Evanston, Philadelphia, Long Beach – USA; vestments – Australia; Torah mantles – Westminster Synagogue, London
	Member of Art Workers' Guild Fellow of the Society of Designer Craftsmen Work purchased by the Victoria and Albert Museum and Royal Scottish Museum and by public and private clients
Publications	*Embroidery for Religion and Ceremonial*, Batsford 1981, paperback 1986; *Church Embroidery*, Mowbray 1982; articles for magazines

Jane Denyer Dip AD 1946–

1972–75	Training at Goldsmiths' School of Art – Dip AD in embroidery
1975–76	St Martin's School of Art – Diploma in Post Graduate Studies
Teaching 1970–72	Full-time teaching (children)
1978 to date	Part-time classes for adults
Exhibitions 1982	Oxford Gallery – embroidery; South-East London Artists – paintings and drawings

1983 Brixton Art Gallery – women artists; Whitechapel Art Gallery – open artists; One-person shows; Premises, Norwich; Cockpit Theatre, London

1984 Centre 181 Gallery, London – paintings; Monson Road Gallery, London – paintings

Isabel Dibden 1952–

1971–72 Training at Manchester Polytechnic

1972–75 Loughborough College of Art and Design – BA 1st Class Hons Embroidery

Teaching 1976 to date Full-time lecturer at Manchester Polytechnic Department of Textiles/Fashion; lecturer at weekend courses, summer schools, day schools

Awards Travel bursary for lecturers in design, awarded by Royal Society of Arts. Used to help finance visit to the USA to study North American patchwork

Exhibitions 1979 & 83 One-person show – Saddleworth Festival of the Arts

Mixed exhibitions include:

1977 'Crafts in Question' – Whitworth Art Gallery, Manchester

1979 Derby Cathedral

1981 'Stitchery' – British Crafts Centre, London

1982–83 'British Needlework' – National Museum of Modern Art, Kyoto and Tokyo Japan

1983 'North West Craftsmen' – Royal Northern College of Music, Manchester; Bees Gallery, Marple Bridge, Cheshire; Great House Gallery, Rivington, Bolton

1984 'Textiles on the Theme of Mazes' – Bath Festival, St James' Gallery, Bath; 'The Leicestershire Exhibition' – The Leicestershire Collection for Schools and Colleges, Woodhouse Eaves, Leicestershire

1975 to date Member of the '62 Group of Textiles Artists – currently Vice Chairman Exhibitions include:

1979 Woodlands Art Gallery, Blackheath; National Museum of Wales, Cardiff

1981 Manchester Polytechnic

1983 Victoria Art Gallery, Bath; DLI Arts Centre, Durham

1984–85 Touring Exhibition, Japan

Works in public and private collections including: Wigan Metropolitan Borough; Trinity College, Carmarthen, Dyfed; Embroiderers' Guild; Leicestershire Education Committee

Commissions 1979 Saddleworth Civic Hall

1982–83 Lord Rhodes of Saddleworth
Domestic interiors, wall hangings, panels, quilts

Publications Articles published in *Embroidery* 1976, 1980, 1982
Featured in *Twelve British Embroiderers*, Gakken Publishing Co, Japan 1984

Ione Dorrington FSDC 1905–1984

Training at Sheffield School of Needlework

1936 Regent Street School of Art – dress design; followed by three years with a West End couturier, cutting and modelling gowns

Teaching and career Hornsey College of Art – lecturer in dress cutting

1960s Technical assistant – embroidery department, Goldsmiths' School of Art
Fellow of the Society of Designer Craftsmen

1974 Member of the Art Workers' Guild

1967 Founder of The New Embroidery Group

Commissions Including: four copes and altar throwover – Ripon Cathedral; cope, chasuble and hanging – St Peter-le-Poer, Muswell Hill, London; banner – the Freemasons'

Company; cope – St Columbus House; London; two copes and a chasuble for a convent in Woking; a cope for Australia

Works exhibited in a number of galleries and sold to private clients. Galleries include the Oxford Gallery, the Seven Dials Gallery, and Leighton House

Exhibition Society of Designer Craftsmen from the late Sixties

1985 Retrospective show – St Mary-at-Lambeth, London

Marjorie Dyer (née Goggs) ATD 1911–

Exhibition 1977 Painting – West of England Academy, Bristol

Commissions 1983 onwards By the Dean and Chapter of Exeter Cathedral – cushions depicting history of the Cathedral from Roman to Modern times; cushions and carpet – St Paul's chapel; long kneelers – chapel of SS Saviour and Boniface; and designs for the chapel of St John the Divine – to be worked by the West Country Embroiderers

Netta Ewing DA ADF (Manchester) FRSA 1944–

1965 Training at Glasgow School of Art – interior design

1965–66 Interior design consultant

Teaching 1966–67 Jordanhill Teacher Training College

1967–69 Teaching art at a comprehensive school

1969–73 Assistant lecturer in three-dimensional design at Dundee College of Commerce

Career 1973–75 Art and Design Fellow at Manchester Polytechnic, Institute of Advanced Studies – research into packaging related to energy and resources conservation

1975–79 Assistant lecturer in three-dimensional design at Carsdonald College of Further Education

Commissions 1967–69 Designed costumes for University Arts Theatre – 'A Satire of the Three Estates'

1979 Mitre and orphrey for Thomas Winning, Archbishop of Glasgow

1980 Altar panel – Gourock Old Parish Church

1981 Design for vestments for priests celebrating mass during Papal visit to Scotland – carried out by Catholic schools

1982 Lectern fall for a synagogue; Glasgow coat of arms – Catholic cathedral; Monstrance veil – Pluscarden Abbey

1979–82 Designed 26 amateur stage shows for Glasgow companies

1984 Founded St Alban's Embroiderers' Guild, Pollockshields, Glasgow; designed four Evangelists' kneelers and Rosary altar frontal

Maria-Theresa Fernandes NDAD ATD 1944–

1967–68 Training at Sir John Cass College, London

1968–71 Manchester College of Art and Design – NDAD with Hons

1975–76 Post-graduate Certificate of Education

1983–85 Cranbrook, USA – weaving course

Awards 1977 & 78 North West Arts grants

1981 British Council

1981 First prize – Third Biennial Competition, Alexandria Museum, Louisiana, USA

Exhibitions Numerous exhibitions in UK and USA including:

1973 One-person shows: Covent Garden Gallery, London; Park Square Gallery, Leeds

1974 'Six Textile Artists' – Sheila David Gallery, London; Whitworth Art Gallery, Manchester

1977 Cartwright Hall, Bradford, Yorkshire

1978 Royal Academy of Arts, London; Bretton Hall, Yorkshire

1979 Leeds Polytechnic

1980	Humberside Art Centre, Lincolnshire
1981	'Common Ground' – Alexandria Museum, Louisiana, USA; Maryland Crafts Council Biennial Travelling Exhibition, USA; 'Artists USA' – World Trade Centre, New York
1982	National Fibre Art Competition, University of Missouri-Columbia, USA; Frederick Community College, Maryland, USA
1983	Woodlands Art Gallery, Blackheath. Exhibits regularly with '62 Group, London; Fibre Art, London; North West Arts Panel, Manchester; Minorities Arts Advisory Service, Manchester; Ethnic Arts Subcommittee, NW Arts; Washington Women's Art Association, DC, USA

Work in public and private collections, including John Barnes Associates, Industrial Designers, Warwickshire; Ministry of Lands and Settlement, Nairobi, Kenya; Werner Oberli, Basle, Switzerland; hospitals and education departments

Rosalind Floyd NDD ATD 1937–

Exhibitions 1978	Commonwealth Institute – Embroiderers' Guild 'Blue, Black, Silver' – Midland Group Gallery, Nottingham
1983	Goldsmiths' College Exhibition Gallery

Mary Fogg 1921–

Training at the Slade School of Fine Art – painting. Malvern School of Art – textiles

Exhibitions	The Quilters' Guild; The Embroiderers' Guild
1979	One-person show at 21 Antiques Gallery
1980s	Beckenham Textile Studio, exhibitions in various places including Bromley Central Library; Woodlands Gallery, Blackheath
1982	The Minories, Colchester
1983	'Quilting, Patchwork and Appliqué' – Waterloo Gallery, London

Mainly works on commissions

Elizabeth Ford NDD 1925–1985

Exhibitions 1978	One-person show – Stoke Polytechnic
1979	One-person show – Ibis Gallery, Leamington Spa; Turks Head Gallery, Alcester

Patricia Foulds (née Beese) NDD ATC 1936–

Continues lectures and courses for embroiderers' guilds and other educational establishments

Exhibition 1985	Centre Internationale d'Art Contemporain, Paris

Hannah Frew Patterson DA 1931–

1947–49	Training at evening classes in graphic design at Glasgow School of Art
Career 1947–49	Window display artist
1949–50	Layout and display in photographic studio
1950	Fashion illustration for women's magazine and newspaper
1950	Advertising layout artist
1951–63	Needlework department of thread manufacturer as a diagram artist, then as knitting, crochet and tatting designer
Further training 1961–63	Day release classes in design at Glasgow School of Art

1963–67	Diploma course at Glasgow School of Art, specialising in embroidery and weaving
1967	Diploma of Art – Newbery Medallist
1967–68	Post-diploma at Birmingham College of Art and Design
Teaching 1968–72	Full-time teaching embroidery at Glasgow School of Art
1972 to date	Part-time teaching embroidery at Glasgow School of Art
1970	Three-month tour of New South Wales, Australia, at invitation of the Embroiderers' Guild, NSW
1969–72	Residential schools for the Embroiderers' Guild
1971, 72 & 74	Summer School, Kirkcudbright; various day schools on specialist subjects and individual lectures
1977–79	Council for National Academic Awards Assessor at Goldsmiths' College
1978	Included in list of Scottish Arts Council lecturers
Exhibitions 1969 onwards	Exhibited nine times with embroidery group of Glasgow School of Art, including touring exhibitions sponsored by the Arts Council
1968	St Paul's Cathedral
1969	York Minster
1972	Scottish Society of Women Artists, Edinburgh; Scottish Crafts Exhibition, Edinburgh
1975	Glasgow Society of Women Artists, Collins Exhibition Hall, Glasgow
1978	Scottish Society of Women Artists, Edinburgh – invited artists
1984	Clarendon Park, Wiltshire
Commissions 1984	*Cardross Hanging*
	Examples or work in various churches in Scotland and in public and private collections
Publication	*Three-Dimensional Embroidery*, Reinhold 1975

Margaret Gaby 1930–

1947–52	Training at Leicester College of Art – fabric design, dress, painting
Teaching 1952–55	Lecturer in dress – Chesterfield College of Art
1963 onwards	Part time at Whitelands College of Education; part time at adult education centres
Exhibitions 1969 onwards	Joined Textile Studio and exhibits every year Fairfield Hall, Croydon; Bromley Central Library; Woodlands Gallery, Blackheath; two-person show with Barbara Siedlecka
	Work in collections in Great Britain and abroad

Elizabeth Geddes NDD 1917–

1978	Retired from teaching
Commissions 1977	Designed and worked an embroidered bed-head for the Queen's bed on the Royal Train
1981	Embroidered a woven altar frontal designed by Joyce Conwy Evans for Canterbury Cathedral. Tapestry woven by Edinburgh Tapestry Company.

Robin Giddings MA 1957–

1976–79	Goldsmiths' School of Art – BA Hons in embroidery
1979–80	Manchester Polytechnic – MA (Distinction) in textiles, guipure lace
1979	Member of the Society of Designer Craftsmen – Licentiate with Distinction
1981	Student member of the '62 Group

Exhibitions 1981 'Stitchery' – British Crafts Centre, London; '62 Group – John Holden Gallery, Manchester

1982 'Superstitchers' – Oxford Gallery; 'One-off Wearables' – British Crafts Centre, London; '100% Pure Silk' – Rufford Craft Centre, Nottinghamshire

1982–83 'British Needlework' – Museum of Modern Art, Kyoto and Tokyo, Japan

1984 'Fabric and Form' – Waterloo Gallery, London

1985 'Material Evidence' – Camden Arts Centre, London

Work in private collections in Britain, Channel Islands and USA; in public collections in Lotherton Hall, Yorkshire, and Leeds City Art Gallery

Frederick Glass 1911–

No art training; taught at the American School in Pernambuco, Brazil

Career Illustrated a book on South American Indians; studied engineering and became a mechanical engineer

1958 Married and began to have an interest in embroidery, making a large canvas panel which led to others; based on own environmental study

Exhibitions Fairfield Halls, Croydon; Eastern Rooms, Rye; Portal Gallery, London; Los Angeles, USA; also in small galleries

Work sold to clients in Australia, Canada, USA and France as well as in Great Britain

Lucy Goffin Dip AD 1947–

1963–64 Training at Hammersmith College of Art and Building – pre-diploma course

1964–66 Apprenticed to Michael Casson

1968–70 Harrow College of Art – Diploma in Ceramics, Grade A

1970 Worked in Gwyn Hanssen Studio, Achères, France

Career 1971–72 With theatrical costumier Jean Lamprell Ltd

1972 Technical assistant – West Surrey College of Art

1972–76 Lecturer in ceramics – West Surrey College of Art

1979 Lecturer in textiles – West Surrey College of Art

1975 Member of British Crafts Centre work selection committee

1976 Selection Committee, Member for Textiles, Crafts Council

1983 Elected member of Visual Arts Panel, South East Arts

Exhibitions These include:

1970 The Ceylon Tea Centre

1973 'The Craftsman's Art' – Victoria and Albert Museum; two-person exhibition with Mo Jupp, British Crafts Centre

1974 'Everyman a Patron' – Crafts Advisory Committee Gallery, Waterloo Place, London

1977 Schweitzer Heimatwark Gallery, Zurich; Musée des Arts Decoratifs, Louvre, Paris; Kantonales Gewerbemuseum, Bern; British Crafts Centre

1979 'Silk' – Charles de Temple, London

1979–80 'British Craftsmen of Distinction' – Galerie Kraus, Paris

1981 Quilters' Guild, Covent Garden, London; 'Making Good' – South East Arts touring exhibition starting at Sussex University

1982 'The Makers' Eye' – Crafts Council; 'One-off Wearables' – Crafts Centre, Covent Garden; British Needlework, Museum of Modern Art, Kyoto and Tokyo, Japan; British Contemporary Crafts, Ohio, USA; 'In Store' – Crafts Council, London

1983	'Quilting, Patchwork and Appliqué 1700–1982', Crafts Council Gallery; Quilters Guild National Exhibition; British Art – 'New Directions' – Puck Building, New York, USA
1985	British Crafts Centre – selected hangings
Publications	Articles on her work in newspapers and periodicals
Special projects 1977	Charles I Coat of Arms for the Banqueting House, Whitehall, London, commissioned by Her Majesty's Government, Department of the Environment
1981–84	Embroidery designs for Jean Muir's Spring and Autumn Collections
1982	British Council visit to Japan to give series of lecture/slide shows 'British Textile Art Today'
1982	'Meet the Makers' – Crafts Council tour to Clwyd, North Wales

Linda Gomm Dip AD HDD 1951

1969–70	Training at Canterbury College of Art – Foundation course
1970–73	Training at Goldsmiths' School of Art – Dip AD in embroidery
1973–74	Central School of Art – HDD Textiles
Teaching 1975 onwards	Adult education centres including colleges of education and Bucks College of Art
Exhibitions	Exhibited with the '62 Group from 1974 onwards, including work in travelling exhibitions in Great Britain and Japan
1975	South London Art Gallery
1978	King's Lynn Festival
1979	Greenwich Theatre Gallery
1981	Guildhall Gallery, Winchester
1982	'Superstitchers' – Oxford Gallery

Esther Grainger 1912–

Continuing to work making large hangings, eventually to exhibit

Jennifer Gray NDD ATC 1931–

1981	Retired from teaching
Group project	Designed and oversaw working of Beverley Minster Festival banners
Publication	*Canvas Work*, Batsford paperback 1985

Sylvia Green ARCA 1915–

Teaching 1982	Retired from the Central, formerly Stanhope, Institute; also from the ILEA where she had taught part time
1983	Founded a class for ecclesiastical embroidery and general work in Highgate Literary Institute
1979 to date	Tutor for classes in ecclesiastical embroidery at the Royal School of Church Music, Canterbury
Commissions 1978	Completed red altar frontal – St Michael's, Highgate
1979	White stole, burse and veil; red stole, burse and veil – St Michael's, Highgate
1974–84	Set of four pennants: two designed by Sylvia Green and two by Beryl Dean and kneelers designed by Sylvia Green, worked by students – The Lady Chapel, All Saints, Newland, Forest of Dean
1979–83	Eleven kneelers 'The Creation' designed by Sylvia Green, embroidered by

individual members of the St Michael's Embroidery Group – St Michael's, Highgate

Since 1980   Major work designing and making, with student help, a patchwork altar frontal and dossal in appliqué – All Saints, Newland, Forest of Dean

Margaret Hall Dip AD ATD 1946–

1967–70   Training at Goldsmiths' School of Art. Dip AD in embroidery

1970–71   Bristol Polytechnic and Bristol University – ATD

Teaching and work 1970–73   Embroidered dresses for Roger Vivyan Ltd

Part-time lecturer at Clifton College for Boys; Bristol Polytechnic, Faculty of Art and Design, and other teaching posts

1974 to date   Part-time lecturer, Goldsmiths' School of Art

1977–79   The Barry Summer School; Chief Examiner, The Associated Examining Board for the General Certificate of Education, in embroidery

1977   Summer schools in London, Ontario, Canada

1981   Courses in the USA and in Great Britain

Exhibitions   Work in group shows in Great Britain and abroad

1974   1st and 2nd prizes in the revival of 'Art in Needlework' for gold work

1976   Commonwealth Institute with the Embroiderers' Guild

1976   One of three, Rochdale Public Library

1977   One of two, Redbourne Art Gallery

1983   Goldsmiths' College Exhibition Gallery

Elizabeth Hammond ARCA 1926–

1940–46   Training at Maidstone School of Art – Industrial design and NDD, dress and embroidery

1946   Awarded a Royal Exhibition to the Royal College of Art

1946–49   Royal College of Art – design school

Teaching   Six years in a school of dance and drama – art, craft and costume; part-time teaching – general drawing and embroidery

To date   Associate lecturer at Medway College of Design, Rochester

Exhibitions   Paintings and embroidery in many places, including the Royal Academy and British Watercolour Society

Commissions   Mainly ecclesiastical
Mothers' Union banner – Canterbury

1974–75   Designed *Canterbury Hanging*; purple hanging for Lent – St Peter's, Rochester

1976–77   Hanging – Rochester Cathedral

Pauline M Hann DA 1949–

1967–71   Training at Duncan of Jordanstone College of Art, Dundee – DA in printed textiles and embroidery

1971–72   Post-diploma at Duncan of Jordanstone College of Art

1972–73   Dundee College of Education – Teaching certificate in secondary education

Teaching 1973 to date   Lecturer in design at Duncan of Jordanstone College of Art

Awards 1970   BMK Carpets Scholarship to Denmark and Holland

1971   BMK Carpets Travel Scholarship to Paris

1972   Nairn Flooring Travel Scholarship to Denmark and Sweden

1982	Grampian Television Award
Exhibitions	Group shows:
1970	Batik exhibition, City Art Gallery, Dundee
1971	Exhibition by Scottish art colleges, Craft Centre, Edinburgh
1972	Three-man show, Scottish Crafts Centre, Edinburgh, and Fair Maid's House, Perth
1973	Scottish Craftsmen, Nice, France
1974	Crafts in Tayside and Region; Scottish Crafts Biennale, Edinburgh
1975	Three-man show, Fair Maid's House, Perth
1977	Dundee Art Society 50th anniversary
1978	Art Workshop, Tayport, Fife
1980	Founder Chairman of Embryo – Dundee Creative Embroiderers Inaugural Exhibition, Bonar Hall, Dundee in 1981
1982	Embryo – Edinburgh Festival, Fringe exhibition
1981–83	Embryo – Fair Maid's House, Perth, and Scottish College of Textiles, Galashields
1983	Invited to be a member of the New Scottish Embroidery Group
1985	'Stitchin' time' Embryo, The Orangery, Holland Park, London
Commissions	Carried out for Dundee Leisure Centre, Brecken Cathedral and the Tayside Region
	Work in the collection of Dundee City Art Gallery and in private collections in Great Britain, USA and Australia

Diana Harrison MA 1950–

1967–71	Training at Goldsmiths' School of Art – Diploma in embroidery
1971–73	Royal College of Art, London – MA in printed textiles
Teaching 1973–75	Lecturer at Mid-Warwickshire College of Further Education, Leamington Spa
1974 to date	Lecturer at the West Surrey College of Art and Design
Exhibitions 1977	Whitworth Art Gallery, Manchester; Victoria and Albert Museum, London
1978	Third International Exhibition of Miniature Textiles, London; 'Tapestries of Today', London
1980	Ten years of $401\frac{1}{2}$, Commonwealth Institute, London; Approaches to Metals and Cloth, British Crafts Centre; Fourth International Exhibition of Miniature Textiles; 'Textile Classics', Midland Group, Nottingham
1982	'Fabric and Form' – Crafts Council Gallery, London, also touring abroad
1982–83	'Quilting, Patchwork and Appliqué 1700–1982' – Minories, Colchester – touring exhibition of the Crafts Council
1983	British Needlework, the National Museum of Modern Art, Tokyo and Kyoto, Japan; 'Designers Choice' – Westminster Gallery, Boston, USA
Awards 1972	Sanderson Travel Scholarship
1973	Courtaulds Textile Prize RCA
	Work in collection of: Brunel University, London; Southern Arts Association; Brighouse Art Gallery; Crafts Council; Reviews of work in various magazines Museum of Modern Art, Kyoto, Japan

Wendy Hawkin B Ed 1941–

	Training at Newland Park College of Education
1973–76	Reading University – Bachelor of Education, painting and art main subjects

Teaching 1976 to date	Comprehensive school, primary, middle and secondary as well as high schools, adult education and day courses; Member of the '62 Group
Commissions	Ecclesiastical embroidery
Exhibitions 1978	'Blue, Black and Silver' – Midland Group, Nottingham
1978	King's Lynn
1979	'62 Group
1981	Guildhall Gallery, Winchester
1982	Derby Cathedral. Exhibitions with the '62 Group to date
	Work in public and private collections

Rozanne Hawksley (née Pibworth) Des ARCA 1931–

1948–51	Training at the Southern College of Art, Portsmouth
1951–54	Royal College of Art, School of Fashion
1980–82	Goldsmiths' School of Art – Advanced Diploma
Teaching	Part time at Brighton, Guildford and Portsmouth Colleges of Art; The American Needlework Center, Washington DC; full-time lecturer in dress at the South Bank Polytechnic
Career	Freelance designer
Exhibitions 1980–84	'62 Group shows
1980	Embroiderers' Guild – Commonwealth Institute
1981	'British Women's Art' – House of Commons
1982	Printmaking – Waterloo Gallery, London
1983	Goldsmiths' College Gallery, London
1984	Felt Exhibition – Bury, Lancashire
1985	Whitespace Gallery, Islington, London; 'Material Evidence' – Camden Arts Centre, London

Maureen Helsdon NDD ATD FSDC 1923–

1975–85	Local exhibitions and work sold to private clients

Jennifer Hex DA 1938–

1956–60	Training at Glasgow School of Art – printmaking
1960–61	Jordanhill College of Education
Teaching 1961–80	Taught art in Ayrshire and Argyll secondary schools
1970	Taught in Kintyre; worked on textiles, made prints and began serious interest in embroidery
Exhibitions 1961–70	Prints shown at the Royal Scottish Academy, Scottish Society of Artists in Edinburgh and the Royal Glasgow Institute of Art in Glasgow; also a one-person show in Edinburgh and several group exhibitions in Glasgow and other places
1970 onwards	Textiles with the Modern Embroidery Group of Glasgow School of Art, various places
1974	Craft Biennale, Edinburgh
1980 to date	Left teaching to learn weaving. Currently a part-time weaver and freelance embroiderer. Exhibits from time to time

Kate Hobson-Wells BA Hons 1953–

1973–76	Training at Loughborough College of Art and Design – embroidery
1976–77	MA textile course at Manchester Polytechnic – embroidery

Teaching and career 1978 onwards	Various part-time and freelance teaching jobs, which include Glasgow School of Art; Loughborough College of Art; Manchester Polytechnic; Sheffield Polytechnic
1981 onwards	Workshops and lectures – Australia; Quarry Bank Mill, Styal; and embroiderers' guilds throughout the country
1978	Member of the '62 Group; member of the British Crafts Centre
Exhibitions	With the '62 Group including the Commonwealth Institute, London; National Museum of Wales, Cardiff; Lincoln; Blackheath and Covent Garden
1981	'Stitchery' – British Crafts Centre
1982	Harvey Nichols; '100% Pure Silk' – Rufford Craft Centre, Nottinghamshire
1983	'Contemporary Cotton'
1979	One-person show – Jews Court, Lincolnshire; Humberside Arts
1980	Derby Museum and Art Gallery; 'Innate Harmony', London
1981–82	Group show – Textiles North
1982	'Superstitchers' – Oxford Gallery
1982–83	British Needlework, National Museum of Modern Art, Kyoto; Japan
1984–83	One-person show – Gawthorpe Hall
	Work Purchased by National Museum of Modern Art, Kyoto; Lincolnshire Humberside Art and Crafts Collection

Polly Hope 1933–

Trained as a ballet dancer with London Festival Ballet and in films
Chelsea Polytechnic; Slade School of Art

Career since 1960	Lived much of her time in Greece; built and decorated houses; worked in ceramics and other crafts; published three novels under the pseudonym Maryann Forrest
1973	First stuffed pictures and quilted cloth hangings
Exhibitions	Mixed shows: Young Contemporaries; John Moore's, Liverpool; also in dealers' galleries in London, Europe and USA
since 1973	One-person show – Patrick Searle Gallery, London
1974–75	Stuffed pictures on Cyprus War theme, Galerie Iris Clert, Paris
1976	One-person show – British Council Gallery, Athens; Institute of Contemporary Art, London; Wyvern Arts Centre, Swindon
1977	Eighth International Tapestry Biennale at Lausanne, Switzerland, and Gulbenkian Foundation, Lisbon
1977–78	One-person show – Kornblee Gallery, New York
1978	One-person show – University Art Gallery, Albany, New York
1979	One-person show – Redfern Gallery, London; Galerie B14 Stuttgart; Trito Mati, Athens
June 1980	'Sculptures for Weaving'. National Theatre, London, and other galleries
1982	Warwick Trust Gallery, London

Constance Howard MBE ARCA ATD FSDC 1910–

Teaching 1975 to date	Freelance lecturing and teaching
1978–81	Assessor for CNAA
1978	Lecture tour of Australia and New Zealand
1979 to date	Lecture tours of Canada and the USA
1981	Slot in Jan Beaney's TV series 'Embroidery'

Exhibitions 1977	Society of Stained Glass Designers, Fishmongers Hall – a hanging to commemorate the Silver Jubilee
1981	'Stitchery' – British Crafts Centre; London, Ontario, Canada
1983	Kyoto and Tokyo – Fine Art Museums; Guildford House, Guildford; York City Art Gallery
1984	Art Workers' Guild Centenary – Brighton Art Gallery
1985	Two-person show – Oxford Gallery
1985	Retrospective show – Goldsmiths' College Exhibition Gallery, London
Commission 1973–84	Hanging – Northampton Museums and Art Gallery, assisted by Karen Spurgin
Publications	*Constance Howards' Book of Stitches*, Batsford 1979
	Twentieth-Century Embroidery in Great Britain to 1939, Batsford 1981
	Twentieth-Century Embroidery in Great Britain 1940–1963, Batsford 1983
	Twentieth-Century Embroidery in Great Britain 1964–1977, Batsford 1984
	Twentieth-Century Embroidery in Great Britain from 1978, Batsford 1986

Edith John 1914–

1976	Retired from teaching
1976–84	Freelance lecturing and teaching
Commissions 1980	Red pulpit fall and lectern fall – Christ Church, Doncaster
1981	Green banner – Church of Edward the Confessor, Croydon
1983	Fair linen cloth – Christ Church, Doncaster

Diana Jones NDD ATD 1932–

Exhibition 1985	Quilts in the Bank of Ireland, Dublin
Publication	Patterns for Canvas Embroidery, Batsford paperback 1985

Sister Kathleen (Kathleen Snelus) 1903–

Commissions 1980–82	Mitre-Bishop of Fulham; worked burse from design by Beryl Dean for All Saints, Newland, Forest of Dean
1982	Lectern fall, figures adapted from ninth-century manuscript

Margaret Kaye ARCA 1912

1977	Retired from teaching
Exhibitions 1977–1985	New Ashgate Gallery, Farnham, Surrey – twice yearly mixed shows
1978	Royal Academy; Guildford House, Guildford; Rye Art Gallery, Kent; Thursley, Surrey
1979	Royal Academy; Menuhin School
1980	Contemporary church embroidery – Northampton
1982	Derby Cathedral
1983	Hambledon Gallery, Blandford
1985	One-man show, New Ashgate Gallery, Farnham
Commissions 1980	Farnworth Parish Church – altar frontal
1981	Arnington – altar frontal

Nancy Kimmins (née White) NDD 1922–

1982	Made an emeritus member of the Embroiderers' Guild

Commission 1978   Participation in group commission for Winchester Cathedral with Barbara Siedlecka and Moyra McNeill

Wendy Lees ATD 1923–

1940–45   Training at Leeds College of Art – drawing, design and printmaking ATD
1950–52   Part-time training: Birmingham College of Art and Mid-Warwickshire School of Art
1975–76   London University Institute of Education – aesthetics
1976–77   Goldsmiths' School of Art – Advanced Diploma in Textiles
Teaching 1945–46   Full time: Levenshulme High School, Manchester
1947–53   Mid-Warwickshire School of Art
1971–84   Gipsy Hill College of Education (now School of Teacher Education and Music, Kingston Polytechnic)
1957–71   Also part-time teaching and short courses
Exhibitions 1968   Group shows include: 'Pictures' for Schools, Royal Academy
1970   New Embroidery Group at Foyle's Art Gallery
1970–76   'Contemporary Hangings'
1972   Lincoln Cathedral Festival
1970–77 & 81   Member of and exhibited work with the Society of Designer Craftsmen
1975 & 80   'Pictures for Schools' – National Museum of Wales
1982   Johnson Wax Kiln Gallery, Farnham
1983   Guildford House, Guildford
1972, 76 & 83   Embroiderers' Guild
1983   USA, Australia and Japan
1984   Society of Designer Craftsmen, Seven Dials, London
One-person shows include:
1979   'Stitched Image' – University of London
1980   Kingston Polytechnic, Gispy Hill – 10th anniversary of Polytechnic
Commissions   Among these:
1969   The Principal, Plymouth College of Art
1978   Panel for the Director of the Merton Festival
1981–83   Textile hangings for Elvin Hall, University of London Institute of Education
Work in collections of education authorities and in private collection
Publications   Articles in magazines including *Embroidery*

Janet Ledsham Dip AD 1944

1962–66   Training at Manchester College of Art and Design – Dip AD, painting
1966–67   Manchester Polytechnic – post-graduate course in textiles
Teaching 1968–74   Art teaching in England and Northern Ireland
1976–83   Full-time Lecturer II, embroidery, Ulster Polytechnic
1982–84   Lectures at St Mary's Training College, Belfast Embroiderers' Guild
1983 to date   Senior Lecturer, Ulster Polytechnic/University of Ulster
Awards 1979   Rachel Kay Shuttleworth Trophy
1980   Royal Dublin Society of Crafts (Embroidery)
Exhibitions 1980   Two-person show – Octagon Gallery, Belfast
1980   Group shows – Commonwealth Institute

1980 to date	With the '62 Group at Lincoln, Winchester, Manchester, Hampton Court, Seven Dials Gallery London, Bath, Durham; Clarendon Park, Wiltshire
1984	Japan – touring exhibition
1984–5	Arts Council Gallery Belfast – touring exhibition
1984	Fifth International Biennial of Miniature Textiles, Hungary
1984	International Exhibition of Miniature Textiles, Strasbourg – touring Europe
	Work in private and public collections

Malcolm Lochhead DA 1948–

1966–70	Training at Glasgow School of Art – embroidery and weaving
Teaching 1971–75	Teaching art in schools
	Lecturer in design at Queen's College, Glasgow, responsibility for embroidery
Commissions	The Shrine of St Mungo, Glasgow Cathedral; various church embroideries; embroidered panels for domestic interiors; stage costume and embroidered gowns for television
1980s	Designs for embroidery for eight chairs in the Chapel of St Andrew, Glasgow; Church furnishings for St John's Church of Scotland, Paisley, Renfrewshire
Publications	Articles written for *Embroidery* magazine on symbolism

Vicky Lugg NDD 1939

1958–61	Training at Portsmouth College of Art – NDD in painting and wood engraving
1978	C & G in embroidery
Teaching	In secondary schools
1970s to date	Part-time art tutor at Guildford College of Technology; teaching C & G embroidery part-time at Goldalming, Surrey, as well as freelance work; tutor – Young Embroiderers, Embroiderers' Guild
	Member of Embroiderers' Guild, Practical Study Group, New Embroidery Group
Commissions	Include work for the Embroiderers' Guild
Exhibitions 1982	'Superstitchers' – Oxford Gallery Oxford
1983–84	New Embroidery Group – Leighton House, London
1983–85	Group show – Guildford House, Guildford
Publication	Contributing author of *Needlework School*, Practical Study Group, Windward Press 1984

Sian Martin BA Hons ATD 1949–

1971	Training at Birmingham College of Art and Design, Faculty of Textile Design – BA Hons
1972	Postgraduate year in the same college
1973	University of Leicester – ATD; Membership of the '62 Group and exhibited regularly since 1975
Teaching	In secondary schools, C & G Embroidery adult courses, weekend and summer schools
	Included in the Clive Gunnell HTV programme *Source of Inspiration* on four female artists living and working in the Sedgemoor area of Somerset
Exhibitions	Independent and one-person shows
1974	Quorn Community College, Leicestershire
1975	Countesthorpe Community College, Leicestershire

1976	The Craft Gallery, Market Harborough
1979	Bridgwater Arts Centre, Somerset
1980	Sherman Theatre, Cardiff
1981	Brewhouse, Taunton
1982	Rural Life Museum, Glastonbury
	Work has been sold to Leicestershire, Derbyshire, Essex and Avon County Councils and St James Gallery, Margaret Buildings, Bath have a changing display of work
Publications	Articles for *Embroidery* magazine

Enid Mason NDD ATD 1928–

1945–49	Training at Harrogate School of Art – hand embroidery
1949–50	Bromley College of Art – machine embroidery
1951	Leeds College of Art – ATD
Teaching and work 1951–52	Designer for J & P Coats, Glasgow
1952–55	Hull College of Art
	Work for the Needlework Development Scheme
Late 1960s	Part-time lecturer at Alsager College of Education, Cheshire
	On Art and Craft Committee for the WI North Federation Lincolnshire
Publications	*Ideas for Machine Embroidery*, Mills and Boon, 1961, second edition 1969 *Embroidery Design*, Mills and Boon 1968, second edition 1970

Kirsty McFarlane DA 1935–

1952–56	Training at Glasgow School of Art – embroidery and weaving
Teaching and career 1957–64	In secondary schools
1964–70	Lecturer in art at Cragie College of Education, Ayr
1970–73	Assistant Adviser in Primary Art, Renfrewshire
1973–78	Lecturer in art at Hamilton College of Education
1978	Volunteered for redundancy – working freelance
1982	January – became the Weaver in Residence at the Paisley Museum and Art Gallery. This was the first of such appointments
Exhibitions	In group shows with the Modern Embroidery Group, Glasgow School of Art
1979	'Innate Harmony' – London Gallery
	Member of the Scottish Crafts Centre and The Scottish Society of Women Artists
	Work purchased by Dundee Museum and Art Gallery; the Gracefield Art Centre, Dumfries; the County Collections, Dumbartonshire, Lanarkshire and Renfrewshire; also by collectors in Great Britain and abroad

Moyra McNeill (née Somerville) NDD FSDC 1930–

| | Workshop tours in Australia |
| *Commission 1978* | Joint commission with Barbara Siedlecka and Nancy Kimmins – five copes for Winchester Cathedral |

Work purchased by public and private collectors including:
The Victoria and Albert Museum, London; Switzerland, Australia and the USA

1983–84 Designed the *Croydon Hanging*, worked by women in the area
Publication *Machine Embroidery: Lace and See-Through Techniques*, Batsford 1985

Jan Messent 1936–

1957 St Mary's College, Bangor, North Wales – qualified as secondary school teacher; no formal art training but taught art and English for five years in secondary schools in Yorkshire and Staffordshire
Exhibitions Group shows with the Berkshire Branch of the Embroiderers' Guild
1981 Work including drawings, photographs and embroideries from her book *Embroidery and Nature* – Foyle's Art Gallery, London
Commissions Mostly for private collectors, but also for the Berkshire and Oxfordshire Schools Museum Service and the Knitting Craft Group
Publications *Designing for Embroidery from Ancient and Primitive Sources*, Studio Vista 1976; *Embroidery and Nature*, Batsford 1980; *Embroidery and Animals*, Batsford 1984; *Embroidery and Architecture*, Batsford 1985; *Stitchery and Embroidery Design*, Search Press 1981–82

Many articles on Creative Knitting and Crochet for *Art and Craft* and also leaflets, project folders and commentaries for the Knitting Craft Group

Renate Meyer NDD 1930–

1947–52 Training at Polytechnic Regent Street – NDD painting
Teaching from 1974 Adult education, Bromley and Beckenham – painting
Exhibitions Among these:
1975 One-person show – Ben Uri Gallery, London; oil paintings but all based on threads, work shown at all the '62 Group exhibitions
1982 Crafts Council Showcase, ICA; three-dimensional 'Apples and Stitchery' travelling exhibition, West Yorkshire circuit; Falcon House Gallery, Boxford; Battersea Arts Centre; 'Women and Textiles' – House of Commons

Member of the '62 Group since 1977 and exhibits regularly with them
Publications Bodley Head Picture Books (7)

Lesley Miller (Mrs Henderson) DA 1937–

1955–59 Training at Glasgow School of Art – embroidery and weaving
1959–60 Jordanhill College of Education
Teaching 1960–68 Various teaching posts, including Glasgow and the Orkney Islands
1968 Lecturer in visual arts at Callendar Park College of Education, Falkirk
Exhibitions 1968–82 Work shown in group exhibitions including the Glasgow School of Art Modern Embroidery Group, and other shows
1984 Three-person show, Portfolio Gallery, Linlithgo
Commissions 1959 Pulpit fall – Glasgow; gold Bible cover – Victoria and Albert Museum, London
1970s Hanging – Glasgow Art Gallery, chosen by the organiser
1978 onwards Various small commissions

Eleri Mills BA Hons 1955–

1974–77	Training at Manchester Polytechnic – BA Hons in Embroidery
Teaching 1977–78	Appointed Artist in Residence and part-time lecturer at Crewe and Alsager College
1978	Working from own studio in Manchester on commissioned pieces and exhibiting work regularly; work included on the Index of Craftsmen, Crafts Council
Exhibitions 1978	'Innate Harmony', St John's Wood, London
1979	Prescote Gallery, Banbury
1980	Royal Northern College of Music, Manchester; Victoria and Albert Museum Craftshop, London
1981	British Crafts Centre, London, 'Textiles North' – Touring Exhibition
1982	Royal Exchange Craft Centre, Manchester; 'Superstitchers' – Oxford Gallery, Oxford
1983	'British Needlework' – Kyoto and Tokyo, Japan; 'Prestcote at the Bluecoat' – Liverpool
Commissions 1979–80	Central Toxicology Laboratory, ICI, Alderley Edge, Macclesfield
1982	Rachel Kay Shuttleworth Collection, Gawthorpe Hall, Burnley; Greater Manchester Transport; North West Arts
1983	Panel *In My Craft or Sullen Art* (see figure 249)
1984	National Farmers Union Mutual and Avon Insurance, Headquarters, Stratford-upon-Avon; Embroiders' Guild Collection, Hampton Court
Publications	*Crafts* no. 44 Exhibition review May/June 1980; 'British Needlework' Catalogue; National Museum of Modern Art, Kyoto, Japan 1982; *Twelve British Embroiders*, Diana Springall, Gakken, Japan, 1984; *British Craft Textiles* Ann Sutton, Collins Publishers 1985

Belinda Montagu 1932–

1948–52	Training at the Byam Shaw School of Art – drawing and painting
1950–51	Central School of Art and Crafts – fresco painting
Teaching	Lectures and classes in adult education; C & G Parts I and II at Southampton College of Art
Career 1952–58	Freelance designer and illustrator. Work for the BBC and ITV making captions and special effects
1959–74	Various design projects for Beaulieu Motor Museum and Bucklers Hard Maritime Museum
1978	Member of the Mid-Wessex Embroiderers' Guild
1978	Member of the Old Sarum Group
Commissions 1979	Commission to design the New Forest embroidery and to organise the working of it; designed cushions presented to HM the Queen on her visit to the New Forest and to the Prince of Wales on his marriage
Publications	*The New Forest Embroidery*, New Forest Association/Michael Russell 1981; *Group Projects in Embroidery* Batsford 1986

Yvonne Morton 1940–

1973–77	Training at Bournemouth and Poole College of Art and Design
Teaching 1977–81	Tutor in embroidery, Bournemouth and Poole College of Art and Design
since 1981	Founded the East Dorset Group of Embroiderers, working towards the C & G examinations; also founded an exhibiting group of professional embroiderers in Dorset; short courses and lectures for groups
Exhibitions	Groups shows with the New Embroidery Group, the Embroiderers' Guild, the West Country Embroiderers

1984	Two-person show 'Grids and Garlands' – Salisbury
Publication	Contributor to *Blandford Book of Handicrafts*, Blandford 1981

Bridget Moss (née Knowles) ARCA 1913–

Commissions 1983 & 84	Large patchwork quilt
1980–84	Silk jackets. Produces two quilts a year

Betty Myerscough (née Frazer) DA 1932–

Teaching 1979 to date	Part time – Chelsea School of Art
Exhibitions 1979 & 80	One-person show in London
1982	Two one-person shows in Norway
Commissions 1983–84	Large hanging for a recital room, Canterbury; large panel for St Theresa's Church, Biggin Hill, commissioned by an architect

Annwen Nicholas NDD 1943–

1960	Training at Cardiff College of Art
1962–65	Goldsmiths' School of Art – NDD, embroidery
Teaching and career 1965–76	Lecturer at Manchester Polytechnic
1967–80	Assessor C & G
1965–79	Glamorgan Summer School
To date	Part-time teaching in adult education – various courses for teachers
1974–77	External examiner for BA course at Ulster Polytechnic – embroidery
1979–80	Examiner for B Ed, London University – art
1979 to date	Member of the Craft Panel, North West Arts
1980 to date	Examiner for the C & G – embroidery
Exhibitions 1976 & 79	One-, two- and three-person shows in Manchester; mixed shows – Manchester and annual exhibitions; other exhibitions throughout the country
1979	'Twelve Manchester Artists' – Kirkaldy AV Gallery
Commissions 1968	St Stephen's, Astley
1970	Manchester Diocesan Architects – St Mark's, Blackley, Manchester
1969 & 72	Building Design Partnership – Manchester, Church of the Good Shepherd, Skelmersdale New Town
1976	St Clement's, Salford
	Work purchased by local education authorities, architects and private clients
Publications	*Embroidery in Fashion*, with Daphne Teague, Pitman 1973; articles in *Embroidery* magazine, *Creative Embroidery* and others

Margaret Nicholson 1913–

Teaching 1978	Retired from full-time teaching
1978–80	Part time, London College of Fashion; lecturer on many courses; moderator, intermediate and advanced examinations in embroidery, C & G
1982	Member of Standing Advisory Committee, Associated Examining Board

Dorothea Nield 1917–

	Judging for the Royal School of Needlework and the Women's Institutes
Publication	Section on Lace – *Textile Crafts*, Pitman 1977

E Kay Norris NDD FSDC 1922–

1983	Retired from teaching
Exhibitions Late 70s	Society of Designer Craftsmen
1980–85	West London Craftsmen, held in different places around London
Commissions 1978	Set of stoles for Devizes School, Wiltshire
1979	Chasuble for Marlborough College
1982	Altar frontal and pulpit fall – St Martin's Hospital chapel, Bath

Joan Openshaw 1905–

1960	Training at Weston-Super-Mare Technical College – C & G
1961–74	Member of Somerset Guild of Craftsmen and Somerset Embroiderers' Guild and Harrogate Branch
Exhibitions 1961	With the Embroiderers' Guild at the Royal Watercolour Society
1966–67	Melbourne Embroiderers' Guild Galleries, Australia
1975	Heirloom Exhibition, London
1983	Preston Embroiderers' Guild
Commissions	Mainly ecclesiastical for England and overseas

Irene Ord DIP AD 1946–

1965–67	Training at Margaret McMillan College of Education – Certificate in Primary Education.
1969–70	Carlisle College of Art and Design. Slater Trust Travelling Scholarship
1970–73	Goldsmiths' School of Art – embroidery and textiles, Dip AD
1981	Crafts Advisory Council special project grant for exhibition at Winchester Guildhall 1981; On register of Crafts Council as listed craftsman
Teaching 1967–69	Full-time and part-time teaching
1974 onwards	Part-time teaching – freelance, primary, secondary and further education
Exhibitions 1974 onwards	Has exhibited regularly in galleries throughout England and Wales
1976	Elected member of the Society of Designer Craftsmen
1982	'Superstitchers' – Oxford Gallery; 'Design Gap' – Interior Design International; British Crafts Centre; Anatol Orient
	Member of the '62 Group and exhibits regularly
	Works sold to public and private clients

Beryl M Page (née Sheaves) ARCA ATC 1914–

1933–36	Training at Leeds College of Art
1936–37	Birmingham College of Art
1937–39	Croydon School of Art. Scholarship to Royal College of Art
1957–58	Teaching certificate at Goldsmiths' School of Art
Teaching and career 1939–45	War service with the Ministry of Works
1945–57	Part time at St Albans, Harrow and Rochester Colleges of Art
1947–48	With Hardy Amies
1958–60	Kingsdale Comprehensive School
1960–65	Leicester College of Art – Lecturer in Fashion and Textiles
1972–83	Hertfordshire CC part-time classes

Exhibitions 1974	Atelier Gallery, St Albans
1975	St Albans Gallery
1976	Letchworth Museum, Four Hertfordshire Embroiderers
1977	Luton Art Gallery; Maynard Gallery, Welwyn Garden City
1979	Luton Art Gallery, with Charles Page
1980	Commonwealth Institute; Hemel Hempstead Arts Centre
1982	Dower House Gallery, Berkhampstead, with Charles Page
1983	Bury St Edmunds Art Gallery
1984	Hampton Court
Commissions	Masonic banner and cushion for the St Albans Lodge; banner for New Greens Church, Leicester

Jane Page 1933–

1951–55	Training at the Royal School of Needlework, then worked in Hasselblad House, Sweden, meeting many craftsmen
1961–64	Goldsmiths' School of Art – embroidery and design
1964	For three months – Konts Facksolan, Stockholm
Teaching 1964–65	Bristol College of Art
1965–68	Derby College of Art
1970 onwards	In-service courses for teachers of domestic subjects – Hertfordshire Education Department; peripatetic teacher of children in several Hertfordshire schools; Classes for C & G examinations in embroidery, for teachers
	Member of the Society of Designer Craftsmen and the New Embroidery Group
Exhibitions	In a number of places, with groups and alone
Commissions 1967	Designs for kneelers – Derby Cathedral
1968	Designs for kneelers for a church in Beverley, Massachusetts, USA
1969	Set of vestments – rebuilt church, Clifton, Bristol
1971	Altar frontal – Thames Pilots' Church, Gravesend
1960–80s	Private commissions
1985	Stole for Chelsea Old Church
	Work bought by Devon and Kent Schools Loans Collection and by other public and private collectors

Beryl Patten DIP AD 1951–

1970–73	Training at Manchester Polytechnic, Department of Textiles/Fashion – embroidery, Dip AD
1973–74	Birmingham Polytechnic – Department of Textiles/Fashion
Teaching 1974 to date	Lecturer in art and design, Department of Textiles/Fashion, Bolton Technical College
Career 1973 to date	In partnership with Judy Barry, designing and carrying out ecclesiastical commissions, with sufficient of these to preclude exhibition work *See Judy Barry entry*

Pamela Pavitt (née Willard) NDD ATD 1925–

Teaching 1981	Retired from primary school teaching
1982	Textile Conservation Centre; Croydon Adult Education Centre
Work 1983 onwards	Development of machine-knitting techniques combined with machine embroidery

Herta Puls 1915–

Training as a radiographer and medical technician

1939   Came to England from Hamburg

1962–66   Studied embroidery and textile design at Newport College of Art part time

1966–68   West of England College of Art, Bristol – part time

1969–70   London College of Fashion – Advanced examination of the C & G – distinction, first prize Merchant Taylors Company, also silver medal

Teaching 1971–78   Freelance lecturer for ILEA specialising in Kuna Indian mola techniques

to date   Day schools and short-courses on mola techniques and others

Exhibitions   Embroiderers' Guild, Commonwealth Institute; Welsh National Eisteddfod

1972 onwards   '62 Group exhibitions; One-person show – Arts Centre of Cwmbran, Gwent

Work in public and private collections in Great Britain, Germany and USA

Publication   *The Art of Cut Work and Appliqué*, Batsford 1978

Paddy Ramsay BA Hons 1949–

1971   Training at Birmingham Polytechnic

Career 1971–73   Embroidery designer – Bellville Sassoon, London

1973–74   Embroidery designer – Marie-Paule (Haute couture) Montreal, Canada. Also freelance

1974 onwards   Working from own studio in Montreal; then London, Ontario; then Edmonton, Alberta

1975   Won competition to design a Christmas hanging for the entrance of University Hospital, London, Ontario. It is hung at Christmas each year

1977   Won fashion competition at University of Alberta, Edmonton

1981   Returned to live in Britain

1983   First prize in Rachel Kay Shuttleworth competition for embroidery, Gawthorpe Hall, Padiham, Lancashire

1985   Craftsperson in Residence Woodhorn Church Museum, Ashington, Northumberland. Member of '62 Group; Society of Scottish Artists; Guild of Lakeland Craftsmen; Embroiderers' Guild

Teaching 1975–77   Part-time lecturer, Fanshawe College, London, Ontario; teacher at Embroiderers' Guild, London, Ontario

1982   Part-time lecturer, Sunderland Polytechnic

1984   Part-time lecturer, Cumbria College of Art, Carlisle

1984 onwards   Workshops and short courses

1985   Part-time lecturer Cleveland College of Art; College of Arts and Technology, Newcastle upon Tyne

Exhibitions 1974–77   Canadian Embroiderers' Guild

1976   Festival of Arts, London, Ontario

1978   University Art Gallery, University of Alberta, Edmonton

1983 & 84   Guild of Lakeland Craftsmen: Dacre Hall, Brampton, Cumbria; Old Windebrowe, Keswick, Cumbria; New Embroidery Group: Leighton House, London; Chelsea Craft Fair, London

1983   Gossipgate Gaslight Gallery, Alston, Cumbria; Gawthorpe Hall, Padiham, Lancashire; Ulverston Point Gallery, Cumbria; Guild of Lakeland Craftsmen, Kendal; Holly House Gallery, Tynemouth; Sunderland Arts Centre, Sunderland

1984   One-person show – Calouste-Gulbenkian Gallery, Newcastle upon Tyne; 'Material Things', Museum and Art Gallery, Carlisle; Shipley Art Gallery, Gateshead; Textile Group of the Guild of Lakeland Craftsmen, Brewery Arts Centre, Kendal; Society of Scottish Artists, RSA, Edinburgh

| 1985 | Woodhorn Church Museum, Ashington, Northumberland; Guild of Lakeland Craftsmen, Dacre Hall, Brampton, Cumbria; MPAA, Burnley, Lancashire; Cleveland Crafts Centre; One-person show – Van Mildert College, University of Durham |
| *Commission 1980* | A series of embroideries on Elk Island National Park, Alberta – private client; Work in private and public collections in Britain, Canada and USA |

Sue Rangeley DIP AD ATD 1948–

	Training at Loughborough College of Art and Design – Foundation year
1967–70	Lancaster Polytechnic, Coventry – three-year course in fine art, Dip AD
1970–71	Brighton Polytechnic – ATD
Teaching and career 1971–75	In schools
1975	Left teaching and went to Fosseway House; part-time at Birmingham Polytechnic and other colleges
1976–78	Dress designs for Bill Gibb
1983	Awarded Southern Arts bursary
Exhibitions 1976 & 80	Among these: Embroiderers' Guild, Commonwealth Institute
1978	Prescote Gallery, near Banbury, Oxfordshire
1979	'Craftsmen of Distinction' – Charles de Temple, London; mixed show – Charles de Temple, Paris; Crafts Council 'New Faces' – British Crafts Centre, London
1980	Crafts Southwest, touring; Prescote Gallery – Edinburgh Festival
1982	'Fashion as Art' – clothing show, Boston, USA; 'Superstitchers' – Oxford Gallery
1983	'Quilting, Patchwork and Appliqué 1700–1982'; Mixed show – Westminster Gallery, Boston, USA
Commissions	Quilts, screens, cushions, mainly for private houses; individually designed clothes for weddings and evening wear

Dorothy Reglar (née Darch) NDD 1944–

1961–63	Training at the West of England College of Art, Bristol – NDD in fashion
1963–64	Post-graduate year at Birmingham College of Art – embroidery
Career and teaching 1964–72	Bellville Sassoon – designing and organising embroidery for the firm
1964–72	Part-time teaching at Hornsey College of Art
1970–82	Block teaching at Birmingham Polytechnic – fashion embroidery with students on the textile/fashion course
	Now, freelance, and works on a commission basis for embroidered clothes. Still has connections with Bellville Sassoon
	Travelling to the following places has influenced her design of clothes:
1976	Turkey
1977	Rhodes
1981 & 84	India
Exhibition 1978	Birmingham Art Gallery
	Former member of the '62 Group

Catherine Riley MA 1952–

| *Training 1970–71* | City of Leicester Polytechnic – Foundation studies Diploma |
| *1971–74* | City of Manchester Polytechnic Dip AD (1st Class Hons) – in embroidery |

1974–75	City of Manchester Polytechnic, MA in Fine Art
Exhibitions 1974	'Embroidery rules OK' – NWAA Manchester; 'Embroidery rules OK' – MPAA Blackburn
1975	One-person 'Sheep Show' – Sheila David Gallery, London; Northern Young Contemporaries – Whitworth Gallery, Manchester; Young Contemporaries, London
1976	'3 am' – Peterloo Gallery, Manchester
1977	'Young Calderdale' – Bankfield Museum, Halifax
1977	One-person 'Frog Show', NWAA Manchester; 'Crafts of the 70s' – Whitworth Gallery Manchester; Piece Hall Gallery, Halifax – joint show with Ray Elliot
1979	'Press View' – Crafts Coucil, London; work purchased by George Melly for Arts Council Collection
1981	'New Faces' – British Crafts Centre; mixed exhibition, V & A Crafts Shop, London
	Work featured in many periodicals and books, including *Crafts, Interior Design, Jewellery Today, Farmers Weekly, The Subversive Stitch* and *Textile Crafts*
1980–81	Received a Crafts Council grant
1980 to date	Part-time lecturer at Manchester Polytechnic 1980

Christine Risley NDD, FSIAD 1926–

Teaching 1982	Lectures at University of Western Ontario, Beal College, the Embroiderers' Guild and the Guild of Stitchery in Toronto and London, Ontario
1984	Lectured Highland Craftpoint, Inverness
Professional other than teaching 1981	Adjudicator for the Embroiderers' Guild 'Celebration' Exhibition, London, Ontario, Canada
1982–85	External Assessor Belfast Polytechnic BA (Hons) Textiles; and Birmingham Polytechnic BA (Hons) Textiles
1983	External Assessor Loughborough College of Art BA (Hons) Textiles
1985	Elected a Fellow of the SIAD
Exhibitions 1981	London Regional Art Gallery, Ontario, Canada
1982	National Museum of Modern Art, Kyoto, Japan
1983	Goldsmiths' College Gallery. Staff Exhibition
1984	St James's Gallery Bath for the Bath Festival; Guildford House Gallery
1985	Retrospective show – Goldsmiths' Exhibition Gallery
Work in public places 1980	Slides of current work in the Index of Craftsmen at the Crafts Council, Waterloo Place, London
1984	Wallpaper design of 1957 used for V & A poster 'wallpaper, four centuries of design'
Publication	Leaflet on own work for the Embroiderers' Guild, 1984

Pamela Anne Rooke NDD 1932–

Commissions 1978	Green chasuble and stole – Parish Church of Llanstephan
1982	Pulpit fall – St Andrew's, Ferring-by-Sea, West Sussex

Pat Russell FSDC 1919–

1978	Consultant on colour and design for church interiors; design consultant to Worcester Cathedral
1980	Awarded a grant by the Crafts Advisory Committee for the pursuance of own work

Exhibitions	Ecclesiastical work and calligraphy in many galleries including:
1985	Art in Jewish Ritual, Manor House Society, London
Commissions	Many for cathedrals and churches in Great Britain, including:
1979	Frontals – St Martin's Worcester; cope – Dean of St Paul's Cathedral, London
1980	Set of six copes for Lichfield Cathedral; set of copes and two large banners in St Paul's Cathedral, London
1981	800th anniversary of Wells Cathedral: set of five copes, design echoing Wells' double arch; frontals for four sides of nave altar, with detachable orphreys to mark seasons, two double-sided banners
1982	'Tree of Life' cope – Dean of Lichfield; frontal – St John's College Chapel, Oxford
1983	Baptism of Christ banner – St John's, Kidderminster; High Mass set – Tewkesbury Abbey
1984	Green festival cope – St Peter's Wolverhampton; dossal curtain – St Matthias, Malvern Link
1985	900th anniversary of Worcester Cathedral: frontals for Crypt Chapel; designs for kneelers for Crypt Chapel; festival cope with Greek inscription – Dean of Worcester
	Set of Stations of the Cross – St Martin's Worcester; banner with Pascal Lamb – St John's Kidderminster; frontals – St Edward's School, Oxford; frontal – Chantry Chapel, Tewkesbury Abbey
Publications	*Lettering for Embroidery*, Batsford, new edition 1985 Articles in *Embroidery* magazine

Vera Sherman NDD 1917–

Training at the Regent Street Polytechnic – NDD in painting; post-graduate course in sculpture

Career	London correspondant for the Italian magazine *D'Ars*; awarded Premio Internazionale Europa Arte for extensive and meritorious artistic activities
1966–76	Organiser of the touring exhibitions of 'Contemporary Hangings', 'Fabric and Thread' and 'Contemporary Pictures in Fabric and Thread'
	Work in public and private collections in Great Britain, Australia, Europe and the USA
Publication	*Wall Hangings Today*, Mills and Boon, 1972

Jennifer Shonk BA 1954–

1972–75	Training at Loughborough College of Art and Design – BA Hons in textiles/embroidery
1975–76	Post-graduate diploma in History of Art and Design at Birmingham Polytechnic
1976–77	Post-graduate Certificate in Education at Birmingham Polytechnic
1981	Uncompleted MA research degree (part time) at Birmingham Polytechnic
Teaching 1978–80	Manchester Polytechnic – visiting lecturer in textiles
1978–80	Birmingham Education Department – part-time work in schools
1979–82	Mid-Warwickshire College of Further Education – part-time lecturer in textiles and three-dimensional construction
From 1980	Gloucestershire Education Authority – part-time work in schools and colleges
Exhibitions 1975	Midland Group Gallery, Nottingham
From 1975	The Warwick Gallery; also with the '62 Group
1976	Textural Art Gallery, London (Inaugural Exhibition)
1977	'Food Art' – Kettles Yard Gallery, Cambridge University

1979	'62 Group at the National Museum of Wales, Cardiff
1980	Embroiderers' Guild at the Commonwealth Institute, London
1982 & 83	Beaumanor Hall, Leicestershire (Leicestershire Collection for schools and colleges)
	Private commissions have been undertaken for clients in England, Scotland, Northern Ireland, Germany and the USA

Eirian Short NDD 1924–

1985	Retired from teaching
Exhibitions 1979, 81 & 85	Tolly Cobbold/Eastern Art
1982	Two-person show – Cardiff
1983	Goldsmiths' College Exhibition Gallery, London
1985	Retrospective show – Goldsmiths' College Exhibition Gallery

Barbara Siedlecka NDD ATD 1931–

	Training at Leicester College of Art – NDD in graphic design
	Leicester College of Art – ATD
Teaching 1955	Lecturer at Leek School of Art
1956–61	Layout artist, art editor, freelance illustrator
1969	Fabrics incorporated into artwork
1970	Joined Beckenham Adult Education Centre, Textile Studio
1975	Member of the '62 Group
To date	Part-time lecturer at Beckenham Adult Education Centre; in charge of the Textile Studio 1978 onwards; also freelance illustrator and textile artist working for advertising using textile techniques – Unilever, Jaeger, Paton and Baldwin
Exhibitions	Work shown in group shows in Great Britain and abroad including the '62 Group
Commissions 1975–76	Wall hangings designed for the London Borough of Hounslow. Work carried out with assistance from Alison Barrell, M Gabay, Nancy Kimmins and Marjorie Self
1978–79	Designed five festival copes for Winchester Cathedral – carried out by Moyra McNeill, Nancy Kimmins and students; fashion illustrations for Jaeger's hand knitting yarns, for National Press advertising, using yarns of the firm
	Work purchased by public and private collectors in Great Britain and abroad, including education authorities in Kent, Derbyshire and Leicestershire; also the Embroiderers' Guild, Japan and the USA
1985	Design approved for a large textile hanging as a focal point for the 1988 Lambeth Conference, Canterbury – units made by women throughout the world

Lilla Speir (née Hilda Norfolk) 1915–

Exhibitions 1978	One-person show – Gracefield Art Gallery, Dumfries; guest craftswoman, Women Artists' Exhibition, Royal Scottish Academy, Edinburgh
1980	One-person show – Broughton Gallery, Biggar, Lanarkshire. Quilts, small hangings
1981	Group show – Philip Francis Gallery, Sheffield
1982	Studio exhibition – past and present quilts. Corresponding with the Dumfries Festival

Millicent Spiller ATD 1923–

1939–42	Training at Slade School of Art, University of London – painting
1942–43	London University Institute of Education – ATD course
1968–69	Part-time classes in embroidery at Goldsmiths' School of Art
1977–79	C & G Part I, Windsor and Maidenhead Adult College
Teaching 1943–58	Art in schools and training colleges including Corsham School of Art near Bath and the Froebel Institute, London
1974	Art examiner, London University

Anne Spring NDD ATD 1939–

1955–59	Training at Nottingham College of Art and Crafts – printed textiles and pottery
1959–60	Leicester College of Art and Crafts – ATD
Teaching 1960–62	Art teacher at Boots College of Further Education, Nottingham
1983	At present teaching part time at a primary school (Lois Weedon)
Exhibitions 1963–70	Exhibiting member, Midland Group of Artists
1964	Two-person show at Midland Group Gallery – paintings and embroideries by Anne and Peter Spring
1975	Craft '75 at British Crafts Centre – represented Midland Group
1977	'Fabric Hangings' – Oxford Gallery
1977	'Fabric Hangings' Prescote Gallery, nr Banbury
1979	Visual Arts Grant Award, East Midlands Arts
1983	'Fabric Wall Hangings' – Oxford Gallery
1983	'Fabric Wall Hangings' – Prescote Gallery, nr Banbury
Commission 1981	Fabric hanging – February Festival, Civic Offices, Milton Keynes

Diana Springall NDD ATC FSDC 1938–

1959–63	Training At Goldsmiths' School of Art – NDD in painting
1963–64	Goldsmiths' School of Art – ATC
1975	London University Diploma in History of Art and C & G in embroidery
Teaching and lectures	
1968–79	Principal lecturer, art department, Stockwell College of Education (closed 1979)
1973 onwards	Lecture tours to the USA and Canada. Attended the World Crafts Council seminars
1975–76	'12 Living British Craftsmen' Victoria and Albert Museum – demonstrations
1978	Visited Kyoto and other places to study embroideries
1978	Member of the World Crafts Council
1978–85	Chairman of the Embroiderers' Guild
1980	Took part in the series of programmes on embroidery for BBC TV
Commissions	For ecclesiastical and secular work include:
1967–72	A number of embroideries for the Kent Education Authority, Maidstone
1973	Burse and veil for St James's Church, Westgate-on-Sea, Kent
1973	Trinity frontal for Farningham Church, Kent
1974	Kneelers designed for St Anne's Chapel, Lincoln Cathedral
1975–79	Designed five panels for Chester Town Hall – worked by the local community
	Many works for private clients, including:
1974	*White Relief* for the late Margaret Sandford, Kent
1978	*Wood Grain Relief* for Mr and Mrs I Joyce, Edenbridge, Kent

1983	*Jessica* – a hanging for a school for mentally and physically handicapped children – Bermondsey, London
Publications	*Canvas Work*, Batsford, 1969; revised edition 1980; *Embroidery*, BBC Publications 1980; *Twelve British Embroiderers*, Gakken, Japan 1984

Gay Swift NDD 1938–

1955–57	Training at Barnsley School of Art
1957–59	Harrogate College of Art – NDD in embroidery
Teaching 1960–62	Youth clubs, recreational classes
1962–65	Harrogate School of Art – embroidery
1963–68	Shipley College – embroidery and drawing
1966–72	Jacob Kramer College, Leeds – embroidery to fashion students
1974	Craven College, Skipton – recreational, the mentally handicapped
Exhibitions	With various mixed groups, including the '62 Group
1964	One-person shows – Barnard Castle, Redditch, Barnsley
1975	One-person show – Ilkley
	Work in a number of private collections and local education authorities
Publications	*Machine Stitchery*, Batsford 1974; *The Batsford Encyclopaedia of Embroidery Techniques*, Batsford 1984

Margaret Elaine Swales BA Hons 1956

1975–78	Training at Birmingham Polytechnic – BA Hons in Fashion/Textiles (specialising in embroidery), 1st Class Hons
Experience and teaching 1977	Industrial practice – Louis Grosse Limited
1979	January to September at Robert Hirst (menswear manufacturers), designing and pattern cutting
1979–80	Until September – Staveley Crafts, design and sales
1980–	Part-time lecturer in embroidery at Harrogate College of Art and Adult Studies; and Selby College of Further Education (C & G embroidery); freelance embroiderer
Exhibitions 1982	January to February at the Darlington Art Centre; Northern Arts Gallery; Aquarius Gallery, Harrogate
Commissions	Cope for the Rev Peter Dunbar, St John's Church, Knaresborough; private commissions

Linda Taylor BA Hons ATD 1951–

1973	Training at Birmingham Polytechnic – 1st Class Honours degree in textiles/fashion, specialising in embroidery – ATD
Teaching 1973–81	Lecturer in textile department of Bournville School of Art; also a visiting lecturer at this time on Foundation Studies at Loughborough College of Art and Design; visiting lecturer teaching C & G embroidery at Kidderminster College of Further Education
1981	Visiting lecturer in textile design on the DATEC course at the North Worcestershire College of Further Education, Bromsgrove
Exhibitions since 1973	Has taken part in many exhibitions
	Work in private collections in England, Ireland, France and Scandinavia

Diana Thornton BA Hons 1956–

1975–78	Training at Goldsmiths' School of Art – BA Hons degree in embroidery and textiles
1978 to date	Part-time technical assistant in machine embroidery, Goldsmiths' School of Art; some commissions
Exhibition 1983	Goldsmiths' College Exhibition Gallery

June Tiley ARCA 1925–

Commissions 1978	Masquerade, touring exhibition: Welsh Arts Council; Craft section National Eisteddfod; 'Textiles – a broader definition' – University of Wales, Aberystwyth
1983	Lecturer at the World Crafts Council Conference, Shannon, Ireland

Veronica Togneri DA 1938–

1956–60	Training at Glasgow School of Art – embroidery and weaving
1960–61	Post-diploma scholarship
Career 1962	Set up own workshop at Campbeltown, Argyll
1969	Lived on Isle of Colonsay, Argyll – weaving rugs
Exhibitions	Exhibits with the Modern Embroidery Group of Glasgow School of Art
1960	With the Modern Embroidery Group, Scottish Arts Council Gallery, Glasgow and other places
1968	'Fabric Collage' – Saltire Society, Edinburgh
1970	'Modern British Hangings', Scottish Arts Council Gallery, Edinburgh and other places in Great Britain
	One-person shows:
1970	'Woven Rugs' – Scottish Crafts Centre, Edinburgh
1974	Patchwork and Embroidery – Corran Halls, Oban
Award 1983–84	Received a Craft Fellowship award from the Scottish Development Agency to develop silk patchwork
To date	A number of exhibitions of drawings, paintings, and designs for stained glass

Margaret Traherne ARCA 1919–

Exhibition	Southover Gallery, Lewes
Commissions 1977	Group of banners, façade of Burlington House, Jubilee Exhibition at the Royal Academy of British Art 1953–77
1978	Dyed and draped fabric hangings – Brunel University, Middlesex
Exhibition 1979	One-person show, mixed media, including glass and textiles – Brunel University
	Works also in many places, stained glass and textiles among these: Manchester Cathedral; Liverpool Metropolitan Cathedral; National Museum of Wales; Victoria and Albert Museum, London; Leicester Art Gallery; Abbott Hall Gallery, Kendal

Lorna Tressider NDD ATC 1938–

1955–59	Training at Bromley College of Art – NDD in painting
1959	Landscape award, Royal Academy
1960	Goldsmiths' School of Art – ATC course. Studied embroidery and continued and attended evening classes. Distinction
1961	C & G – embroidery
Teaching 1961	Lecturer at Berridge House College of Domestic Science, London

1962–65	Part-time lecturer at Harris College of Art, Preston
1965–67	Teacher training college in Liverpool
1965–67	Part-time lecturer at Liverpool Polytechnic
1967	Senior lecturer in charge of embroidery at Liverpool Polytechnic
1970	Part-time lecturer at Liverpool Polytechnic
1980 to date	Part-time lecturer at Dyfed College of Art, Carmarthen
Lecturing and examining	
1968	Assessor – Dublin Society of Arts
	Lecturer – Society of Designer Craftsmen panel
	Assessor and speaker – Merseyside and Conway Embroiderers' Guild
Exhibitions	In group shows throughout career. One-person shows:
1970	Bluecoat Gallery, Liverpool Arts Council
1974	Camden Arts Centre, London
1975	Exhibition sponsored by the *Liverpool Daily Post and Echo*
1976	Welsh Arts Council
Commissions 1967	Ecclesiastical vestments and altar frontals for Liverpool Catholic Cathedral
1969	Lenten array for Mossley Hill Church
1971	Motifs for dress designer Bill Gibb
1978	Three panels on *Space* – British Airways Hotel, Manchester
	Work purchased by private and public collectors
Other work 1976	Sabbatical year – visited India
1984	Visited India collecting embroideries and living in villages, recording way of life and embroidery

Dorothy Tucker B Ed Hons 1948–

1967–70	Training at Brighton College of Education – Cert Ed
1970–71	University of Sussex, School of Education – B Ed Hons
1974–76	Oxford College of Further Education – C & G Fashion Part I
1976–78	Goldsmiths' School of Art – Advanced Diploma in embroidery and textiles
Teaching 1974–76	Art and needlework in a comprehensive school in Oxford
1979 to date	Part-time lecturer at Roehampton Institute and part-time tutor for the ILEA; short courses and lectures for the Embroiderers' Guild and Practical Study Group
1983 to date	Teaching C & G classes at Blackheath Art School, London
1980	Member of Society of Designer Craftsmen, the British Crafts Centre, the Embroiderers' Guild and Practical Study Group
Exhibitions 1980 & 85	Practical Study Group
1982	'Superstitchers' – Oxford Gallery, Oxford
Commission	Heraldic banner for the Freemasons, Penge
Publications	Articles in *Embroidery* magazine; contributing-author of *Needlework School*, Practical Study Group, Windward Press 1984

Stephanie Tuckwell Dip AD ATC 1953–

1971–75	Training at Goldsmiths' School of Art Dip AD in embroidery and textiles
1975–76	Brighton Polytechnic – ATC
1976–77	West Midlands Arts and Crafts Fellow, awarded in conjunction with the University of Aston, Birmingham

Teaching and career 1978–79	Freelance work, part-time teaching in adult education, youth clubs, a psychiatric day centre and family workshops
1979 to date	Freelance work
	Part-time teaching, London College of Fashion – embroidery department Epsom School of Art – fashion department
	On the Index of Craftsmen (Crafts Council)
	Member of the '62 Group
Exhibitions 1977	Aston University, Birmingham
1979	Warwick County Museum
1980	Munich Crafts Fair – one of six British Craftsmen representing Great Britain for the Crafts Council
1982	South London Artists at the South London Art Gallery
1983	'Makers '83' and 'Printed and Painted Textiles' – British Crafts Centre
	Work in several private collections in England and Australia; Oxford County Museum, Aston University;
	Work sold in several places including Heals, Liberty's and the Victoria and Albert Museum Crafts Council shop

Ruth Tudor ATD 1921–

1939–43	Chester School of Art – Drawing, Industrial Design (embroidery/weaving) examinations
1943–44	Liverpool School of Art, ATD
Teaching 1944–46	Full time Tinstall Grammar School
1962–65	Part time Lady Verney Grammar School High Wycombe; College of Art and Design High Wycombe
1965–84	Penzance School of Art
	Member of Embroiderers' Guild; Red Rose Guild; Cornwall Crafts Society
Exhibitions 1980	Embroiderers' Guild, Commonwealth Institute London
1982–85	Red Rose Guild, Manchester; Foyle's Gallery, London
1983	Newlyn Orion Gallery Penzance; Falmouth Art Gallery
Commissions 1968 onwards	Church vestments
1980	Altar frontal – Anthony, Cornwall
	Work sold to Avon Education Authority
	In churches and in private collections

Valerie Tulloch 1922–

1939	Grantham – received as school prize *Modern Embroidery*, Mary Hogarth, Studio 1933; a significant influence; entered Civil Service
1950–53	Training at Kingston-upon-Thames School of Art – dress making and pattern cutting
1954–57	Kingston-upon-Thames School of Art – embroidery
1958–63	Leamington Spa School of Art – embroidery, C & G Bronze Medal – Merchant Taylors' Prize and Pearsall Prize – embroidery
1966	Birmingham College of Food and Domestic Arts – C & G Teachers' Certificate
Teaching and career 1967–68	Part time at Mid-Warwickshire College of Further Education, School of Art Leamington
1968 to date	North Hertfordshire College, Hitchin
	Day courses, summer schools and teachers' courses

1969–70	ILEA classes for the Embroiderers' Guild
1969–71	Elstow Crafts Centre, Bedfordshire
1977–79	Founder chairman of North Hertfordshire and Bedfordshire Branch of the Embroiderers' Guild
Publications 1967	Embroiderers' Guild leaflet No 12
1967–70, 78 & 80	Articles for *Embroidery* magazine with Kit Pyman
1977	Needlework and embroidery section in *Things to Make and Do*, Readers' Digest; Search Press booklets, *Art of Embroidery* (Hamlyn)
Exhibitions 1966–84	Embroiderers' Guild at the Commonwealth Institute, branch and area, group shows – Midlands and Hertfordshire
1969–76	'Contemporary Hangings'
1971 & 76	Foyle's Art Gallery, London; Hitchin Museum and Art Gallery, own and students' work
1979–80	Bedford Central Library – two-person show
1983	Hitchin Museum and Art Gallery – two-person show
	Work in public and private collections in Great Britain and abroad

Audrey Walker 1924–

1944–48	Training at Edinburgh College of Art – painting
1948–51	Slade School of Fine Art, London University – painting
1965	Began to embroider and attended part-time classes at the London College of Fashion
Teaching	Art in secondary schools and Whitelands College of Education
1975 to date	Head of Textiles/Fashion BA Hons degree course, Goldsmiths' School of Art
Exhibitions	With the '62 Group since becoming a member in 1967
1981	'Stitchery' – British Crafts Centre
1982	The Oxford Gallery and other galleries
1983	Goldsmiths' College Exhibition Gallery
Commission 1973	'Monarchy 1000' – a large commemorative panel for the Pump Room, City of Bath
	Work in the Victoria and Albert Museum, the National Gallery of New South Wales, the Department of the Environment, education departments and colleges of education; also in private collections

Julia Walker BSc 1936–

1955–58	Training at Manchester University – botany: studied textiles in local creative embroidery classes
Teaching and career 1958–62	Hornsey High School
1977	Member of Beckenham Textile Studio
1981	Member of Tunbridge Wells Embroiderers' Guild and member of New Embroidery Group
Exhibitions 1970	One-person show Bourne Hall, Ewell
1974	Group show – Rio de Janeiro
1982	Group shows: Bourne Hall, Ewell; Beckenham Textile Studio; Bromley Library
1983	With Embroiderers' Guild in Japan
1984	Woodlands Art Gallery, Blackheath
Commissions	Decorative panels, wall hangings and quilts for private collections

Mary Ward DA 1945–

1962–66	Training at Glasgow School of Art – embroidery and weaving
Teaching 1967–73	Lecturer in art
1968–72	Part-time lecturer in embroidery at Glasgow School of Art
1973 to date	Discontinued teaching in order to pursue own work
Exhibitions 1975	Two-person show with Kirsty McFarlane
until 1983	Annually with group shows, including the Glasgow School of Art Modern Embroidery Group
1981	Broughton Gallery, Biggar – group show
	Now doing private commissions only and exploring new ways of working
	Work purchased by Argyll County Council, Lanark County Council and Strathclyde Region, and by public and private collectors in Great Britain and Australia

Stewart Warren Dip AD 1946–

	Trained at Goldsmiths' School of Art – Textiles/Fashion/Embroidery – Dip AD
Teaching 1971–78	Full-time lecturer, Totley College of Education; Sheffield Polytechnic
1978	Joined Verina Warren in a freelance career; initially exhibited marquetry and inlaid frames and boxes, developed during recent years concentrating on assembling, framing and the presentation of Verina's embroideries, with combinations of fabric, thread and painted card mounts
To date	Lectures and demonstrates to embroiderers' guilds

Verina Warren Dip AD 1946–

1964–68	Trained at Goldsmiths' School of Art – Textiles/Fashion/Embroidery – Dip AD
Teaching 1969–75	Full-time lecturer, Loughborough College of Art
	Part-time lecturer, Canterbury College of Art, Manchester College of Art
1973	Set up own studio
	Lecture tour of Chicago – Hot Springs, Arkansas – Boston, Mass, for the 'National Standards Council of American Embroiderers'
Exhibitions	(only the first exhibition is listed at each gallery, as they are often repeated in successive years)
1973	Oxford Gallery – Oxford
1974	'New Faces' – British Crafts Centre, London
1975	Yaw Gallery – Michigan, USA; North West Arts – Manchester; Yew Tree Gallery – Derbyshire; Park Square Gallery – Leeds; Design Council – London
1976	Midland Group Gallery – Nottingham; Design Centre – London
1977	Boadicea – London; Booth House Gallery – Yorkshire; Cornhill Gallery – Lincolnshire; Goosewell Gallery – Yorkshire; Locus Gallery – London
1978	De Beerburght Gallery – Holland; 'Objects' – Victoria & Albert Museum – London; Craven Gallery – Lancashire; Lantern Gallery – Manchester
1979	Black Horse Gallery – Norwich; Doddington Hall – Lincolnshire; Derby Cathedral – Derbyshire; Kunstindustrimuseum – Norway
1980	DLI Arts Centre – Durham
1981	Sudbury Hall – Derbyshire; Rufford Craft Centre – Nottinghamshire; Castle Museum – Nottingham; Textiles North – Travelling Exhibition; Shipley Art Gallery – Tyne and Wear; Museum and Art Gallery – Derby
1982	Distlefink Gallery – Victoria – Australia; Museum of Modern Art – Kyoto – Japan; Gallery on the Green – Boston – USA

1983	Leicestershire Collection (Schools and Colleges) – Leicestershire; 'Embroidery '83' – York Minster – Yorkshire
1984	St James's Gallery – Bath
1985	University of Durham – Co. Durham; Elaine Potter Gallery – San Francisco, USA

Work in public collections

Museum of Modern Art – Kyoto, Japan; National Gallery of Victoria – Melbourne, Australia; The Embroiderers' Guild – Victoria, Australia; Victoria and Albert Museum – London; The Embroiderers' Guild – Hampton Court, London; Lincoln and Humberside Arts Association – Lincolnshire; East Midlands Arts Association – Loughborough; Abbot Hall Museum – Cumbria; Derbyshire and Wiltshire County Museums Collections Service

Awards	East Midlands Arts Association, Craftsman Award, in recognition of excellence of work
Television references	BBC 1 Pebble Mill at One. Interview and demonstration
	Slot in Jan Beaney's TV series 'Embroidery'
	Exhibits on a regular bi-annual basis in both America and Austalia
Publications	*Landscape in Embroidery*, Batsford 1986

Crissie White DA 1939–

Training 1956–60	Glasgow School of Art – Diploma in embroidery and weaving
1960–61	Jordanhill College of Education – teachers' certificate
Teaching 1961–64	Art teacher at Augustine's Secondary School, Glasgow
1964–74	Lecturer in embroidery and weaving at Duncan of Jordanstone College of Art, Dundee
1974 to date	Senior Lecturer in charge of embroidered and woven textiles, Glasgow School of Art

Lectures and courses

1963–64	Lecturer in embroidery, evenings, Glasgow School of Art
1966–67	In-service courses for teachers
1964–84	Various lectures in Scotland
1967–70	Visits to USA – East and West coasts
1973	Visits to Denmark, Sweden and Finland to see art schools and craft establishments
Exhibitions 1961–84	With Embroidery Group of Glasgow School of Art; two Scottish Arts Council touring exhibitions; Embroiderers' Guild, London; Foyle's Art Gallery, London; Regent Gallery, Glasgow; Strathclyde University; Collins Gallery; Arts Centre, Edinburgh; Royal Glasgow Institute of Fine Arts; English Speaking Union, Tapestries by Scottish Weavers, Edinburgh; Kelvin Grove Art Gallery; Glasgow School of Art
1972	'Contemporary Weavers' – Scottish Arts Council
	Embroideries in collections in Scotland, England, USA and Switzerland
Commissions 1978	Crafts Advisory Council – hanging for the Department of Surgical Neurology, Dundee Royal Infirmary; *Joseph's Coat of Many Colours*
1980	Pulpit fall for Lent – New Kilpatrick Church, Bearsden, Glasgow
1982	Pulpit fall for Trinity – St Stephen's, Renfield Parish Church, Glasgow
1984–85	Stole for the Moderator of the General Assembly of the Church of Scotland, the Very Rev John Paterson of St Paul's Church, Milngavie, Glasgow

Kathleen Whyte MBE DA 1907–

Commission 1984	Pulpit fall for Prestonkird, Midlothian
Publication	*Design in Embroidery*, Batsford, new edition 1982

Anna Wilson 1907–1985

Training 1915–25	Bedfordshire High School
1926	Agnetendorf im Riesengebirge
1960–64	Part-time student at Goldsmiths' School of Art – embroidery
Career and teaching 1965	Translator of German books
	Further education, Manchester and Cheshire, and Norfolk
Mid-1970s	Many courses for education authorities
Exhibitions 1973	Of her own and students' work in Manchester University Business School
1980–82, 83 & 85	Assembly Rooms, Norwich
Commissions 1970s	Altar frontals – Manchester Cathedral and Church of St Michael and All Angels, Low Moor, Wythenshawe
	Work sold to education authorities and private collectors
Publication	*Enjoying Embroidery*, Batsford 1975

Carrie Robertson Wright DA 1957–

1975–79	Training at Duncan of Jordanstone College of Art, Dundee – Diploma in weaving and embroidery
1979–80	Post-diploma in weaving at Duncan of Jordanstone College of Art
Teaching 1979–82	Teaching part time at Duncan of Jordanstone College of Art
1983	Part-time lecturer at Hertfordshire College of Higher Education
Exhibitions	In Scotland
	Work in private collections in Britain, Canada, USA and South America
1985	'Stitchin' time' – Embryo, The Orangery, Holland Park, London

Mary J Youles, NDD Des RCA 1930–

Training	At Carlisle College of Art, Min of Ed, Intermediate Examination
1949–53	National Diploma in Design (Printing – main. Weaving – additional)
1953–56	Royal College of Art – textiles
1962–65	Part-time courses in Embroidery at Goldsmiths' School of Art
1980–81	One year post-graduate course in textiles – West Surrey College of Art and Design
1956–58	Full-time employment in Yorkshire. Jacquard woven textile designer
Teaching 1958–67	Part-time appointments: Barking Regional College of Technology; Southend College of Art; Gravesend College of Art; Sydenham Comprehensive School
1967–74	Lecturer/Senior Lecturer – Whitelands College of Education (Roehampton Institute)
1974–81	Gloucestershire College of Education
1981	Freelance lecturer and embroiderer
1965–85	Member of the '62 Group (past secretary and chairman)
1982	Member of the Practical Study Group
Exhibitions	Design Centre – London; International Fairs – Stockholm, Brussels, Milan; touring exhibitions – America, Australia, Japan
1965–85	All major '62 Group exhibitions
Commissions	Work purchased for private and public collections, and education authorities

Index